Introduction to English Language Learners and Culturally Responsive Pedagogy

Introduction to English Language Learners and Culturally Responsive Pedagogy

Critical Readings

First Edition

Edited by Daniel J. Gilhooly
University of Central Missouri

cognella®
SAN DIEGO

Bassim Hamadeh, CEO and Publisher
Angela Schultz, Senior Field Acquisitions Editor
Michelle Piehl, Senior Project Editor
Alia Bales, Production Editor
Emely Villavicencio, Senior Graphic Designer
Greg Isales, Licensing Associate
Natalie Piccotti, Director of Marketing
Kassie Graves, Vice President of Editorial
Jamie Giganti, Director of Academic Publishing

Cover images:
Cover: Copyright © 2019 iStockphoto LP/monkeybusinessimages.
Cover: Copyright © 2018 iStockphoto LP/monkeybusinessimages.
Cover: Copyright © 2017 iStockphoto LP/FatCamera.
Cover: Copyright © 2016 iStockphoto LP/gradyreese.
Cover: Copyright © 2015 iStockphoto LP/FatCamera.
Cover: Copyright © 2013 iStockphoto LP/monkeybusinessimages.

Printed in the United States of America.

cognella® | ACADEMIC PUBLISHING
3970 Sorrento Valley Blvd., Ste. 500, San Diego, CA 92121

Brief Contents

Detailed Contents

Acknowledgments

THIS BOOK WOULD NEVER HAVE MADE it into print without the efforts of all the collaborators who participated on this project. I'd like to especially thank my colleagues at the University of Central Missouri, Nabat Erdogan and Christina Kiston; and thanks to Lynn Tarvin, the English Language Development coordinator for Raytown Schools; and the three teachers from KCIA who helped shape this book and currently teach the course the book has been designed for, Danielle Harris, Taylor Hernandez, and Fernando Sergio Navarro Lopez. Each of the contributors brings many years of K–12 teaching experience with culturally and linguistically diverse students to the pages of this book. We hope that this text will help better prepare teachers for the challenges and rewards that working with diverse populations entails.

I would also like to thank Dr. Ann McCoy for her support.

Introduction

T HE FOLLOWING TEXTBOOK IS THE RESULT of a collaborative effort between various stake-holders trying to meet the needs of pre-service and in-service teachers working with culturally diverse students and their families in western Missouri. Many of the chapters were written by professors from the University of Central Missouri. All of the contributing authors bring a range of administrative, teaching, and research experiences to each of the topics. The text is also informed by the work of three K–8 teachers at Kansas City International Academy (KCIA), an urban charter school catering to high-population culturally and linguistically diverse (CLD) students.

In Chapter 1 Daniel Gilhooly and Michelle Amos offer an introduction to working with CLD students. This chapter first introduces readers to the variety of students identified as English language learners and also provides key background information related to working with CLD students. The chapter also provides some practical measures teachers can use to help begin to address the needs of their culturally diverse students. The chapter concludes with *student profiles* that provide pre-service and in-service teachers a starting point to better understanding the academic, cultural, emotional, language, personal, and social needs of their CLD students and their families.

Chapter 2, by UCM assistant professor Nabat Erdogan, provides readers an introduction to some of the key concepts related to second language acquisition. This chapter includes a review of the major concepts, theories, and stages of second language acquisition. The chapter concludes with some practical ways teachers can utilize their understanding of how languages are learned in their classroom teaching.

In Chapter 3, Younghee Shin and Rod Ellis provide insight into issues surrounding corrective feedback and the role it plays in teaching language learners. The chapter helps teachers begin to consider what errors look like and how they might best respond to learner errors.

The authors also include an introduction on how the various theoretical frameworks address error correction. Excellent sample transcriptions of learner errors help readers have a better sense of what errors look like and how various types of corrective feedback work in response.

In Chapter 4, Christina Kitson explores the ways technology can enhance student learning. This chapter provides some background on the various kinds of technologies available to teachers and concludes with some time-tested websites that teachers can use in their classes.

Chapter 5 looks at assessment as it relates to English language learners. Lynn Tarvin brings his expertise as an English language development (ELD) coordinator to frame the various assessments students take from their first day of school until they test out of support services. The chapter provides an introduction to the World-class Instructional Design and Assessment WIDA assessment and offers strategies that help teachers more equitably assess their CLD students.

In Chapter 6, Velma Menchaca presents an interesting overview of issues pertaining to Latino migrant students and their families. The chapter addresses important considerations for teachers working with Latino students and other migrant populations. Specifically, the chapter explores issues germane to culturally relevant teaching when working with Latinos, migrant family involvement, and the unique challenges of secondary school for Latinos and other migrant populations. The chapter provides teachers some insight into the realities associated with the Latino migration experience and schooling.

Katherine H. Au provides some introduction to culturally responsive teaching. In Chapter 7, Au provides teachers a working definition of what it means to be culturally responsive and then frames the chapter via three key questions. The chapter helps teachers consider how cultural differences can be integrated into classrooms and schools so as to benefit all students and communities.

Nan Li provides highly contextualized examples of the eight components of Sheltered Instructional Observation Protocol (SIOP) in Chapter 8. The chapter provides strategies that help teachers consider the ways to develop CLD students' English language repertoires. The chapter is replete with ideas and examples for all teachers to use in their classrooms. Importantly, Li walks teachers through the important process of deciding what language elements students need to develop their academic language proficiency.

In Chapter 9, Lynn Tarvin offers important insights into working with high school newcomer immigrants. The chapter looks at the student profiles of Anai and Roberto, two English learners with differing student biographies and language proficiencies. The chapter offers an important introduction to the types of obstacles these two students face as well as ways to help them develop their English via research-based strategies. The chapter also offers an introduction to systemic functional linguistics and its role in enriching language development.

Our final chapter, Chapter 10, offers readers important considerations when working with a specific group of CLD students and their families. While the chapter focuses on the Karen ethnic group, the chapter models the kinds of background information teachers need to consider when working with diverse populations of students. The chapter reinforces the importance of better understanding the cultural and linguistic backgrounds of their students so as to be better positioned to address students' emotional, linguistic, psychological, and academic needs.

Chapter 1

Getting Started Working With Culturally and Linguistically Diverse Learners

Daniel Gilhooly and Michelle Amos

Glossary

Term/acronym	Meaning	Usage
CLD	Culturally and linguistically diverse	A more nuanced term that views the student as a cultural being and not just a language learner
CRP	Culturally responsive pedagogy	The inclusion of students' culture, beliefs, language, values, and learning styles in instruction
DACA recipient (Dreamer)	Refers to someone who was brought to the United States as a child and is protected from deportation by the Deferred Action for Childhood Arrivals (DACA) policy (Dickerson, 2018)	Used to refer to those brought to the United States illegally by parents but who are often Americanized and have little or no experience with their parents' country of origin
EFL	English as a foreign language	Generally refers to the teaching of English in a non-English-speaking country by a non-native English speaker
ELL EL ELD	English language learner(s) English learner English language development	Generically used in reference to students learning English in a K–12 setting

(Continued)

Term/acronym	Meaning	Usage
Funds of knowledge	"... refers to those historically developed and accumulated strategies (skills, abilities, ideas, practices) or bodies of knowledge that are essential to a household's functioning and well-being" (González & Moll, 1995, p. 446)	The recognition by teachers that culturally diverse students are an asset as they bring unique knowledge and skills into classrooms and schools
Idiom	A word or phrase that contains a meaning different from the literal definition	Common idioms include "up in the air," "hang out," "hit the books," and "dropout"
L1, native language, mother tongue, primary language, home/heritage language	Refers to the language the child was first exposed to, usually, at home	Often used interchangeably to indicate a student's first language
LEP	Limited English proficient	Often used to describe English learners in schools and on state and national policy documents
Newcomer	Often used to describe students who have been in the United States under 1 year and score below 1.9 on WIDA ACCESS test	Often used in schools to refer to a student who is new to English and potentially new to schooling
Refugee	"Someone who has been forced to flee his or her country because of persecution, war, or violence. A refugee has a well-founded fear of persecution for reasons of race, religion, nationality, political opinion or membership in a particular social group" (UNHCR)	A specific subgroup of immigrants, vetted through an extensive process and offered limited federal support with their transition to the United States

I try with school but not easy for me. I just want learning English first, only English. I never understanding teacher speaking in class. Just sitting. My teacher nice for me but I not learning the way I want. Many times I think stopping school. I need help my parent for everything. They need me for speaking, helping with everything and I tired. Many time I think why I come here [the US]. (December Htoo)

T HE INTRODUCTORY QUOTE IS FROM AN interview with December Htoo, a 17-year-old ethnic Karen young man from Myanmar living and attending school in rural Georgia. His words represent some of the frustrations and realities for the growing number of **culturally** and linguistically diverse (**CLD**) students in American classrooms. Moreover, it represents a high level of communicative competence (Hymes, 1972) of an **English language learner** (**ELL**). Despite some language errors, December provides important insights into English language learning, the schooling of CLD students, and the motivations of many students to improve their English language ability. It also demonstrates his and other CLD students' frustrations with an education system that often fails to meet their needs.

December Htoo is one the 4.9 million students labeled ELL who were enrolled in public schools in the United States in 2016, according to data from the National Center for Educational Statistics (NCES). This number represents an increase of 28.9% since 2000, far outpacing the overall increase in public school enrollment, which increased 2.6% in a similar time period. In fall 2015, 9.9% of the total public school enrollments were labeled ELL students; in eight states over 10% of students were ELL; in California, these students represented 22.1% of public school enrollment (Migration Policy Institute, n.d.).

These increases reflect a historical trend. From 1998 to fall 2019, the number of ELL enrolled in public schools increased by 40%, from 3.5 million to 4.9 million (NCES, 2019a). This growth was most notable from 1995–2005, when ELL school enrollment increased by 105% while the general school population growth was less than 10% (National Clearinghouse for English Language Acquisition, 2019). Teachers from rural to urban districts are facing larger numbers of CLD students who have unique backgrounds and linguistic needs to succeed in U.S. schools. It is important to consider that not all CLD students are alike and have a variety of personal stories that have lead them to your community and school.

Who Are the Culturally and Linguistically Diverse Students We Serve?

While the majority of CLD students in U.S. schools are Latinos, there is a growing diversity throughout rural and urban districts across the country. It is important to realize that every family's story is unique. Students may be in your class for a variety of reasons. In rural areas, many migrants work agricultural jobs. Some families follow the seasons harvesting crops. Other families may be working at local pork, beef, or chicken farms or processing facilities. Small enclaves of immigrant communities are building their American experience in small towns in every corner of the country. Other parents or guardians may be in the United States on special visas to study or work at local universities or in medical professions, while others may be working in local restaurants and corporations at all levels of socioeconomic status. Some children are identified as English language learners even though they were born in the United States. Since they only spoke their home language until starting school it is no surprise they need support acquiring English. Other U.S.-born students may speak English with a high degree of proficiency but lack reading and writing skills. A refugee student coming to your school may have not had any prior experience to schooling or English, while their classmate may be on an exchange program living with a host family in your community. The reality is that CLD students come from every region of the world and every level of English proficiency. However, the one characteristic that many CLD students share is their desire and need to acquire English.

Learning languages is a complex process that involves social, cognitive, and academic dimensions, and each can be daunting for learners and their teachers. The reality is that language acquisition is not easy, and schools have to take a holistic approach when it comes to their CLD students. Importantly, acquiring languages is not limited to the classroom. Rather, we learn language in every social interaction we encounter: in the classroom, on the court, in the playground, in the halls and cafeteria, and on the bus. Each of these settings are full of language exchanges where students can and will acquire language, if they are included. Creating a rich and supportive language-learning atmosphere is as much the responsibility of the office professionals, physical education teachers, and bus drivers as it is the English teacher. By following a few simple strategies all members of the school community can help develop students' English language proficiency.

The Basics of Cross-Linguistic Communication

A great starting point when considering cross-linguistic communication is our own language learning experiences. When we begin learning a new language it can feel as if everything we hear is a jumble of incomprehensible fleeing sounds. When we consider our own stories trying to communicate in a foreign country or when learning Spanish in high school it can help inform us on some fundamentals. The following six strategies can help everyone in the school ensure that CLD students are understanding what is being said and feel connected to their school.

1. **Speak slowly.** Most people tend to speak their first language at lightning speed. Think back to your own language learning experiences and how difficult it was to even capture one word when listening to someone speaking the language naturally!
2. **Modify the way we speak.** Be mindful of the words we use and all those idioms that we use in normal everyday communication. Expressions like "hit the books," "hand in your assignment," and "What's up?" will most likely be new expressions to many English language learners. Try as you may, idioms defy logic and can baffle someone listening intently.
3. **Be clear and explicit** when giving instructions.
4. **Be aware of nonverbal communication.** So much of communication is nonverbal, and language learners are always sensitive to our expressions, body language, and gestures. Use these to full effect.

5. **Have fun** with the language differences. Try and speak the child's language, if only to show them that you, too, struggle with language learning. They can laugh at your mistakes and learn to laugh at their own. Cross-cultural and cross-linguistic communication can be frustrating, but with the right attitude it can be a lot of fun for all and beneficial to all students.
6. **Have empathy**. It is never easy adjusting to a new place. Consider all the challenges you might face having to attend school in a language you did not understand and how tough it would be to fit in. Help CLD students get involved with their fellow students.

As we consider how to address the arrival of a new CLD student into our classroom it is important to have some understanding of the broader context related to working with diverse student populations. This is especially true in contemporary American society where issues of immigration, diversity, and globalism have become so polarized. This chapter aims to provide in-service and pre-service teachers the necessary context for the historical and legal issues that have shaped American policy and perspectives related to working with CLD students and families.

Serving All Students: ELL Performance in U.S. Public Schools

Students who are labeled as ELL are underperforming compared to their native English peers. Trend data based on the National Assessment of Educational Progress (NAEP) show that while average scores have increased or remained steady in both groups, the gap in performance has stayed the same or widened slightly. For example, in 2017, the average scale score for grade 4 reading was 225 for non-ELL students and 189 for students labeled ELL, an increase from 223 and 188, respectively, in 2007 (NCELA, 2019b). Comparative data for both reading and mathematics follow:

	2007		2017		Trend		Gap		
	ELL	**Non-ELL**	**ELL**	**Non-ELL**	**ELL**	**Non-ELL**	**2007**	**2017**	**Change**
Grade 4 reading	188	223	189	225	+1	+2	35	36	+1
Grade 4 mathematics	217	242	217	242	none	none	25	25	none
Grade 8 reading	222	263	226	268	+4	+5	41	42	+1
Grade 8 mathematics	245	282	245	284	none	+2	37	39	+2

NCES data from 2015–2016 also show that Hispanic students have lower high school completion rates (79.3%) than their Caucasian peers (88.3%). This is especially significant as, since 1994, fewer than half of all public school students are White, and the percentage of those who are Hispanic has increased to 27.4%, or 13.9 million students.

It is no wonder that many ELLs are underperforming when we consider that most state and federal exams are not intended for CLD students and many teachers are unprepared to work with culturally and linguistically diverse populations. It is important that teachers working with these students help develop students' language repertoires while also helping them develop their academic development. We believe that an important first step in understanding students is having some sense of the historical and political decisions that have impacted and shaped the diversity of American society.

Legal Decisions

Although debates about immigration, language, and bilingualism in schools today often focus on Spanish speakers, German immigrants in Nebraska initiated the first pivotal case related to **heritage language** instruction in schools. In 1924, the case *Myers v. Nebraska* was filed in response to the Simon Act of 1919, which made it illegal in Nebraska for any public or private school to provide foreign language instruction before the eighth grade (Sudbeck, 2015). The law was challenged by parochial schools, and in 1924, the Supreme Court struck down the decision, which stands as one of the first decisions that provides protection for language minorities.

Nearly 60 years later, the *Lau v. Nichols* case of 1974 was a decision that directly impacted the teaching of CLD students. The case was taken up by Chinese students against the San Francisco Unified School District (Sugarman & Widess, 1974) and set a major precedent for the teaching of ELL students. At the center of the complaint was the failure of the schools to address the language needs of the roughly 1,800 Chinese complainants who did not speak English as a first language. The Supreme Court decision in favor of the students later established the **Lau Remedies**, which provided a basic framework to guide schools in addressing the needs of their English language students (ELL).

The landmark decision of the 1982 case *Plyler v. Doe* has had a major impact on immigrant children's education (Olivas, 2012). The Supreme Court decision holds that states cannot constitutionally deny students a free public education based on their immigration status. In short, schools cannot demand documentation proving American citizenship to register for school. Interestingly, the Court's decision was pragmatic, concluding that excluding children from education would have harmful effects on society. The Court stated, "By denying these children a basic education, we deny them the ability to live within the structure of our civic institutions, and foreclose any realistic possibility that they will contribute in even the smallest way to the progress of our nation" (*Plyler v. Doe*, 1982).

These cases represent only a few of the major legal cases that have impacted CLD students, their families, and the teachers and schools working to accommodate them. While the courts have had direct effects on the education of CLD students, national policies have also shaped American immigration and the ethnic diversity of American schools.

Immigration Policy

In September 2019, at a naturalization ceremony in Kansas City, Missouri, 383 people from 84 countries became naturalized as U.S. citizens. Similar ceremonies take place throughout the country periodically each year and are a testament to the growing diversity of the U.S. population. However, such diversity of immigrants is relatively new in the United States. A multitude of legal decisions have altered U.S. immigration policy and deserve some attention. We focus on the following immigration decisions to better inform teachers on the role national policies have had on immigration and the diversity of U.S. communities and schools.

The **Naturalization Act** of 1906 required that all immigrants speak English in order to become naturalized citizens (Ragsdale, 2013). This act alone may have precluded many living in the United States to attain citizenship. In 1924, the **Johnson-Reed Act** was signed into law by President Coolidge and established a race-based quota system that restricted Italian, Jewish, Polish, and Asians from immigrating to the United States (Ngai, 1999). The law was not replaced until 1965, and it has played a role in shaping American perspectives on immigration (Ngai, 1999). An earlier act, the **China Exclusion Act of 1882**, specifically prohibited Chinese immigration until 1943 with the Magnuson Act, which only allowed 105 Chinese to immigrate per year, and that act was not abolished until 1965.

President Lyndon Johnson signed the **Immigration and Nationality Act** in 1965, which would "transform the United States into a society of diverse cultures, religions, and ethnic groups (Ragsdale, 2013, p. 172). Much of the diversity would come from the growing number of refugees that would be admitted in the 1980s and 1990s.

FIGURE 1.1 Uncle Sam and anti-Italian immigration, 1903.

Source: https://digitalcollections.nypl.org/items/c146bf32-7fda-68d3-e040-e00a1806693f.

Refugee Students

While much of the public and policy attention on immigration has focused on border cross-ings along the U.S.-Mexican border, refugees from across the globe have been resettling to the United States since the end of WWII. Since the **Refugee Act** of 1980, the United States has resettled more refugees than any other country in the world. Initially, in the 1980s and early 1990s, the refugee resettlement program resettled majority Vietnamese, Laotian, and Cambodian populations due to the U.S.'s involvement in the Vietnam conflict. In the 1990s, refugees from post-Soviet countries represented the largest groups resettled. The largest groups resettled over the past 20 years have been from Burma, Iraq, Somalia, Bhutan, and the Democratic Republic of the Congo.

According to Igielnik and Krogstad (2017), more than three million refugees have been invited to live in the United States since 1975. Annual refugee arrivals are typically between 40,000 and 70,000, though these numbers have declined to a low of 22,500 for 2018 under the Trump administration (MPI, n.d.). The immigration experience is often very traumatic; however, ref-ugee families face particularly severe traumas on their journey from their native countries to the United States. Those traumas include but are not limited to loss of family and friends to war, rape, and other physical violence; persecution or the fear of persecution; disruption of school-ing; displacement from their native homes; economic deprivation; protracted stays in refugee camps; loss of citizenship, and a host of other deprivations and traumas. Importantly, trauma continues as families try and adapt to their new lives in the United States. Recognizing the last-ing impact of these experiences is key to providing trauma-informed care in the classroom.

While refugee families tend to place a high value on education, they often lack the skills to support their children's academic success (Gilhooly, 2015; Matthews, 2008). Teachers, administrators, and support staff each play a major role in helping students and families suc-ceed but too often do not have the skills to support them. Later in this chapter we outline some important considerations for teachers and administrators when a new CLD student arrives in their classroom and school.

In addition to refugee children, a new category of "immigrants" has emerged in the CLD community that has its own set of unique challenges teachers need to recognize. Dreamers (DACA recipients) have become the focus of much political and media attention in recent years. Teachers need to be aware of the unique immigration limbo of these recipients.

What Is DACA?

Much of the public and policy debates of the past years have focused on those who have become known as dreamers or DACA recipients. Deferred Action for Childhood Arrivals (DACA) is a U.S. immigration policy that was established under the Obama administration, which allows some individuals in the United States who were brought to the country unlawfully as children to receive a renewable 2-year period of deferred action from deportation (Dickerson, 2018). This allows recipients to be eligible for a work permit or to pursue higher education. While many have called for an end to the program and the deportation of those covered by the policy, others harken back to the Supreme Court decision of *Plyler v. Doe*, acknowledging that children should not be punished for the actions of their parents. Regardless of where an individual teacher stands on the debate, it is important to recognize that the loss or the fear of loss of such a protection has an impact on children and families. Families throughout the United States live in fear that a parent, grandparent, spouse, or other family member may be deported. As a response to such stress, students' attitudes toward school may be affected.

Getting Started: How We View Our Students Matters

Too often teachers, classmates of CLD students, parents of classmates, and others working with CLD students assume a **deficit perspective** on the learning environment where ELL students are placed. Most teachers have good intentions but only are able to see the struggles and obstacles facing the student. Teachers readily identify what their CLD students cannot do but often do not consider the wide range of experiences, knowledge, perspectives, styles of learning, values, and languages these students and families bring with them into our schools and communities. In short, teachers do not always see their students in terms of the **funds of knowledge** (González et al., 2006) they bring to the classroom and wider community. While identifying student needs is an important consideration, teachers must see beyond these limitations by acknowledging the assets these students bring. This change of perspective can be transformative for teachers and students.

A salient example of this is represented by the following two cases. Hser Htoo, a 17-year-old and a junior in high school, struggled academically and linguistically but was a very capable artist who often drew for enjoyment. He had notebooks filled with drawings, cartoons, and other designs. Once his teacher perceived him as a talented artist, she began to make her assignments more pictorial than language based. Expressed admiration for his skills did not go unnoticed, and Hser Htoo began to show his art and feel pride in his ability. Assignments that allowed him to showcase his ability made them much less of a frustration, and he worked with enthusiasm. Purely pictorial assignments slowly merged with short, written texts or speech bubbles in his native Karen and later in English. Over time, Hser Htoo became a more proficient and confident English writer. The drawing in Figure 1.2 demonstrates how such pictorial assignments can act as a means for students to often describe some of their anxieties, fears, and experiences. Hser Htoo's drawing of his first day on the school bus demonstrates his artistic skills, but his speech bubble lets us in on the range of emotion he was feeling.

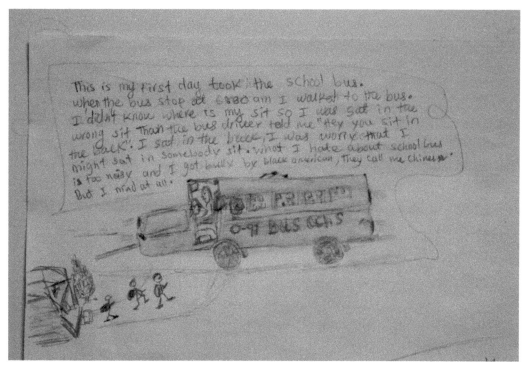

FIGURE 1.2 First day of school on the school bus.

Source:

The second example is of Hector, a 13-year-old from El Salvador. Hector struggled in math, and his teacher was desperate to find ways that she could be more culturally responsive in her approach to working with him on his math. She began trying to find out more of Hector's story so as to help integrate some of his funds of knowledge. When talking to the district's Spanish language interpreter she learned that Hector's family owned a small grocery store back in El Salvador and had recently opened a small convenience store not far from school. His teacher decided to visit the store to see if she could learn more about Hector. When she walked into the store she was surprised to see Hector working behind the register. After many visits she came to realize that Hector had many responsibilities at the store. He was an interpreter for his parents and various vendors and customers. He helped his father take care of inventory and helped with submitting various orders. He also helped his parents clean and stock shelves. She soon realized that Hector had many real-life math skills but that he associated math with Spanish since he always communicated with his father in Spanish. She came to realize what Hector lacked was the language of math in English. He had the ability but was unable to express himself. In response, she created math lessons that integrated concepts he was aware of from working at his family store. She also provided him experience with some of the authentic texts he was using at the store. She was able to collect various forms and applications that gave him real-world experience.

In both cases, teachers took an asset approach to how they viewed their student. By incorporating a CLD student's assets (home language, skills, funds of knowledge) into lessons, a teacher also sets an important precedent in the classroom and represents an example of **culturally responsive pedagogy (CRP)**. Other teachers, classmates, and parents will begin to recognize that their CLD classmates are valuable additions to the learning experience and the wider community. We suggest that teachers learn as much as they can about the unique backgrounds via student biographies, presented later in this chapter.

While respecting and integrating students' home culture and learning styles is important, it is also important that we acknowledge students' home language. Too often teachers and schools have "English-only" policies that result in students having a negative perception toward their home language. Students' home language needs to be seen as an asset, especially in a globalized world where speaking multiple languages is beneficial. Teachers also need to inform themselves about their students' home language so as to better understand the issues the student may be facing learning English. Most importantly, teachers need to inform parents that promoting the child's L1 at home is a positive attribute in the child's cognitive, emotional, and academic development. Too often parents wrongfully perceive of their language practices as obstructing their child's English development. The reality is that literacy skills in the learner's L1 are important in helping development L2 literacy skills. Importantly, the child will benefit by speaking their home language so as to develop healthy, communicative relationships with their parents and grandparents.

Teachers can help promote students' L1 in their classroom to the benefit of all students. By using books or other curricular material in students' home language, they will demonstrate respect for their language and help bridge the school-home divide. CLD students will begin to see the advantages associated with knowing an additional language and may begin to feel pride in their heritage language. Importantly, by incorporating languages like Spanish into the curriculum, all students will benefit from learning new words and phrases and the CLD student will benefit from his or her position as expert.

The Balancing Act

Like learning a new language, learning a new culture can be fraught with frustrations and misunderstandings. Some students may have very little experience with American culture and the norms of American schools. Consider all the school idioms that we use every day. Expressions like "hand in" and "exit ticket" are sure to confuse an English language learner. Other students may feel very American and reject their home culture and the values of their parents and grandparents. Incorporating the strategies addressed in this and later chapters will help teachers begin to be more culturally inclusive in their teaching practices. However, we must be sensitive to the individual person's needs and their process of acculturation.

The reality is that some CLD students do not want to be identified as anything but "student" and may resist being associated as representatives of their heritage culture. This creates a problem for the teacher who is hoping to be culturally responsive. Moreover, when a student has a negative attitude toward their home culture there invariably may be difficulties at home as they struggle with parental expectations. So, should a teacher incorporate the students' home culture and language when a student is resisting?

The answer to this and other questions related to CLD students depends on the individual student and the awareness of their teacher. The key lies in the teacher's ability to make each child feel pride in his or her cultural heritage. While culture may include ethnic pride or linguistic pride, it also includes a host of other attributes. This means that the teacher continually demonstrates a positive response to that culture and uses the child as a cultural insider rather than as a representative. This takes away the burden of being the poster child for any given culture. This may also address one of the reasons that some children do not like being identified as a cultural representative in the first place: It makes them feel that their identities are limited to a few stereotypes.

In practice, this demands some mindfulness on the part of teachers. Teachers have to first assess where the student stands in terms of their identity. Rather than making students representatives, we need to find subtler ways of legitimizing their home culture. For older students, questions about culture and identity can be parts of the curriculum. Discussions about the pros and cons of various cultural norms can help all students better understand their own identities and that of their families. For teachers, a genuine sense of interest, wonder, and curiosity is needed.

The teacher must be willing to learn more about other cultural values and beliefs. Ideally, teachers can draw from their own cross-cultural experiences or be willing to learn about the cultures of those children in their school. This would include some insight into the history, language, and culture (music, religion, famous popular personalities, geography, food, dance, film, arts). Ideally, these cultural expressions would all find their place in lessons and on the walls of classrooms and schools. This knowledge can also help teachers help students have a more positive association with their heritage culture. Students may take pride when they realize all the positives associated with their heritage. Negative perceptions of self and home can lead to children losing self-esteem and distancing them from their families. Creating student biographies is an important first step in better understanding your CLD student's individual story.

Student Biographies and Needs Assessment

Biographically driven, culturally responsive teaching is an important step in learning more about CLD students and being able to effectively address their needs (Herrera & Murry, 2016). Through student biographies, teachers begin to contextualize the CLD student's singular story. This information will help teachers better understand and address a student's academic, emotional, language, psychological, and social needs. By creating such biographies, teachers will begin to also view students as individuals and not simply categorize or stereotype them based on their ethnic or national background. The following eight considerations can provide teachers a starting point when creating student biographies.

Creating Student Biographies

1. Basic biographical information
   - Age: How old was the student when they arrived in the United States?
   - Country of birth:
   - Siblings: Are there siblings in school that might be able to assist you with information?
   - Parents or guardians: How can you make contact with parents?
   - How long has the student been in the country, the state, and the city?
   - Ethnicity: Students may come from an ethnic minority group from their home country. For example. Do not assume that someone who is "from Thailand" is ethnically Thai.

2. L1 considerations
   - What language(s) does the student speak at home?
   - What is their level of L1 proficiency in speaking, listening, reading, and writing?
   - What language system is the student's L1: alphabetic, syllabic, pictographic?
   - What is the directionality of the L1: left to right; right to left; top to bottom?
   - What is the word order of the L1: subject-object-verb; subject-verb-object?

3. Parental considerations
   - How can you contact the student's parent or guardian?
   - What is the parents' preferred language of communication?
   - What experience do the parents have with the U.S. education system?
   - Do parents know their role in supporting their children?
   - What are the parental funds of knowledge (González et al., 2006)?
   - What is the parents' literacy ability in their L1 and/or English?

4. Child's attitude toward home culture
   - In what ways does the child demonstrate pride or shame of home culture and language?
   - Has the student experienced trauma in their home country or on route to the United States?
   - How can teachers help promote pride in students' heritage culture and language?

5. Prior experiences with school
   - Does the child have any experience with school? Do parents have any formal education?

6. Political context
   - What was the child and family's experience in their home country?
   - What stressors/traumas might the child and/or family be under in the United States (fear of deportation, persecution of family members in the home country, deportation of family members)?
   - How are U.S. policies and the public rhetoric impacting immigrant families?

7. Language needs assessment   *(Continued)*
   - Begin to identify demonstrable language needs in English and establish goals accordingly.
   - Document characteristics of the learner's proficiency in speaking, listening, reading, and writing.

8. Asset perspective
   - What talents does the child demonstrate?
   - What are the student's interests inside and outside of school?
   - Who are the child's friends?
   - Who are the child's heroes?
   - What does the student do after school?
   - What are their responsibilities in the home?

Working with CLD students can be a rewarding and fascinating experience for teachers willing to include these students in their classrooms. We also encourage in-service and pre-service teachers to utilize our first-day checklist (appendices A and B) to help them start their experience with CLD students on the right foot.

The following "Tips for Teachers" section also provides some important insights for both pre-service and in-service teachers who prepare to work with CLD students and their families.

TIPS FOR TEACHERS!

What's in a Name?

There are a wide variety of naming conventions used across cultures. Do not assume that a student's name on the roster follows the same naming practices as in the United States. Look at a few naming practices from various cultures. Too often students get stuck with a name assigned to them, which offers teachers a perfect time to begin to recognize students' unique cultural conventions.

Deegala Dorage Mayuri Silva (Sri Lanka Singhalese): The first two names are paternal lineage names. The student's "personal name" is Mayuri and the family name is Silva.

Eh Taw (Love Truth) and Paw Htoo (Flower Gold) (Karen): These two ethnic Karen siblings do not share a "family name"; family names or surnames are not used in their culture.

Kim Mi Hyun (Korean): In Korean culture the family name proceeds other names.

Pedro Maria Rodriquez Lopez (Mexican): In this example, Lopez represents the father's first surname and Rodriquez is also a surname. According to Mexican naming conventions, a person's first surname (Rodriguez, in this case) is the father's first surname, and the second surname (Lopez, in this case) is the mother's first surname.

*Remember, some students may feel uncomfortable referring to their teacher as Ms. Julie or Mr. Brown as teachers are usually referred to with a title in many cultures.

Comprehensible Input and Working With Parents

A major consideration when working cross-culturally and cross-linguistically is to make ourselves understood. Here are a few tips when talking to CLD students and parents.

- Laughing at our mistakes: One way that can help set a relaxed mood is to demonstrate that language mistakes and miscues are funny and nothing to be ashamed of when speaking a new language. Teachers can model this by trying to say things in the student's L1. This should evoke a chuckle and set a friendly tone.

- Even though the school provides an interpreter, maintain eye contact with the parent in your discussions. Too often, teachers speak with the interpreter and not the parent.

- Parents often speak more English then they reveal. Be an empathetic language partner and speak slow and clear but not so slow and loud as to offend.

- Avoid idioms and other Americanisms that may be new to students and parents.

Questions to Consider

1. Consider the introductory quote from December Htoo and list all the frustrations that CLD students face in school and society. What are your thoughts on his belief that language should be addressed first? Consider how you might feel in his shoes.
2. Consider one of the legal decisions related to CLD students and try and find more information about that particular decision and how it relates to working with CLD students and families.

3. Create an activity you might employ whenever you have a new CLD student that will help that student feel included. Make sure the activity includes some means for everyone to learn how to pronounce the student's name.
4. Discuss any cross-cultural experiences that you have had and how they have affected your views on cross-cultural and cross-linguistic communication.
5. Consider one of the following student profiles. Identify the key issues and ways you might address the needs of the particular student and teacher.

Student Profiles

The following CLD student profiles are from teachers writing about their students in the first week of a new semester. These also represent excellent student biographies, as each demonstrates how well informed the teacher is of their student. The names and other information have been changed in order to maintain anonymity.

Student Profile 1: Edgar and Attendance

Edgar (prefers to be called Eddy) Mario Lopez is an outgoing and rambunctious 15-year-old sophomore in high school. He was born in the United States to Mexican parents. Edgar speaks Spanish at home with his parents and grandmother but English with his younger siblings. He has very limited Spanish writing proficiency. He is taking Spanish 1, and his teacher told me that he has a very difficult time spelling and that his Spanish grammar is very poor. He has been identified as an ELL since he arrived in the district and receives English language support three times each week, but I don't know what he is doing. It is supposed to be aligned with my classes, but since he is bussed to another school for ESL, I've never met his teacher there. He is a class clown, and his attendance has been poor the first weeks of school. His ninth-grade teacher indicated that his attendance started to slide at the end of last school year, and she said he was with the "wrong crowd" and was "maybe in a gang." No prior records of him exist because he has only been in the district the past 2 years. I'm not sure of the gang thing, as I don't see any signs, but I don't know. One of his friends in class said he thought something was going on at home, but he wasn't sure. *What can I do to get Edgar to school?*

Student Profile 2: Issues of Motivation

Asnage, pronounced "Az Na Jae," Normand is 12 years old and in sixth grade. He and his family are from Haiti. Asnage's L1 is Haitian Creole. His language proficiency in his L1 is mostly conversational. He is literate in French Creole and speaks this language at home with relatives. Asnage generally appears to show a positive attitude toward his L1 and home culture. When given the chance, he likes to talk about places in Haiti. However, he exclusively uses English at school and has been hesitant to talk about what life was like in Haiti. Asnage and his family are refugees from Haiti after the earthquake in 2010. They arrived in the Midwest in 2012 after 2 years with an aunt in Miami. As a sixth-grade student, Asnage has only been at our middle school for 7 months. His mom comes to all our parent-teacher conferences and is involved, and he is at grade level or above in math. He is polite and quiet but very unmotivated. Everyone seems to like him, but he seems tired every day and too laid back. His English writing makes all his classes but math difficult, and he seems to be giving up with school. *What do I need to do to motivate Asnage?*

Student Profile 3: Missing Your Best Friend

June, pronounced the same as the month, Paw, pronounced like a cat's "paw," is ethnic Karen, 11 years old, and in fifth grade. Her parents are from Burma (Myanmar), but she was born in a Thai refugee camp. According to the translator at school, she speaks Karen at home with her mom, grandma, and siblings, is the oldest of five, and is really active at her Karen church. She has lived in the United States for 3 years. June is very quiet but excels in drawing and singing. She often wears her Karen shirt to school. Her previous teachers held her back so that she should be in sixth grade. She is disappointed and pretty despondent this year because she is no longer in class with her cousin, Moo Moo (like the sound of a cow!). Moo Moo is a model student in all her subjects and helps out with June Paw and other Karen kids. *Why were these two kids separated? How can I reach June? She seems a million miles away!*

Student Profile 4: Identifying Issues Related to English Acquisition

Sofia is a 6-year-old kindergartner from Mexico. I am not sure when she and her family arrived in the United States, but I know she now lives with her mom and younger brother. She is a joy in class but demonstrates a few language issues I have identified in week one. Some errors I found are in pronunciation, vocabulary, speaking, writing, and grammar. When pronouncing words, Sofia says her words long and slow. Her "v" is often replaced with "b." Her vocabulary is also still developing. On the district-wide assessment, vocabulary is one of her lowest scores. She has used the word "fork" when talking about a spoon and often must ask what a word means. When speaking, her words are often out of order, and her writing is also. She will write sentences that say, "The dog funny. The dog brown." When writing she leaves out verbs, like /is/, and often mixes up the words "he" and "she." Some errors are common in kindergarten, and others are due to her first language, I think. *How can I begin to address her needs when I have 16 other kids in class?*

References

Dickerson, C. (2018). What Is DACA? And how did it end up in the Supreme Court. *New York Times*. https://www.nytimes.com/2019/11/12/us/daca-supreme-court.html

Georgis, R., Gokiert, R. J., Ford, D. M., & Ali, M. (2014). Creating inclusive parent engagement practices: Lessons learned from a school community collaborative supporting newcomer refugee families. *Multicultural Education, 21*(3/4), 23–27.

González, N., & Moll, L. C. (1995). Funds of knowledge for teaching in Latino households. *Urban Education, 29*(4), 443–470.

González, N., Moll, L. C., & Amanti, C. (Eds.). (2006). *Funds of knowledge: Theorizing practices in households, communities, and classrooms*. Routledge.

Herrera, S. G., & Murry, K. G. (2006). Mastering ESL and Bilingual Methods: Differentiated Instruction for Culturally and Linguistically Diverse (CLD) Students. *Education Review/Reseñas Educativas/Resenhas Educativas*.

Hymes, D. (1972). On communicative competence. *Sociolinguistics*, 269–293.

Igielnik, R., & Krogstad, J. M. (2017, February 3). *Where refugees to the U.S. come from*. Pew Research Center. https://www.pewresearch.org/fact-tank/2017/02/03/where-refugees-to-the-u-s-come-from/

Ladson-Billings, G. (1995). Toward a theory of culturally relevant pedagogy. *American Educational Research Journal, 32*(3), 465–491.

Matthews, J. (2008). Schooling and settlement: Refugee education in Australia. *International studies in Sociology of Education, 18*(1), 31–45.

Migration Policy Institute. (n.d.). *ELL information center*. https://www.migrationpolicy.org/programs/ell-information-center

Migration Policy Institute. (2019, June 13). *Refugees and asylees in the United States*. https://reliefweb.int/report/united-states-america/refugees-and-asylees-united-states

National Center for Educational Statistics. (n.d.). *Fast facts: Back to school statistics*. https://nces.ed.gov/fastfacts/display.asp?id=372

National Center for Educational Statistics. (2018). English language learners in public schools. *The Condition of Education 2018*. https://nces.ed.gov/programs/coe/pdf/Indicator_CGF/coe_cgf_2018_05.pdf

National Center for Educational Statistics. (2019a, February). *Indicator 8: English language learners in public schools*. https://nces.ed.gov/programs/raceindicators/indicator_RBC.asp

National Center for Educational Statistics. (2019b, May). *English language learners in public schools*. https://nces.ed.gov/programs/coe/indicator_cgf.asp

National Clearinghouse for English Language Acquisition. (2019). *English learner trends from the nation's report card*. https://ncela.ed.gov/files/fast_facts/ELs-NAEP_Card.pdf

Ngai, M. (1999). The Architecture of Race in American Immigration Law: A Reexamination of the Immigration Act of 1924. *Journal of American History*, 86(1), 67–92. https://doi.org/10.2307/2567407

Olivas, M. A. (2012). *No undocumented child left behind:* Plyler v. Doe *and the education of undocumented schoolchildren*. New York University Press.

Plyler v. Doe, 457 U.S. 202, 230 (1982)

Ragsdale, S. (2013). Immigrants in the United States of America. *Advances in Historical Studies*, 2(3), 167–174.

Rhodes, R. L., Ochoa, S. H., & Ortiz, S. O. (2005). *Assessing culturally and linguistically diverse students: A practical guide*. Guilford.

Roberts, C. (1994). Transferring literacy skills from L1 to L2: From theory to practice. *Journal of Educational Issues of Language Minority Students*, 13, 209–221.

Sudbeck, Kristine M. (2015). Educational Language Planning and Policy in Nebraska: An Historical Overview. *The Nebraska Educator: A Student-Led Journal*. 25. http://digitalcommons.unl.edu/nebeducator/25

Sugarman, S. D., & Widess, E. G. (1974). Equal protection for non-English-speaking school children: *Lau v. Nichols*. *Calif. Law Review*, 62(1), 157–182.

UNHCR, the UN Refugee Agency. What is a Refugee? Definition and Meaning: USA for UNHCR. (n.d.). https://www.unrefugees.org/refugee-facts/what-is-a-refugee/

Chapter 2

Second Language Acquisition
From Theory to Practice

Nabat Erdogan

Glossary

Term/acronym	Meaning	Usage
Audiolingual method	A language teaching or learning method that emphasizes speaking and listening as the most essential language skills and relies on drilling, repetition, and memorization in language learning	Earlier known as the Army method, it was used specifically for Army personnel during World War II so that they could learn foreign languages faster.
Behaviorism	An environmentalist theory that views language learning as a process of habit formation through experience and nurture	Widely used as Skinner's behaviorism in the research literature
BICS	Basic interpersonal communicative skills	Conversational fluency in a language that takes about 2 years for second or foreign language learners to attain
CALP	Cognitive academic language proficiency	Academic proficiency in oral and written modes of a language that takes about 5–7 or more years for second or foreign language learners to achieve
CPH	Critical period hypothesis	A hypothesis that claims that full native-like language proficiency can only be achieved between ages 0–13, before puberty
Creative aspect of language use	An expression used by Noam Chomsky to explain the innovative uses of language	Used to refer to the ability to produce new and innovative utterances by language speakers

(Continued)

Term/acronym	Meaning	Usage
CUP model	Common underlying proficiency model	A model of bilingualism that claims that cognitive and academic proficiencies are interdependent and transferrable across languages
FDH	Fundamental difference hypothesis	A hypothesis that claims that children and adults acquire languages differently since children have direct access to universal grammar (UG) and adults do not
Fossilization	A concept used in SLA literature to explain permanent errors in adult second language.	Used to refer to the process in which incorrect linguistic features become permanent errors in adult second language, despite adequate motivation to learn, continuous exposure to the L2 input, and ample opportunities for communicative practice
Innateness theory	A theory proposed by Noam Chomsky that claims that humans are born with a natural propensity for language learning.	Used to claim the existence of innate properties of language that enable children to master their native language and its abstract rules quickly and effortlessly
Input	Information received through listening or reading in a language	Used to describe the language that the learner is exposed to
LAD	Language acquisition device	A built-in mechanism that contains language universals or universal grammar and predisposes humans to a systematic acquisition of language, as proposed by Noam Chomsky
Language acquisition theory	An SLA theory proposed by Stephen Krashen that is based on five fundamental tenets.	Includes five hypotheses: (a) the acquisition-learning hypothesis; (b) the natural order hypothesis; (c) the monitor hypothesis; (d) the comprehension hypothesis; (e) the affective filter hypothesis
Natural approach	A language teaching or learning approach proposed by Stephen Krashen and Tracy Terrell that stresses the importance of authentic language input and interaction.	Views language as a vehicle for communicating meaning and messages and emphasizes the importance of teaching L2 communicative abilities
Negative transfer	Linguistic transfer that occurs when structures of L1 and L2 do not overlap, which leads to systematic errors in L2	Used to refer to the linguistic transfer that results in systematic errors in L2

Term/acronym	Meaning	Usage
Output	Spoken or written piece of information that is produced in a language	Used to describe the language that is produced by the learner
Positive transfer	Linguistic transfer that occurs when the features of L1 and L2 are similar, which facilitates L2 learning	Used to refer to the linguistic transfer that facilitates L2 learning
Prism model	A language acquisition model that focuses on four major developmental processes—sociocultural, linguistic, academic, and cognitive—involved in the acquisition of L1 and L2	Used to predict the major school factors that affect learners' second language acquisition
Productive skills	Language skills required to produce speaking (oral language) and writing (written language)	Used to refer to speaking and writing
Receptive skills	Language skills required to receive and understand listening and reading	Used to refer to listening and reading
Silent period	The period during which the learner does not produce language	Used to refer to the preproduction stage of L2 acquisition that usually lasts up to 6 months
SLA	Second language acquisition	Used to denote (a) a process of learning or acquiring a language other than native; (b) an academic field that studies the process of learning or acquiring second or foreign languages
Tabula rasa	A Latin phrase meaning "blank slate"	A term frequently used by behaviorists to claim that all children are born with a "blank slate" (i.e., without any built-in mental content) and that all knowledge (including language learning) comes from experience and nurture
UG	Universal grammar	The blueprint for the grammar of any language; a Chomskyan theory that asserts that all humans are born with a predetermined listing of language universals that are contained in the so-called "language acquisition device"

What Is Language Acquisition?

Language is a complex system that is acquired (or learned) and used by humans to communicate with one another. All linguistically or cognitively unimpaired humans acquire their native or first language (L1) in early childhood. They do it through social interaction, without any formal education. Learning a second language (L2), however, can occur informally, in a natural environment, or formally, through classroom instruction. The process of learning or acquiring a language other than the first language is called **second language acquisition** (SLA). SLA is also the name of an academic field that studies the process of learning or acquiring a second or foreign language.

Whether it be a first, second, or foreign language, acquisition of a language in general requires extensive exposure to the target language. Many documented cases of children raised by animals or locked in solitary confinement for long years report that those children who were isolated from human contact could never learn to speak properly or perfectly (Corballis, 2017; Newton, 2003). Such cases once again point to the fact that humans need to be in society to be able to learn and speak a language. But how is language acquired or learned? What are the theories behind the acquisition of language? We will look into different language acquisition theories to answer these questions in the next section of this chapter.

Theories of Language Acquisition

Language acquisition and development theories have been the focus of research for many decades. Most of these theories have originated from the disciplines of philosophy and linguistics and later influenced the development of first and second language acquisition theories. Language acquisition theories have mostly centered around the distinction between "nature" and "nurture," in other words, innateness and environmental factors. While innatists believe that humans have biologically endowed abilities to learn languages, environmentalists insist that nurture—education and training—is the key to language learning.

One of the most widely known environmentalist theories is **behaviorism.** Developed by Skinner, the behaviorist approach to learning was based on the premise that all humans are born with a **tabula rasa** or **blank slate,** and that language learning is a process of habit formation (Griffiths, 2008; Sanz, & Igoa, 2012). According to behaviorists, language is learned through "mimicry, memorization, and analogy" (Carrasquillo, 1994, p. 7). The behaviorist approach to language learning and teaching brought about the **audiolingual method,** initially known as the **Army method,** which was designed specifically for Army personnel during World War II so that they could learn foreign languages faster (Danesi, 2003). Proponents of the audiolingual method believed that speaking and listening are the most essential language skills and emphasized the importance of drilling and memorization in language learning. However, in the 1960s, with the emergence of nativist theories of language acquisition, the behaviorist approach to language learning started to fade away. The prominent American linguist Noam Chomsky's **innateness theory** began to challenge the behavioristic views.

Chomsky argued that behaviorism could not alone account for language acquisition since input cannot provide all possible structures that humans are able to create (Carrasquillo, 1994; Karmiloff & Karmiloff-Smith, 2002). Chomsky viewed language learning as a creative process that does not depend solely on habits and conditioning. He claimed the existence of innate properties of language that enable children to master their native language and its abstract rules in a short period of time. According to Chomsky, it is because of these innate properties of language that children are able to create new, grammatically acceptable and comprehensible utterances that conform to the rules that they have internalized subconsciously in their native language. Chomsky (2006) uses the phrase "**the creative aspect of language use**" (p. 6) to describe this phenomenon—a child's use of innovative sentences he or she has never heard before. He explains this innate ability by way of **universal grammar** (UG), the blueprint for the grammar of any language, that accommodates the creative aspect of language use or that of a built-in device known as a **language acquisition device** (LAD). According to nativists, it is this built-in mechanism that predisposes humans to a systematic acquisition of language.

In the late 1970s and early 1980s, the linguist Stephen Krashen, inspired by Noam Chomsky's nativist theory of first language acquisition, proposed one of the most famous and influential second language acquisition theories, which he initially called the **monitor model** (also known as the input hypothesis), but later renamed as **language acquisition theory** (Brown, 2007; Knibbeler, 1989). Krashen's language acquisition theory includes five hypotheses: (a) the acquisition-learning hypothesis; (b) the natural order hypothesis; (c) the monitor hypothesis; (d) the comprehension hypothesis; and (e) the affective filter hypothesis.

According to the **acquisition-learning hypothesis,** humans can either learn or acquire language, and there are clear differences between *learning* and *acquiring*. **Language acquisition** is a subconscious process (which is sometimes described as "picking up" a language) that happens naturally in informal situations or through interaction, while **language learning** occurs consciously, mostly in the classroom, through formal instruction. Language acquisition is an implicit process since the focus is on meaning or communication rather than form, whereas language learning is mostly explicit. Even though many might think that acquisition is specific to children, research shows that both children and adults can subconsciously acquire language by the creative construction process (James & Westney, 1981; VanPatten & Rothman, 2015). Table 2.1 summarizes the differences between language acquisition and language learning.

FIGURE 2.1 Stephen Krashen (1972), the founder of the monitor model, also known as the input hypothesis.

Source: Copyright © by University of Southern California (CC BY-SA 4.0) at https://commons.wikimedia.org/wiki/File:Stephen_Krashen.jpg.

The **natural order hypothesis** claims that second language learners acquire the features of the target language in a predictable order. For example, the *-ing* marker (as in *reading*) is acquired earlier than the third-person singular *–s* (as in *reads*). According to this hypothesis, the order of acquisition does not depend on how simple or complicated the

TABLE 2.1 Differences Between Language Acquisition and Language Learning

Acquisition	Learning
Natural	artificial
informal situations (interaction)	formal situations (instruction)
Implicit	explicit
subconscious	conscious
focus on meaning/communication	focus on form

Progressive –*ing* (*reading*)
Plural –*s* (*books*)
Copula *to be* (*Reading is fun*)

Progressive Auxiliary *to be* (*He is reading*)
Indefinite and Definite Articles *a – the* (*a book – the book*)

Irregular Past Tense Forms (*sit – sat – sat; eat – ate – eaten*)

Regular Past Tense Form (*open – opened; count – counted*)
Third Person Singular –*s* (*He reads every day*)
Possessive –*s* (*Tolstoy's novels are interesting to read*)

FIGURE 2.2 Average order of acquisition of grammatical morphemes in English. Adapted from Krashen and Terrell (1983).

Source:

rules of the target language "look." The rules that may look complicated to a linguist or a grammarian may sometimes be acquired late, or vice versa. Although not every language acquirer proceeds in the same order, the variation among them is not extreme. Figure 2.2 describes the average order of acquisition of grammatical morphemes for English language learners (ELLs). This order also mostly holds true for child first-language acquisition (Krashen & Terrell, 1983).

The **monitor hypothesis** asserts that the grammar rules that are learned by language learners only serve as a monitor or editor. Krashen (2013) contends that when language learners initiate an utterance in the target language, the sentence (both in spoken and written form) pops into their mind only thanks to their subconsciously acquired competence. The role of the "conscious monitor" or "conscious learning" in this process is limited to internally scanning the utterance that is about to be produced (or that has already been generated) and consciously making any error corrections. To activate and use this "conscious monitor" successfully, the learner needs (a) to know the rules of the target language, (b) to think about the correctness of the form, and (c) to have enough time to think about grammar rules in order to "monitor" and correct the errors in their speech. Since this self-correction process takes some time, it can decrease the language learner's fluency in production, which means that when conscious learning is involved in language production, **output**—the

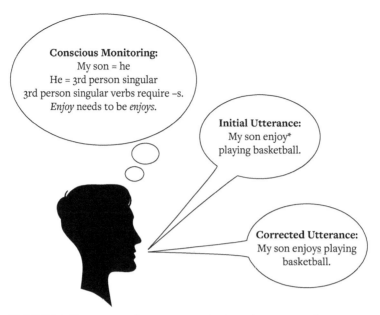

FIGURE 2.3 The process of conscious monitoring in language production.

Source: Copyright © 2018 Depositphotos/tartila.stock.gmail.com.

learner's speech or writing—can be delayed. Based on this rationale, Krashen (2013) asserts that fluency in language production comes from what is acquired subconsciously, in natural communication. Figure 2.3 demonstrates the process of conscious monitoring in second or foreign language production.

The **comprehension hypothesis,** which is described as "the centerpiece of language acquisition theory" (Krashen, 2013, p. 3), is largely employed in second language education. This hypothesis claims that language learners move from i (input) to i+1 (input+1) by enough comprehensible input. **Comprehensible input** is defined as language that is slightly beyond the learner's current level of competence. **Input** is provided to language learners in two forms: through listening and reading. It is important to know that interesting, comprehensible, age-appropriate, and culturally relevant input (listening and reading texts, activities, etc.) can promote the language acquisition process. The language that the learner has already acquired, his or her knowledge of the world, the context of communication, and extra-linguistic support or nonverbal means of communication such as pictures, actions, mimics, gestures, and so on can also help to make language comprehensible.

The **affective filter hypothesis** posits that although comprehensible input is necessary for language acquisition, it is not sufficient since language learners must be open to "input," in other words, have a low affective filter. While affective variables, such as the learner's motivation, attitude (to the target language, to the teachers, to other learners, etc.), anxiety, and self-confidence, do not directly impact language acquisition, they prevent input from reaching the Chomskyan "language acquisition device"—the part of the brain responsible for language acquisition. As a result, the affective filter simply blocks input, and thus hinders acquisition.

Based on **language acquisition theory**, Krashen and Terrell (1983) developed a new philosophy of language teaching which they called the **natural approach**. According to this approach, language is a vehicle for communicating meaning and messages, and successful language instruction should focus on teaching communicative abilities (Salim, 2001). There is no doubt that Krashen's language acquisition theory and the natural approach emerging from this theory have substantially impacted second language learning and teaching; however, they still fail to cover all necessary aspects of language learning. Language learning is not about communicative proficiency only, but also about content or academic proficiency. In this regard, Cummins's **basic interpersonal communicative skills (BICS) and cognitive academic langauge proficiency (CALP) theory** opened a new trend in language learning, teaching, and assessment. Cummins (2008) introduced the distinction between BICS and CALP in order to draw educators' attention to the timelines and challenges that L2 learners encounter as they try to catch up to their peers in academic aspects of the school language. According to this theory, it requires about 2–3 years to attain BICS, in other words, conversational fluency in L2, whereas it takes 5–7 or more years to reach CALP or academic proficiency in oral (listening and speaking) and written (reading and writing) modes of the target language. Achieving BICS in a second language is not enough for academic success in that language. In order for non-English speaking children to succeed in the mainstream classroom, they need to have developed CALP, which is "the ability to deal with context-reduced, cognitively demanding language and content" in English (Faltis, 1997, p. 192). Cummins (2001) posits that literacy and academic proficiency in L1 can promote the attainment of CALP in L2 since it is assumed that the cognitive and academic proficiencies underlying literacy skills in L1 and L2 are interdependent and transferrable, which means that a language learner who has strong literacy skills in his or her L1 does not have to learn or relearn the same skills in L2, but just needs to transfer and apply those skills to L2. Cummins (2001) calls this interdependence between L1 and L2 cognitive and academic proficiencies a **common underlying proficiency (CUP) model** of bilingualism.

Cummins's BICS and CALP theory urged many researchers, educators, and test developers to think about the importance of academic English insomuch that newly developed language proficiency assessments were designed to measure language learners' academic English as well as their communicative English. For example, one of the most widely used English language proficiency assessments, Assessing Comprehension and Communication in English State-to-State (ACCESS) for ELLs, is based on this principle. Developed by the WIDA (World-Class Instructional Design and Assessment) Consortium and administered in 38 U.S. states now, ACCESS for ELLs claims to assess social and instructional English as well as the content language (i.e., the language associated with language arts, mathematics, science, and social studies within the school context across the four language domains (speaking, listening, reading, and writing). In order to pass this language proficiency assessment, ELLs need to receive robust language and content instruction, which means that all educators (English as a second language (ESL) teachers as well as classroom and content teachers, and sometimes even special education teachers in case the learner receives both special education and ELL services) share the responsibility for the education of ELLs.

Krashen's language acquisition theory and Cummins's BICS/CALP theory gave rise to the emergence of another very influential language acquisition model, the **prism model,** which recognized and considered broader aspects of language acquisition and learning. Developed by Collier and Thomas in 1990s, the prism model asserts that there are four major developmental processes—sociocultural, linguistic, academic, and cognitive—that all children experience in school, and these developmental processes need to be supported at school for language acquisition and learning to take place both in L1 and L2 (Collier & Thomas, 2007). This model emphasizes the importance of bilingual education and the need to develop both students' L1 and L2 acquisition and learning for their overall achievement in schools. Figure 2.4 visually demonstrates the sociocultural,

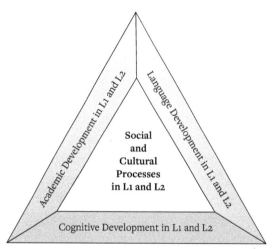

FIGURE 2.4 The prism model developed by Collier & Thomas (2007).

Source: Adapted from Virginia P. Collier and Wayne P. Thomas, "Predicting Second Language Academic Success in English Using the Prism Model," International Handbook of English Language Teaching, ed. Jim Cummins and Chris Davison, pp. 334. Copyright © 2007 by Springer Nature.

linguistic, academic, and cognitive components of the prism model that drive the acquisition of L1 and L2.

The eight dimensions (four processes, each in L1 and L2) of the prism model are interdependent and must work together for the student to receive the greatest benefit. Social and cultural processes occurring in each student's everyday life in all contexts (home, school, community, etc.) are central to that student's acquisition of language. It is on this level where Collier and Thomas's prism model overlaps with Krashen's language acquisition theory; both theories focus on affective factors surrounding language learners in their everyday lives. The *language development* piece of the prism model focuses on linguistic processes, which involve both subconscious and conscious aspects of language development. This component justifies both nativist and environmentalist theories of language acquisition and teaching. It is suggested that students' L1 oral and written systems must be developed in order to assure their cognitive and academic success in L2. The language development component strongly encourages bilingual education. The third component of the model, *academic development,* claims that academic knowledge and conceptual development transfers from the first language to the second language. This component supports Cummins's common underlying proficiency (CUP) model, which is based on the rationale that literacy-related aspects of a bilingual student's proficiency in L1 and L2 are common or interdependent across languages. The academic development piece of the prism model underscores the importance of developing bilinguals' academic knowledge and skills in both L1 and L2. The *cognitive development* component of the model highlights the crucial role of cognitive development in children's L1 for their academic success in L2.

To provide effective language and content instruction for English learners requires more than knowing different theories of language acquisition. Educators working with ELLs also need to be knowledgeable about the stages and approximate time frame of second language acquisition, as well as learner characteristics in each stage of L2 acquisition—the concepts that are discussed in the next section of the chapter.

Stages of Second Language Acquisition

It is important for educators to know every ELL's language acquisition stage for effective curriculum design, instruction, and assessment for the learner. According to extensive research and analysis of L2 learners' language developmental processes (Haynes, 2007; Hill & Miller, 2013; Krashen & Terrell, 1983), there are five stages of acquisition of a language other than the native language: (1) preproduction; (2) early production; (3) speech emergence; (4) intermediate fluency; and (5) advanced fluency.

Learners in the **preproduction stage** of L2 acquisition have minimal comprehension and very limited vocabulary. They usually repeat what their teacher says and do not produce language. They mostly use gestures (nodding, pointing, etc.), movements, or pictures to communicate and show comprehension. Learners are mostly silent in this stage. However, it does not mean that this stage is unproductive and the students are not learning. Learners at this stage of L2 acquisition are in the process of improving their receptive (listening and reading) skills in the target language. This stage, also known as the **silent period** in SLA literature, usually takes up to 6 months. However, depending on other affecting factors, it can also last longer than 6 months for some language learners. During this time period, teachers of silent students can feel challenged and think that they need to force their learners to speak in L2. However, forcing silent students to speak can raise the students' affective filter and completely inhibit their participation in class. Therefore, teachers of beginner ELLs need to be patient and give the students the time they need to become ready to produce the target language. It is recommended that teachers give the learners in this stage of L2 acquisition the questions that allow the students to draw or show their answers. For example, prompts such as "Show me ..."; "Circle the ..."; "Where is ... ?" and so on are appropriate for the students in this stage of SLA (Hill & Miller, 2013).

In the **early production** stage of second language acquisition, learners already have somewhat improved vocabulary and comprehension, and they can understand and use about 1,000 words. Learners in this stage are able to speak in one- or two-word sentences. They use easy grammatical forms (for example, present tense) and familiar phrases. This stage can last from 6 months to 1 year. At this stage, students are just becoming ready to participate in whole-class activities; therefore, it is recommended that teachers give them frequent opportunities to do so. In addition, the students in this phase of L2 acquisition can respond to yes/no, either/or, who, what, and how many questions. Knowing and applying these tips can help teachers scaffold and support ELLs' language and content learning during the early production stage of SLA.

Learners at the **speech emergence** stage have good comprehension of receptive language (listening and reading) and can produce simple sentences. At this stage, they have already developed a vocabulary of about 3,000 words that they can understand and use in their speech and writing. Although their sentences may not always be grammatically correct, they are still comprehensible. Moreover, learners at this stage can already understand short and simplified academic texts with some support and scaffolding. These learners should be encouraged to participate in discussions (preferably, small-group discussions) and writing activities in literacy-rich content area (math, social studies, science, etc.) classrooms. Learners at the speech emergence stage can respond to why and how questions with short and one-sentence answers. The approximate time frame for this stage is 1–3 years.

The **intermediate fluency** stage is characterized by learners who have excellent listening and reading comprehension and increased understanding of academic texts in content areas. These learners already possess a vocabulary of about 6,000 words that they actively use in their productive language. They make few grammatical errors in their speech and writing. They can use more complex sentences and grammatical structures. At this stage, learners feel more confident to participate in whole-group discussions in the classroom. They can answer the questions that require more than a one-sentence response. Hill and Miller (2013) recommend that teachers ask these students questions starting with "What would happen if ... ?" or "Why do you think ... ?" that require the explanation of their thoughts using more than one sentence. It takes language learners 3–5 years to reach this stage of L2 acquisition.

The last stage of L2 acquisition is the **advanced fluency** stage. Learners at this stage have already acquired near-native proficiency in L2. They can understand and produce complex academic language. They can participate in all classroom activities (discussions, collaborative work, presentations, etc.) as their native-speaking peers. It can take a language learner 5–7 or more years to get to this level of language proficiency. This stage is when learners are very close to acquiring or have already acquired cognitive academic language proficiency (CALP) in L2. Table 2.2 summarizes the characteristics of each SLA stage.

Knowing English learners' second language acquisition stages can guide educators when selecting the most effective language teaching methods, strategies, and materials for their learners. However, teachers of ELLs should not forget that there are also other important factors, such as the ones discussed in the next two sections of the chapter, that affect learners' acquisition of English.

Age and Second Language Acquisition

Second language acquisition literature has focused on many factors, such as motivation, attitude, intelligence, and personality, that affect language learning. Age, however, is probably one of the most influential and widely discussed factors with regard to language learning. There are several hypotheses suggesting that children learn languages better than adults. One of the most popular hypotheses regarding this concept is the **critical period hypothesis** (CPH) initially proposed by Penfield and Roberts (1959) and later improved by Lenneberg (1967). Although this hypothesis was first proposed in regard to the acquisition of native language by children, later researchers also considered the possibility of the same critical period for L2 acquisition (Stewart, 2003). The CPH claims that there is a genetically or biologically determined time frame for language acquisition, and humans can only achieve full native-like competence in a language within this period, which starts at birth (age 0) and ends at puberty (between ages 9–13 depending on gender, individual factors, and so on). According

TABLE 2.2 Stages of Second Language Acquisition. Adapted From Hill and Miller (2013).

Stages of SLA	Characteristics	Approximate time frame	Recommended prompts and questions
Preproduction	The language learner • has minimal comprehension and very limited vocabulary; • usually repeats after others; • is developing his or her receptive skills in L2; • does not produce language; and • mostly uses gestures, movements, or pictures to communicate and show comprehension.	0–6 months or some-times longer based on individual factors	Show me ... Circle the ... Where is ... ? Who has ... ?
Early production	The language learner • has somewhat improved vocabulary and comprehension; • can understand and use about 1,000 words; • is able to speak in one- or two-word sentences; and • uses easy grammatical forms and familiar phrases.	6 months–1 year	Yes/no questions Either/or questions Who, what, and how many questions
Speech emergence	The language learner • has good listening and reading comprehension; • can produce simple sentences; • can understand and use about 3,000 words; • makes grammatical and pronunciation errors; and • can understand short and simplified academic texts with some support and scaffolding.	1–3 years	Why ... ? How ... ? Explain ... Questions with short and one-sentence answers
Intermediate fluency	The language learner • has excellent listening and reading comprehension; • has increased understanding of academic texts in content areas; • can understand and use about 6,000 words; • makes few grammatical errors; and • uses more complex sentences and grammatical structures.	3–5 years	What would happen if ... ? Why do you think ... ? Questions with more than a one-sentence answer
Advanced fluency	The language learner • has already acquired near-native proficiency in L2; • can understand and produce complex academic language; and • can participate in all classroom activities as his or her native-speaking peers.	5–7 years or more	Decide if ... Retell ...

Adapted from Jane D. Hill and Kristen Miller, "Stages of Second-Language Acquisition," Classroom Instruction that Works with English Language Learners. pp. 11-24. Copyright © 2013 by McREL International.

to this hypothesis, after the critical period ends, a person can never reach full native-like mastery of any language, at least in the phonological aspects or native-like pronunciation of the target language (de Groot, 2011). This hypothesis urges schools and educators to design effective second language development programs as well as ensure strong L2 instruction for children as early as possible, particularly in the elementary grades, for the students' ultimate attainment of the second language. The CPH also has implications for parents with regard to providing L2 learning opportunities for their children at early ages.

Another hypothesis closely related to the CPH is the **fundamental difference hypothesis** (FDH) proposed by Bley-Vroman (1989). According to FDH, there is a "fundamental difference" between child and adult language acquisition that lies in the rationale that children have direct access to universal grammar (UG) whereas adults do not. In other words, children acquire L2 parameters subconsciously and implicitly, without paying much attention to form or grammar of the language, while adults rely on their knowledge of L1 grammar and use their problem-solving skills to consciously transfer their L1 knowledge to the L2 production. Stewart (2003) asserts that adult learners' L2 grammar is less native like and less uniform across individuals than that of children because adults vary in their ability to use their problem-solving skills when transferring their L1 grammar knowledge to L2. Moreover, language transfer may not always be successful. The phenomenon known as **negative transfer** can also adversely affect adult L2 acquisition. Negative transfer occurs when structures of L1 and L2 do not overlap, which leads to systematic errors in L2. For example, if adjectives follow nouns in a learner's first language (such as *manzana roja* (*apple + red*) in Spanish), the learner may tend to carry over the same word order to L2 in which this structure is not grammatically acceptable (for example, *apple red* is not grammatically correct in English). However, if the features of L1 and L2 are similar (for example, *manzana roja* (*apple + red*) in Spanish has the same word order as *pomme rouge* (*apple + red*) in French), a **positive transfer** occurs, which facilitates L2 learning.

Negative transfer is not the only limitation that hinders native-like acquisition of L2 by adults. Most adult L2 learners also experience a phenomenon called **fossilization**. First introduced by Selinker (1972), fossilization refers to the process in which incorrect linguistic features become permanent errors in adult second language, despite adequate motivation to learn, continuous exposure to the L2 input, and ample opportunities for communicative practice (Han, 2004). It is believed that negative transfer from L1 to L2 is the potential cause of fossilization (Nakuma, 1998; Selinker, 1972). Some aspects of L2 vocabulary usage, grammar, and pronunciation may undergo negative transfer from L1 and become fossilized in adult oral (speaking) and written (writing) L2 production. For example, if you hear a Russian learner of English repeatedly say *Fank* you* or *Sank* you* instead of *Thank you*, it is most probably an example of a phonological or pronunciation error resulting from fossilization. You may also hear a Russian learner of English use a sentence like *We with wife went to the movies* instead of *My wife and I went to the movies*. This error is an example of fossilized grammar, which results from word-for-word translation from Russian into English. While fossilized features of grammar sound odd, non-native, and sometimes even funny, fossilized pronunciation errors contribute to foreign accent in L2 speech. Such errors can also result in misunderstandings during communication in an L2. After L2 linguistic features are fossilized, it is very difficult to correct them.

Language Learning Settings

Language learning setting or context is another important factor to consider with regard to second language acquisition. Language can be learned (or taught) in two settings: **second language setting** and **foreign language setting**. Most of us have heard the acronyms ESL and EFL that stand for **English as a second language** and **English as a foreign language**, respectively. These terms highlight two different contexts of learning English. To refer to English learned or taught in an English-speaking country, such as the United States of America (USA), the United Kingdom (UK), Australia, Canada, and so on, we use the acronym ESL. For English learned or taught in a country where it is not the primary language of communication, we utilize the acronym EFL. For example, an English instructor in China teaches EFL, while a person teaching English as an additional language to ELLs in K–12 public schools or at college level in the United States teaches ESL. Note that while we use the term ESL in the United States, English can be the learner's third, fourth, or even fifth language. To accurately describe such cases, the term **English as an additional language** (EAL) is also widely used, which can conceptually replace the terms ESL and EFL.

ESL and EFL settings fundamentally differ from each other and thus can promote different aspects of English learning. Since an ESL classroom is in an English-speaking country, ESL students have ample opportunities to practice English (at least its communicative aspects) in the classroom as well as outside the classroom. They are also exposed to English-speaking culture and can explore it without a conscious effort. However, EFL students' exposure to English is often limited to classroom instruction. EFL teachers can be native English speakers as well as non-native speakers of English (which also holds true for ESL context), which means that EFL teachers may share the same cultural values as EFL students, which may decrease the students' opportunities to get exposed to English culture. Moreover, exposure to a target language a few hours a week during school days does not provide enough practice and is not sufficient for communicative proficiency in that language. Thus, compared to ESL students, EFL students usually attain oral fluency in English much more slowly. Therefore, more oral practice is recommended for EFL students. ESL students, on the other hand, may need more emphasis on their academic English in K–12, considering the fact that they have to master the language of content areas (math, science, social studies, etc.) and assuming that they already receive enough input from their peers, teachers, and other English-speaking people around them to improve their communicative skills in English. In short, ESL and EFL students have different needs, and for effective language instruction, it is important for educators to consider the specific needs of students within a certain language learning setting.

Implications From SLA Theory for Language Teaching

The fact that ELL population is rapidly growing in U.S. schools and colleges constantly brings about the discussions regarding the most effective SLA theories, approaches, and models. These discussions lead to the continuous refinement of the existing L2 acquisition theories to address the needs of current ELL populations. Knowing these theories, however, does not suffice to help linguistically and culturally diverse ELLs succeed in schools. The application of this knowledge is as important. By applying the knowledge of SLA theory, teachers can tailor their instruction to meet the unique needs of their ELLs and provide effective language development experiences for the students. Following are some tips that teachers can use to improve educational experiences and outcomes for English learners in K–12 U.S. schools.

TIPS FOR TEACHERS!

- Know your language learners. Gather as much information as you can about their native language background, L1 literacy proficiency, previous schooling experiences, learning styles, and so on. This information can guide you when selecting effective strategies and materials to use with your ELLs. Consider the checklist from Chapter 1.

- Find out how long your ELLs have been in the United States and in a U.S. school. This information can help you determine whether a learner is going through the silent period in case the child does not speak or interact in the classroom. Remember that being in the silent period does not mean that the student is not learning. Irrespective of the language acquisition stage, ELLs are still involved in receptive acquisition of language, which means that they listen to the target language (in some cases, they can also read in the target language) in the classroom. Learners in the early language development stages need some time before they feel ready to produce in L2. Teachers of these students need to be patient and understanding so that the learners do not feel forced to produce L2 output, which can raise their affective filter.

- Observe carefully and identify each English learner's language acquisition stage. Provide materials and activities that are comprehensible, interesting, and appropriate for their L2 acquisition stage.

- While providing linguistically appropriate and comprehensible materials, make sure you do not "water down" the curriculum and lower your expectations for your beginner ELLs. Irrespective of their language acquisition stage, English learners have to learn the same content standards as their native-speaking peers. What should be modified for ELLs is not the content itself, but the language of the content.

- The fact that some ELLs have good conservational fluency in English does not necessarily mean that their academic English is also strong. Remember that while it takes 2–3 years to attain basic interpersonal communicative skills (BICS) in a second language, it takes 5–7 or more years to reach cognitive academic language proficiency (CALP) in an L2.

- Pay close attention to your students' oral and written output for possible negative transfer. Remember that school-aged ELLs, especially those who have well-established literacy and oral skills in their L1, can also demonstrate evidence of negative transfer in English. It is important to correct such errors as early as possible.

- Provide a lot of visual support to your ELLs. Visuals can help ELLs with comprehension and, consequently, promote English language acquisition.

- Create a warm and welcoming environment and a friendly atmosphere for your students. This can help to lower all students' affective filters and encourage the students to take linguistic and academic risks without fear of embarrassment or ridicule.

- Regard each student as an individual "case." Knowing the specific linguistic and academic needs of every student in your classroom will help you optimize your teaching and maximize student learning.

In conclusion, we should not forget Margo Gottlieb's famous quote: "Every learner is a language learner, and every teacher is a language teacher." Educators, school administrators, and all other stakeholders who play a crucial role in students' education, should not ignore the fact that language is an integral part of the school curriculum, either as a subject or as a medium of teaching and learning. For this reason, neglecting the importance of language and language learning can result in irreparable detriment to the quality of education in K–12. In order to avoid this consequence, ELL education should be given the importance it deserves in U.S. schools.

Questions to Consider

1. How are environmentalist and nativist theories of language acquisition different?
2. What is Krashen's language acquisition theory about? How many hypotheses does it have, and what does each hypothesis claim?
3. What is the difference between basic interpersonal communicative skills (BICS) and cognitive academic language proficiency (CALP)? Provide examples for each.
4. What developmental processes does the prism model include? Explain each process with relevant examples.
5. What is the critical period hypothesis (CPH)?
6. What is *fossilization* and how is it related to the phenomenon known as *negative transfer*?
7. Explain ESL and EFL settings in your own words.
8. Discuss different SLA theories. Which of them do you find most effective and why? Or do you think that there is a piece of truth in each of them? How?
9. Discuss different stages of second language acquisition. Consider your own second/foreign language learning journey. Have you ever reached the advanced fluency stage in a language other than your native? If yes, what strategies have you used? If not, why do you think that you could not reach the highest stage in that second/foreign language? What were the obstacles?
10. What are the challenges of being in the preproduction stage of L2 acquisition? Refer to your own second/foreign language learning experiences and provide some advice to fellow students, future teachers, or your colleagues in regard to how they can help students at this stage of second language acquisition.
11. Xavier is a fourth-grade ELL. His class is learning about adjectives this week. One of their assignments is to describe nouns with adjectives. When Xavier's teacher checks his work, she notices that Xavier has constantly placed adjectives after nouns, such as *book interesting, story funny,* and so on. What linguistic term explains this phenomenon? Discuss what kind of problem Xavier might be experiencing and how you could help him if you were his teacher.
12. Leyla is a high school student in Turkey. She learns English at school. One of her assignments is to watch the American version of *The Good Doctor,* read the subtitles while watching, take notes of unfamiliar words, and look up those words in the English-Turkish dictionary. Is Leyla learning English as ESL or EFL? Is she learning or acquiring English? Discuss these questions and provide a rationale for your responses.

References

Bley-Vroman, R. (1989). What is the logical problem of foreign language learning? In S. Gass & J. Schachter (Eds.), *Linguistic perspectives on second language acquisition* (pp. 41–68). Cambridge University Press.

Brown, H. D. (2007). *Principles of language learning and teaching* (5th edition). Pearson.

Carrasquillo, A. L. (1994). *Teaching English as a second language: A resource guide.* Garland.

Chomsky, N. (2006). *Language and mind.* Cambridge University Press.

Collier, V. P., & Thomas, W. P. (2007). Predicting second language academic success in English using the prism model. In J. Cummins & C. Davison (Eds.), *International handbook of English language teaching* (pp. 333–348). Springer.

Corballis, M. C. (2017). *The truth about language: What it is and where it came from.* University of Chicago Press.

Cummins, J. (2001). The entry and exit fallacy in bilingual education. In C. Baker & N. H. Hornberger (Eds.), *An introductory reader to the writings of Jim Cummins* (pp. 110-138). Multilingual Matters.

Cummins, J. (2008). BICS and CALP: Empirical and theoretical status of the distinction. In B. Street & N. H. Hornberger (Eds.), *Encyclopedia of language and education,* Vol. 2 (2nd ed.) (pp. 71–83). Springer.

Danesi, M. (2003). *Second language teaching: A view from the right side of the brain.* Kluwer Academic.

de Groot, A. (2011). *Language and cognition in bilinguals and multilinguals: An introduction.* Psychology Press.

Faltis, C. (1997). Bilingual education in the United States. In J. Cummins & D. Corson (Eds.), *Encyclopedia of language and education,* Vol. 5 (pp. 189–197). Kluwer.

Griffiths, C. (2008). *Lessons from good language learners.* Cambridge University Press.

Han, Z. (2004). *Fossilization in adult second language acquisition.* Multilingual Matters.

Haynes, J. (2007). *Getting started with English language learners: How educators can meet the challenge.* Association for Supervision and Curriculum Development.

Hill, J., & Miller, K. (2013). *Classroom instruction that works with English language learners.* Mid-continent Research for Education and Learning (McREL).

James, A., & Westney, P. (1981). *New linguistic impulses in foreign language teaching.* Gunter Narr.

Karmiloff, K., & Karmiloff-Smith, A. (2002). *Pathways to language: From fetus to adolescent.* Harvard University Press.

Knibbeler, W. (1989). *The explorative-creative way: Implementation of a humanistic language teaching model.* Gunter Narr.

Krashen, S. (2013). *Second language acquisition: Theory, applications, and some conjectures.* Cambridge University Press.

Krashen, S. D., & Terrell, T. D. (1983). *The natural approach: Language acquisition in the classroom.* Alemany.

Lenneberg, E. (1967). *Biological foundations of language*. Wiley.

Nakuma, C. (1998). A new theoretical account of "fossilization": Implications for L2 attrition research. *International Review of Applied Linguistics in Language Teaching, 36*(3), 247–256.

Newton, M. (2003). *Savage girls and wild boys: A history of feral children*. St. Martin's.

Penfield, W., & Roberts, L. (1959). *Speech and brain mechanisms*. Princeton: Princeton University Press.

Salim, B. (2001). *A companion to teaching of English*. Atlantic.

Sanz, M., & Igoa, J. M. (2012). *Applying language science to language pedagogy: Contributions of linguistics and psycholinguistics to second language teaching*. Cambridge Scholars.

Selinker, L. (1972). Interlanguage. *International Review of Applied Linguistics, 10*(2), 209–231.

Stewart, J. (2003). Is there a fundamental difference? The availability of universal grammar in child versus adult second language acquisition. In J. M. Liceras, H. Zobl, & Goodluck, H. (Eds.), *Proceedings of the 6th Generative Approaches to Second Language Acquisition Conference* (pp. 308–314). Descargado.

VanPatten, B., & Rothman, J. (2015). What does current generative theory have to say about the explicit-implicit debate. In P. Rebuschat (Ed.), *Implicit and explicit learning of languages* (pp. 91–116). John Benjamins.

Chapter 3

Corrective Feedback

Younghee Sheen and Rod Ellis

Glossary

Term/acronym	Meaning	Usage/example
CF	Corrective feedback	Feedback learners receive when an error is made in oral or written production.
Explicit feedback	A direct error correction	No! No! That is wrong. You need to say, "I took the pencil, not 'taked' the pencil."
Fossilization	A term used to describe a language error that persists over a learner's lifetime	Often used to refer to a language error that is repeated by a learner over an extended period of time
Implicit feedback	Indirect error correction	Any of a variety of CF techniques that aim for students to recognize their error and self-correct: "Is it 'taked' the pencil?"
Input	Information received from the target language	Often used to describe the words spoken or written by the teacher to the language learner
Input providing	Learners supply the correct form either explicitly or implicitly	A type of CF that provides the correct form to the learner: "It is 'took' the pencil."
Metalinguistic feedback	Feedback that contains either comments, information, or questions related to student's error, without explicitly providing the correct form	Feedback that aims to get the learner to consider and resolve their language error without giving them the correct form
Offline feedback	Feedback that is withheld until after the learner is finished speaking	A type of feedback that does not interrupt a student's speech so as to not offend or interrupt a learner

(Continued)

Term/acronym	Meaning	Usage/example
Online feedback	Feedback that follows immediately after error is made	A type of feedback that aims to make the learner aware that they made an error when the error is made
Output	A term that refers to any spoken or written piece of information produced in the target language	Often used to refer to the words learners produce orally or in written text
Output prompting	An attempt to elicit the correct form from learner	Any of a variety of CF techniques that forces learners to reprocess their original output
Prompts	A CF strategy that aims to elicit a self-repair or correction from learner	Any CF strategy that leads to the learner self-correcting
Recasts	A repetition of the learner's error	A type of implicit feedback that repeats the learner's error in an attempt to make the learner aware of the correct form. The error is often highlighted by the teacher's emphasis on the error: "You TAKED the pencil."
Self-correction	When a learner self-corrects in response to either CF or due to his or her own realization of an error	The goal of corrective feedback
Sociocultural theory	A theory in education that focuses on the social aspects of learning	A theory in second-language acquisition that sees languages are learned via social interaction
Uptake	Term used to describe learners' responses to the corrective feedback	Often used to describe the written or spoken language produced in response to CF
Utterance	Oral language or vocalizations	Often used to refer to a learner's speech
ZPD	Zone of proximal development	The difference between what a learner can do with and without assistance.

ORRECTIVE FEEDBACK (CF) REFERS TO THE feedback that learners receive on the linguistic errors they make in their oral or written production in a second language (L2). Both oral and written CF have attracted considerable attention in recent years because of their significance for the development of theories of L2 acquisition and because they have held an important place in L2 pedagogy. We begin with a brief description of what oral and written CF entail and then move on to consider a number of theories of L2 learning where CF holds a central place. We will then consider the key issues that surround the provision of CF in language pedagogy. Finally, we review the empirical research that has investigated oral and written CF.

Types of Corrective Feedback

Oral CF can involve both on-line attempts to make learners aware that they have produced an utterance that contains an error (i.e., the feedback is provided more or less immediately following the utterance that contained an error) and off-line attempts (i.e., the feedback is withheld until the communicative event the learner is participating in has finished). Oral CF can be input-providing (i.e., the learner is supplied with the correct form) or output-prompting (i.e., it can attempt to elicit a correction from the learner). Oral CF can also be implicit as when the teacher simply requests clarification in response to the learner's erroneous utterance or explicit as when the teacher directly corrects the learner and/or provides some kind of metalinguistic explanation of the error.[1] A common form of CF is a recast. Recasts can be conversational and implicit when they take the form of a confirmation check as a response to a failure to understand the learner's utterance or didactic and more explicit when the learner's erroneous utterance is reformulated even though it has not caused a communication problem (see Ellis & Sheen, 2006; Sheen, 2006). Definitions of these different types of oral CF are provided in Table 3.1.

TABLE 3.1 A Taxonomy of Oral CF Strategies

	Implicit	Explicit
Input-providing	• Conversational recasts (i.e., the correction consists of a reformulation of a student utterance in the attempt to resolve a communication problem; such recasts often take the form confirmation checks where the reformulation is followed by a question tag as in "Oh, so you were sick, were you?").	• Didactic recasts (i.e., the correction takes the form of a reformulation of a student utterance even though no communication problem has arisen). • Explicit correction only (i.e., the correction takes the form of a direct signal that an error has been committed and the correct form is supplied). • Explicit correction with metalinguistic explanation (i.e., in addition to signaling an error has been committed and providing the correct form, there is also a metalinguistic comment).
Output-prompting	• Repetition (i.e., the learner's erroneous utterance is repeated without any intonational highlighting of the error). • Clarification requests (i.e., attention is drawn to a problem utterance by the speaker indicating he/she has not understood it).	• Metalinguistic clue (i.e., a brief metalinguistic statement aimed at eliciting a correction from the learner). • Elicitation (i.e., an attempt is made to verbally elicit the correct form from the learner by, for example, a prompting question). • Paralinguistic signal (i.e., an attempt is made to non-verbally elicit the correct form from the learner).

TABLE 3.2 A Taxonomy of Written CF Strategies

	Direct	Indirect
Metalinguistic information	• Provision of the correct form with brief grammatical explanation.	• Use of error code (e.g., symbols such as VT to signal a verb tense error or WO a word order error are inserted into the text). • Use of brief grammatical explanation (e.g., error types are numbered in the text and then a brief explanation of each type of error is provided at the end of the text).
No metalinguistic information	• Provision of the correct form only. • Reformation of the entire sentence or paragraph.	• Errors are indicated but not located and the correct form is not supplied (e.g., a cross is placed in the margin next to the line where an error has occurred). • Errors are indicated and located but the correct form is not supplied (e.g., an error is underlined in the place in the text in which it occurs).

Written CF almost always involves off-line (i.e., delayed) corrections of the errors that students have committed in a written text. As with oral CF, this can involve both input-providing feedback (usually referred to as "direct correction") and output-prompting feedback (referred to as "indirect correction"). Direct correction involves supplying learners with the correct form or reformulating the entire text; indirect correction involves indicating that an error has been committed either in the margin of the text or within the text where the error occurs. Both direct and indirect written CF may or may not be accompanied with metalinguistic information. However, the distinction between implicit and explicit CF does not apply in the case of writing; all written CF is necessarily explicit (i.e., the student knows he/she has been corrected—see Sheen, 2010). A description of these written CF strategies is provided in Table 3.2.

Theoretical Positions

Corrective feedback is addressed in just about every theory of L2 acquisition. However, in this section we will consider only those theories that view CF as making a major contribution to L2 acquisition (i.e., we will not consider theories that claim that CF has no or only a very limited role). We feel this is justified given the very substantial empirical evidence now available that shows that CF can affect acquisition (see later sections in this chapter).

Cognitive Theories of Corrective Feedback

The main cognitive theoretical perspectives are the Interaction Hypothesis (Long, 1983, 1996), the Output Hypothesis (Swain, 1985, 1995) and the Noticing Hypothesis (Schmidt,

TABLE 3.3 Three Hypotheses That Inform Cognitive Accounts of Corrective Feedback

Hypothesis	Description
Interaction Hypothesis	This claims that the negotiation of meaning that occurs when a communication problem arises results in interactional modifications that provide learners with the input needed for L2 learning.
Output Hypothesis	This claims that learners also learn from their own output when this requires them to "stretch their interlanguage in order to meet communicative goals" (Swain, 1995, p. 127).
Noticing Hypothesis	This claims that L2 learning is enhanced when learners pay conscious attention to specific linguistic forms in the input to which they are exposed.

1994, 2001). Table 3.3 below provides a brief account of these hypotheses. They come together in what Long (1991) termed "focus on form," of which CF is one manifestation. They also figure in skill-acquisition theory (Johnson, 1996), which emphasizes the importance of learners receiving feedback in the context of the real-life behaviors they are trying to learn. However, rather than examining these different theories in detail, we will offer a composite account of how cognitive theories see CF as facilitating L2 acquisition.

Cognitive theories emphasize the fact that CF assists acquisition when the participants are focused primarily on meaning, commit errors and receive feedback that they recognize as corrective. In this way, learners receive information not just about linguistic form but also about form-meaning mappings (i.e., they are able to see how a particular linguistic form realizes a particular meaning in context). An example will make this clear:

S1: What do you spend with your wife?
T: What?
S1: What do you spend your extra time with your wife?
T: Ah, how do you spend?
S2: How do you spend.

(Ellis & Sheen, 2006, p. 581)

Here Student 1 (S1) asks the teacher a question about how he spends time with his wife but erroneously uses "what" instead of "how." This elicits a request for clarification from the teacher (T), to which S1 responds by extending his original utterance but with the same error. T then recasts S1's utterance and this is uptaken by Student 2 (S2). In this way the learners are able to see that the meaning they wish to convey in this context requires the use of the linguistic form "how," not "what." In this example, corrective feedback occurred as a result of a communicative breakdown. That is, it involved "negotiation of meaning." However, it can also occur when the teacher (or another learner) chooses to focus attention on form even though no communication breakdown has taken place, as in this example also taken from Ellis and Sheen (2006, p. 292):

> S: Korean is more faster.
> T: Is faster.
> S: Is faster than English.

Here the learner makes the common error of double marking a comparative adjective ("more faster"). The teacher clearly understands the learner but goes ahead and provides the explicit correction ("is faster"). This results in the learner's modified uptake ("is faster than English"). In this case, the CF is "didactic" rather than "conversational" and involves "negotiation of form."

In both cases, CF works by causing learners to notice the errors they have committed. In particular, it affords an opportunity for them to "notice-the-gap," i.e., to compare their own production with that provided for them in the CF move. CF may also assist acquisition when learners have the opportunity to repair/correct their initial error following the CF move. This is known as "uptake"; it constitutes one type of "modified output" (as illustrated in the examples above). It may help learners to rehearse the correct form in their short-term memory and consolidate a form-function mapping and thus enable them to incorporate the corrected feature more fully into their interlanguage. However, the role of uptake/modified ouput remains controversial, with some researchers (e.g., Lyster, 1998a) suggesting it is beneficial and others (e.g., Long, 2007) arguing that CF promotes acquisition through the input it provides rather than through opportunities for modifying output.

Cognitive theories also make claims about the type of CF strategy most likely to enhance acquisition but, again, the claims are conflicting. Long (1996, 2007) argues that recasts are especially beneficial in that they provide learners with positive evidence of what is correct as well as negative evidence showing an error has been committed and minimally disturb the focus on communication. Lyster (2004) makes a theoretical case to suggest that what he calls "prompts" (i.e., CF strategies that elicit a self-repair/correction from the learner) are more effective than recasts. Other theorists have argued that explicit feedback (e.g., involving metalinguistic information) is especially effective as it not only induces noticing of an error and its correction but also fosters understanding of the nature of the error.

Cognitive theories seek to account for how CF assists acquisition in interaction. Thus, a key feature of such theories is that the feedback is provided on-line in what Doughty (2001) has called "a window of opportunity" (i.e., at a time that the learner is cognitively primed to attend to the correction). Doughty argues that feedback needs to be attended to more or less immediately if it is to activate the cognitive mechanisms responsible for acquisition.

Cognitive theories have generally sought to account for how oral CF assists acquisition. Constructs such as "negotiation of meaning," "negotiation of form" and "window of opportunity" apply primarily to oral CF. However, cognitive theories can also be applied to written CF. For example, as illustrated in Sheen (2010), the distinction between "input-providing" and "output-prompting" CF is equally applicable to both oral and written CF. So too are the key notions of "noticing" and "noticing-the-gap." Even "uptake/ modified output" can be applied to written CF if learners are given the opportunity to incorporate corrections into a second draft (revision) of their written text. As already noted, written CF is invariably explicit and thus is perhaps more likely to invite metalinguistic understanding of an error.

Cognitive theories, therefore, can account for how CF works in both oral and written communication. The differences between the two media also afford a means of testing some of the claims made about CF (e.g., whether CF can only produce change in the learner's L2 system if it is provided on-line in "a window of opportunity").

Corrective Feedback in Sociocultural Theory

In sociocultural theory (SCT), learning is "participation" rather than "acquisition"; that is, it is mediated by and is evident in social interaction rather than in the mind of the learner. Thus, to explicate how SCT views CF it is necessary to understand how participation in interaction creates affordances for learning. According to SCT, there is no single set of characteristics of social interaction that constitute affordances for all learners. Rather, affordances arise out of the successful tailoring of the interaction to the developmental level of individual learners. They occur when the interaction enables the participants to construct a "zone of proximal development" for the learner—that is, the learners come to be able to perform a language feature through the scaffolding provided by an interlocutor when they are not able to do so independently. The aim of interaction (including corrective feedback) is to assist the learner to move from other-regulation in the zone of proximal development to self-regulation, where the learner is finally able to use a linguistic feature correctly without assistance. According to this view of CF, what constitutes a facilitative form of correction for one learner might not be so for another, either because it is pitched at a level too far in advance of the learner or because it fails to "stretch" the learner by posing a sufficient challenge.

This approach to the mediating role of CF is well represented in Aljaafreh and Lantolf's (1994) study. They developed a "regulatory scale" to reflect the extent to which a tutor's oral feedback on the errors students had made in their writing was implicit or explicit. For example, asking learners to find and correct their own errors was considered an implicit strategy, while providing examples of the correct pattern was highly explicit. An intermediate level occurred when the tutor indicated the nature of an error without identifying it for the learner. Aljaafreh and Lantolf showed how the degree of scaffolding provided by the tutor for a particular learner in oral conferences diminished (i.e., the help provided became more implicit over time). This was possible because the learners assumed increased control over the L2 and therefore needed less assistance. Aljaafreh and Lantolf identified a number of general principles governing the effectiveness of CF: (1) it must be graduated—no more help than is necessary should be provided at any single time; (2) it must be contingent—it must reflect actual need and be removed when the learner demonstrates an ability to function independently; and (3) it is dialogic—it involves dynamic assessment of a learner's Zone of Proximal Development.

An SCT view of corrective feedback is also reflected in Poehner and Lantolf's (2005) account of "dynamic assessment." Some examples from Poehner's (2008) research with advanced learners of L2 French will illustrate this. Poehner asked the learners to construct a past-tense oral narrative in French after watching a short video-clip. They were given no feedback or mediation in this first task. Then they repeated the task after watching a second clip. This time "they interacted with a mediator who offered suggestions, posed questions, made corrections, and helped them think through decisions concerning selection of lexical items, verb tense, and other language difficulties" (Poehner & Lantolf, 2005, p. 246). This interactive assistance, which was provided in English, was "highly flexible, emerging from the interaction between the student and the mediator" (Poehner & Lantolf, 2005, p. 246). For example, in the case of one learner, the teacher initially used quite direct clues (for example, "in the past") and subsequently, when addressing the same linguistic problem, more indirect means (for example, "there's something there with the verb").

In SCT corrective feedback is seen as a key element in how teachers (or other learners) can assist a learner to achieve self-regulation through self-correction and thereby ultimately learn how to use a feature correctly without assistance. Two points need to be emphasized. First, a SCT perspective on corrective feedback rejects the view adopted in cognitive accounts, namely that it is possible to identify specific corrective strategies that are the most effective in promoting learning. Rather, SCT emphasizes the importance of varying the strategies employed to suit the developmental level of the learner. Second, as Aljaafreh and Lantolf's (1994) and Poehner and Lantolf's (2005) studies make clear, CF in this theoretical framework is necessarily oral in nature. It is not clear how written CF can be tailored to the learner's developmental level given that there is typically no opportunity to engage in social interaction when teachers correct and simply return their students' written work.

Pedagogical Positions

The key issues facing teachers and teacher educators were identified by Hendrickson in 1978 while Chaudron (1988) reviewed research that has addressed these issues. These issues are still current today. Here we will focus on what teacher educators and teachers have had to say about these issues, noting that there is considerable disagreement evident in their opinions.

Should Learner Errors Be Corrected?

Hendrickson's (1978) review article focused on oral CF. He argued that teachers should definitely correct learners' oral errors. This conclusion was based on both theoretical grounds (i.e., CF helps learners to engage in the process of hypothesis testing) and on empirical grounds (i.e., studies had shown that students wished to be corrected). However, not all language teaching methods view CF so positively. Ur (1996) summarized the position adopted by different methods. She noted that errors in audiolingualism need to be prevented so that bad habits do not develop and, for this reason, "negative assessment" plays little part in learning and ideally should be avoided. In humanistic methods, "assessment should be positive or non-judgmental" in order to "promote a positive self-image of the learner as a person and language learner," while in skill theory "the learner needs feedback on how well he or she is doing" (Ur, 1996, p. 243). In the post-method era, methodologists are more likely to affirm the need for oral CF, recognizing the cognitive contribution it can make while also issuing warnings about the potential affective damage it can cause. Ur concluded that "there is certainly a place for correction" but "we should not over-estimate this contribution" (1996, p. 255) because it often fails to eliminate errors and concluded that she would rather invest time in avoiding errors than in correcting them.

Similar differences in opinion exist where written CF is concerned as is evident in the debate between Truscott and Ferris (Truscott, 1996, 1999, 2007; Ferris 1999, 2004). Truscott, reflecting the views of teachers who adhere to process theories of writing, advanced the strong claim that correcting learners' errors in a written composition may enable them to eliminate the errors in a subsequent draft but has no effect on grammatical accuracy in a new piece of writing (i.e., it does not result in acquisition). Ferris (1999) disputed this claim, arguing that it was not possible to dismiss correction in general as it depended on the quality of the correction—in other words, if the correction was clear and consistent it could work for acquisition. Truscott (1999) replied by claiming that Ferris (1999) failed to cite any evidence in support of her contention. Writers of handbooks for teachers almost invariably adopt Ferris' (2004) position in arguing that there is a need for teachers to correct their students' written work. However, they also point out the danger of over-correcting and the importance of providing feedback on other aspects of writing (e.g., content and organization) as well as linguistic problems. How to balance content-correction and corrective feedback is a major issue where writing is concerned. Indeed, as Ferris (2003a) noted a common refrain is that teachers focus too much on correcting linguistic errors at the expense of content and organization.

When Should Learner Errors Be Corrected?

In the case of oral CF, teachers are faced with the choice of either correcting immediately following the learner's erroneous utterance or delaying the correction until later. Teacher educators often distinguish between "accuracy" and "fluency" work, arguing that CF has a place in the former but not in the latter. Harmer (1983), for example, argued that when students are engaged in communicative activity, the teacher should not intervene by "telling students that they are making mistakes, insisting on accuracy and asking for repetition etc." (p. 44). Bartram and Walt (1991) similarly argued that students should not be interrupted while speaking. Hedge (2000) listed a number of techniques that can be used in delayed CF (e.g., recording an activity and then asking students to identify and correct their own errors or simply noting down errors as students perform an activity and going through these afterwards). Teachers also appear to favor delayed correction in fluency work. Basturkmen, Loewen and Ellis (2004) found language teachers believed that it was best not to correct students during a communicative activity. However, they also found that the teachers did not always conform to this belief in their actual practice of CF. Rolin-Ianzati (2010) identified two different approaches that teachers of L2 French used when providing delayed feedback following a role-play activity—they either initiated repair by the student or simply reviewed the errors students had made. She argued that initiating repair was a more effective strategy as it led to more self-repair by the students.

When to correct is less of an issue in written CF as correction is nearly always delayed to some extent—unless, as in Aljaafreh and Lantolf's (1994) study, teachers ask students to read out their written text and correct errors orally. However, the issue of timing arises in process writing instruction where students produce multiple drafts. Teachers need to decide whether to stage their feedback, focusing initially on content and organization and only in later drafts on linguistic errors. McGarrell and Verbeen (2007) argue that corrective feedback should be delayed as it constitutes a form of assessment that may deter students from revising their ideas and organization of the text.

Which Learner Errors Should Be Corrected?

A key issue is whether teachers should aim to correct all the linguistic errors in a text or only some. Selective correction is widely promoted by language teaching methodologists (e.g., Byrne, 1988; Edge, 1989; Raimes, 1983; Ferris, 1999). Various proposals—relevant to both oral and written CF—have been advanced regarding which errors to correct. Some methodologists have suggested that teachers should focus only on "errors" and ignore "mistakes" as these are merely performance phenomena (see Corder [1967] for a discussion of this distinction). Another favored approach is to recommend correcting "global" rather than "local" errors (Burt, 1975) on the grounds that the former are more likely to interfere with communication. Global errors are errors that affect overall sentence organization while local errors are errors that affect single elements in a sentence (for example, errors in morphology). Krashen's (1982) proposal that CF should be limited to features that are simple and portable (i.e., "rules of thumb") and therefore "learnable" has also attracted attention from methodologists.

In fact, none of these proposals is easy to implement in practice. The distinctions between an "error" and a "mistake" and a "local" and "global" error are not as clear-cut as Corder (1967) and Burt (1975) made out. There is no widely accepted theory of grammatical complexity to help teachers decide which rules are simple and portable. Hard-pressed teachers may not have the time to ascertain which features are problematic. As Truscott (1996) noted, there is good reason to doubt teachers' ability to engage systematically with selective correction.

A different approach to selective correction, however, does hold out more promise. Teachers can elect to focus on one specific category of error (i.e., adopt what Sheen [2007a] called "focused corrective feedback"). For example, they could correct just past-tense errors at one time and article errors at another. As the review of the research below shows, focused correction has been the approach adopted in experimental studies of both oral and written CF.

How Should Learner Errors Be Corrected?

A feature of teachers' actual practice of CF is its inconsistency and lack of precision. Inconsistency arises when teachers respond variably to the same error made by different students in the same class, correcting some students and ignoring others. Such inconsistency is not necessarily detrimental, however, for, as Allwright (1975) pointed out, it may reflect teachers' attempts to cater for individual differences among the students.

Reflecting this, teacher educators have been understandably reluctant to prescribe or proscribe the strategies that teachers should use. In part this is because they are uncertain as to which strategies are the effective ones. But it also almost certainly reflects their recognition that the process of correcting errors is a complex one, involving a number of competing factors. The approach adopted by Ur (1996) is to raise a number of questions for teachers to consider and then to offer answers based on her own practical teaching experience.

Who Should Correct Learner Errors?

Teachers are often advised to give students the opportunity to self-correct and, if that fails, to invite other students to perform the correction (e.g., Hedge, 2000). Such advice can be seen as part and parcel of the western educational ideology of learner-centeredness.

Some CF strategies automatically place the burden of correction on the learner—for example, signaling an error by means of a clarification request or by simply repeating the erroneous utterance. In the case of written CF, "indirect correction" (e.g., indicating the presence of an error without supplying the correct form or using an error-coding system to signal the general category of an error) constitutes a half-way house—the teacher takes on some responsibility for correcting but leaves it up to the individual student to make the actual correction.

There are, however, a number of problems with learner self-correction. First, learners typically prefer the teacher do the correction for them. Second, and more importantly, learners can only self-correct if they possess the necessary linguistic knowledge. Other (typically teacher) correction will be necessary to enable learners to identify forms that have not yet been acquired. Third, although output-prompting CF strategies signal that there is some kind of problem with the learner's utterance they do not make it clear that the problem is a linguistic one (as opposed to just a communicative one). Thus, there are clear grounds (theoretical and practical) for encouraging self-correction but this will not always be possible, as methodologists such as Hedge acknowledge. This poses teachers a conundrum—should they push the learner to self-correct or provide the correction directly themselves? One solution sometimes advocated to this problem is to conduct CF as a two-stage process: first encourage self-correction and, if that fails, provide the correction. Such an approach is, of course compatible with a SCT view of CF.

Another alternative is peer-correction. Methodologists generally endorse the importance of allowing learners opportunities to correct their fellow learners' oral errors. However, peer correction has been more extensively practiced in the case of writing. Ferris (2003b) reports that first language (L1) writing scholars (many of whom are skeptical of the value of teacher correction) give "nearly unqualified endorsement" (p. 15) to peer-correction. She also notes that many L2 process writing methodologists (e.g., Zamel, 1985) are similarly in favor of peer-correction. However, Hyland and Hyland (2006) advise against "idealizing L2 peer group interactions as sites of constructive interaction, since the reality can be quite different" (p. 6) while Ferris (2003b) herself argues that students need careful training in how to conduct a peer review.

Two points emerge from this brief review of pedagogical positions regarding CF. The first is that CF is a very complex issue with no simple rules-of-thumb available to guide teachers. The second, a corollary of the first point, is that considerable disagreement exists over how best to conduct CF. Hyland and Hyland (2006) rightly point out that CF is "a form of social action designed to accomplish educational and social goals" (p. 10) and for this reason needs to be viewed contextually. Thus there can be no single set of guidelines for conducting either oral or written CF that is appropriate for all instructional contexts. Nor, we would argue, is it likely that research will provide definitive answers to the pedagogical questions that Hendrickson (1978) raised. It can, however, illuminate the issues involved, and suggest possible strategies that teachers can explore in their own contexts.

Research into Corrective Feedback

Studies of oral and written CF have been conducted separately with almost no reference to each other. For this reason we will consider them separately here.

Oral Corrective Feedback

We will focus exclusively on the classroom-based CF research. The research has been both interpretative (i.e., descriptive and ethnographic) and confirmatory (i.e., correlational and experimental) in design.

Much of the earlier research was descriptive. A number of studies (e.g., Allwright, 1975; Chaudron, 1977; Long, 1977) set out to develop typologies of CF strategies with a view to identifying which strategies teachers typically used and how consistent they were in their use of them. This work has carried on into recent times. In an often cited study, Lyster and Ranta (1997), for example, identified the strategies used by teachers in French immersion classrooms in Canada. A feature of this more recent research has been to examine the frequency with which the different strategies are used. Lyster and Ranta reported that recasts were by far the preferred means of correcting students. Seedhouse (1997), who examined classroom repair sequences, also found that teachers generally showed a preference for mitigated, indirect forms of correction (e.g., recasts) rather than more direct forms (e.g., explicit correction). However, other studies have shown considerable variation in teachers' handling of errors both within and across classrooms. Van Lier (1988), for example, showed that the type of repair work reflects the nature of the context which the teacher and learners jointly create. Seedhouse (2004) emphasized that there is "no single, monolithic organization of repair in the L2 classroom" (p. 179), with the type of organization varying depending on whether the pedagogic focus is on accuracy or fluency. Sheen (2004) reported significant differences in the types of CF in four macro teaching contexts (Canada immersion, Canada English as a second language (ESL), New Zealand ESL and Korea English as a foreign language (EFL)). The frequency of recasts, for example, varied significantly from one context to the next. Explicit correction was rare in Canada ESL classes but quite common in New Zealand ESL ones. This descriptive/ethnographic research has provided a useful set of categories for investigating CF and also demonstrated the complexity of CF as an interactional phenomenon.

Recasts have received special attention from researchers. In a descriptive study, Sheen (2006) distinguished a number of different characteristics of recasts. They can occur in a single-move or multiple-move. Single-move recasts can vary in terms of mode, scope, whether they are reduced or not reduced, the number of changes made to the learner's utterances, the type of change and the linguistic focus. For example, the recast in the following sequence can be coded in terms of mode (= declarative), scope (= isolated), reduction (= non-reduced), length (= clause), number of changes (= one change), type of change (= addition), and linguistic focus (= grammar).

> S: I think she'll travel together her boyfriend after the course.
> T: I think she'll travel together with her boyfriend.
>
> (Sheen, 2006, p. 372)

Such a description is useful because it enables researchers to examine the relationship between different types/characteristics of recasts and learner repair (i.e., whether the learner's response successfully incorporates the correction) and acquisition (i.e., whether as a result of exposure to a recast the learner is subsequently able to use the corrected form more accurately). Studies that have attempted this will be considered below.

Reflecting the complexity of CF, research has shown that teachers are often inconsistent and imprecise in how they correct learner errors. Long (1977) noted that teachers often give more than one type of feedback simultaneously and that often their feedback moves go unnoticed by the students. Yoshida's (2008) study helps to explain why teachers vary in the practice of CF. This study used a stimulus recall interview to examine teachers' choice of and learners' preferences for different CF types. The findings shed light on when and why teachers use recasts, elicitation, and metalinguistic feedback. For example, the teachers claimed they used recasts because of the time limitation of classes and in response to learners' differing cognitive styles. On the other hand, the teachers stated they used prompts (e.g., elicitation or metalinguistic clue) when they felt sure that the learner was able to self-correct the error. Also most of the student participants Yoshida interviewed preferred to receive output-prompting CF before recasts so that they had the chance to work out and correct their errors themselves.

Correlational studies have examined the relationship between different types of CF and learner uptake/repair (e.g., Sheen, 2004; Lyster & Mori, 2006) and between uptake and acquisition (e.g., Williams, 2001; Loewen, 2005). This research has been motivated by Schmidt's

(1994) Noticing Hypothesis, Swain's (1995) Output Hypothesis and Long's (1991, 1996) claims regarding the importance of focus on form. Thus, corrective feedback is hypothesized to facilitate acquisition if learners first notice the correction and second repair their own erroneous utterance, especially when this occurs in a context where they are primarily focused on meaning rather than form.

Lyster (1998b) found that learner repair of lexical and grammatical errors was more likely after elicitations, requests for clarification, and metalinguistic clues (all examples of output-prompting CF—see Table 3.1) than other types. Sheen (2004), in the study referred to above reported that New Zealand ESL and Korea EFL produced significantly higher uptake and repair following recasts than Canada Immersion and Canada ESL, suggesting that recasts do not necessarily lead to less uptake in instructional contexts where teachers and students are oriented towards language as form. Lyster and Mori (2006) also reported differences in uptake and repair according to instructional context, in this case two different immersion contexts—French immersion in Canada and Japanese immersion in Japan. They advanced the "counterbalance hypothesis," which predicts that the extent to which different CF strategies lead to uptake/repair is influenced by whether the overall instruction orients learners to attend to form as it did in Japan but not in Canada. Oliver and Mackey (2003) found differences according to the specific contexts found within child ESL classrooms with uptake more frequent in explicit language contexts and least frequent in management-related exchanges. Thus, as with corrective feedback itself, uptake and repair have been shown to be highly variable.

Studies that have investigated the relationship between uptake and acquisition have reported mixed results. Loewen (2005) found that learners' successful uptake in classroom-based communicative lessons was a strong predictor of their ability to subsequently correct their errors in tailor-made tests administered to individual students. Loewen and Philp (2006) investigated the effect of different characteristics of recasts (e.g., linguistic focus, length, number of changes, segmentation) on individual learners' uptake and acquisition, as measured by tailor-made tests. They found that those recasts with explicit linguistic characteristics were more likely to result in both uptake and learning. McDonough and Mackey (2006), however, found no evidence that the learners' repetitions of recasts assisted acquisition although they did find that what they called "primed production" (i.e., the learner correctly produced the corrected form within six turns of the recast that provided it) predicted acquisition.

Classroom-based experimental studies have focused on investigating the effects of two broad types of oral CF—implicit vs. explicit and input-providing vs. output-prompting (see Table 3.1 for the specific corrective strategies involved). Ellis, Loewen, and Erlam (2006) compared the effects of implicit CF in the form of recasts and explicit CF in the form of metalinguistic comments on adult ESL learners' acquisition of regular past tense. In the implicit CF, the teacher simply recast the verb in the past tense as in this example:

> S: Yesterday two boys, Joe and Bill visit their rich uncle
> T: Visited
> S: Visited their rich uncle.
>
> (Ellis et al., 2006, p. 362)

In the explicit CF, the teacher repeated the learner's error and then provided a metalinguistic clue:

> S: Yesterday Joe and Bill ah went to ah Bill's grandmother and visit their grandmother
> T: and visit—you need past tense
> S: Visited, yes.
>
> (Ellis et al., 2006, p. 362)

This study found no effect for either treatment on the immediate post-tests but the students receiving the explicit CF outperformed both the control group and the group receiving implicit feedback on the delayed post-tests. The tests were designed to provide measures of both implicit and explicit L2 knowledge. Sheen (2007b) compared the effects of implicit CF in the form of recasts and explicit CF in the form of explicit correction together with metalinguistic comments on adult ESL learners' acquisition of definite and indefinite articles. Whereas the explicit correction resulted in significant gains in learning in both immediate and post-tests, the implicit did not. Thus, in a classroom context, it would appear that explicit CF is more effective.

Other experimental studies have investigated the relative effects of input-providing and output-prompting CF. Lyster (2004) investigated grade 5 French immersion learners, comparing the effects of recasts (as an input-providing strategy) and a mixture of output-prompting CF strategies (including explicit CF) on the acquisition of gender marking on articles and nouns. Both groups also received initial form-focused instruction (FFI). There was also a group that just received the FFI (i.e., no CF) and a control/comparison group. The FFI-prompt group was the only group to outperform the control group on all eight measures of acquisition. The FFI-recast group outperformed the control group on five out of eight measures while the FFI-only group outperformed control group on four out eight measures. Statistically significant differences were found between the FFI-prompt and FFI-only groups but not between FFI-recast and FFI-prompt groups. Ammar and Spada (2006) investigated learners in grade 6 intensive ESL classes, comparing the effects of recasts and prompts on their acquisition of possessive pronouns. They found that the high proficiency learners benefitted equally from both types of CF but that the prompts were more effective than the recasts with the low proficiency learners. These studies suggest that output-prompting feedback is more effective than input-providing feedback although, clearly, this can only be true for learners who have at least begun to acquire the target feature.

Researchers have also explored the role of computer-mediated corrective feedback involving recasts (e.g., Loewen & Erlam, 2006; Sachs & Suh, 2007; Sauro, 2009; Smith, 2005). Smith (2005) found no relationship between degree of uptake (with or without repair) and the acquisition of L2 vocabulary items by intermediate-level ESL learners, who participated in computer-mediated communication based on jigsaw tasks. Loewen and Erlam (2006) compared recasts and metalinguistic prompts during group text-chat interaction and found that neither type of CF resulted in significantly greater gains in linguistic accuracy than no CF. Sachs and Suh compared enhanced and non-enhanced recasts, reporting no difference in learning gains for these two types of recasts. However, Sauro's (2009) study produced results more favorable to computer-mediated CF. She reported that two different types of CF (recasts and metalinguistic prompts) did not differ in the learning gains they produced but did have a positive effect on learners' short-term development of L2 grammar. There is a need for studies that compare traditional face-to-face oral CF and synchronous computer-mediated CF.

It is not easy to reach clear conclusions about such issues as the importance of uptake/repair or the type of CF most likely to promote acquisition. One reason is that many other variables that interact with the feedback are involved. Sheen (2008), for example, reported that recasts do result in acquisition but only in learners with low foreign language speaking anxiety. Individual difference factors and contextual factors will clearly influence whether, how and when oral CF is effective. For this reason, the idea of an overall "best" CF strategy may prove to be a chimera (Ellis, 2010). Overall, however, there is now clear evidence that oral CF—in one form or another—can benefit acquisition.

Written Corrective Feedback

Teacher feedback received bad press in the 1980s and early 1990s. Ferris and Hedgcock (2005) list the following adjectives that L1 researchers used to describe the nature of teachers' feedback: "exercise in futility" (Knoblauch & Brannon, 1981, p. 1), "arbitrary, idiosyncratic" (Sommers, 1982, p. 149), "overly directive, removing students' rights to their own texts" (Ferris & Hedgcock, 2005, p. 186), and "short, careless, exhausted, or insensitive comments" (Connors & Lunsford, 1993, p. 215). However, Ferris, and Hedgcock (2005) pointed out that this negative view of teacher feedback arose from critiques of feedback directed at justifying a grade or at providing very general comments to assist students when revising their drafts and ignored the fact that written CF can serve other functions.

Descriptive studies that have examined the relationship between teacher feedback and students' revisions have employed analytic models (Hyland & Hyland, 2001). For example, Ferris (1997), in a study that employed such a model, found that students were able to revise 73% of the grammatical errors teachers corrected. She further reported that her students (1) revised consistently and successfully following feedback involving form, (2) revised less successfully following comments about content or questions seeking further information, and (3) revised or did not revise irrespective of whether the teacher attempted to hedge on critical comments.[2]

A number of studies of students' perceptions have been conducted using survey and self-report data (e.g., Cohen & Cavalcanti, 1990; Ferris, 1995; Hedgcock & Lefkowitz, 1994, 1996; Leki, 1991). These studies have consistently shown that learners value teacher feedback highly and believe that it helps improve their writing. More specifically, students prefer comments that explain specific problems in their texts and make concrete suggestions about how to revise them. Conversely, they report that teachers' short, general comments are not very helpful, especially when these take the form of content-related questions.

Leki (1991) found that most students desired to be corrected by their teachers. Hedgcock and Lefkowitz (1994) also reported that both ESL and foreign language (FL) learners have a positive attitude toward written CF. In comparing ESL and FL students, however, they noted that whereas FL students tend to prefer CF directed at grammar, the lexicon and mechanics of their written texts to feedback directed at content and style, ESL students expressed a preference toward feedback on the content and organization of their writing. In other words, the learning context may determine how learners respond to the CF they receive. Furthermore, as Conrad and Goldstein (1999) rightly pointed out, students may differ individually in their reaction to feedback depending on such factors as language aptitude, learning style, personality, and motivation. Hyland's (2000) case study showed how a learner's own values and preferences influenced the use made of the CF received from the teacher.

These different assumptions about written CF and learners' differing preferences may explain why teachers practice CF the way they do. However, according to a recent study by Lee (2009), a considerable gap exists between teachers' beliefs and their practice of CF. She reported that while teachers reported they were selective in correcting errors, they often adopted a comprehensive approach to correcting errors. They also indicated a preference for indirect CF but in practice frequently used direct correction.

Discussions of written CF have centered on whether or not it is effective in helping improve learners' linguistic accuracy. In a controversial paper, Truscott (1996) concluded that written grammar correction has no effect on L2 acquisition and, in some cases, may even be harmful and thus should be abandoned. Truscott emphasized the fact that teachers' feedback is unsystematic and arbitrary and concluded that teachers could serve L2 writers better by helping them with the content of their writing and by providing reading activities that will enhance writing abilities. He argued for the complete abandonment of written CF. As noted earlier in this chapter, this conclusion has been challenged by a number of L2 writing researchers and practitioners (e.g., Chandler, 2003; Ferris, 1999, 2004).

This debate has spawned a number of empirical studies of written CF using quasi-experimental designs to investigate if CF is effective and which types of CF are more effective. These studies fall into three major categories: (1) studies that have examined the effect of CF on learners' revised texts; (2) studies that have compared different types of CF—e.g., feedback on form vs. feedback on content, direct CF vs. indirect CF, error codes vs. underlining; and (3) studies that have investigated the effect of CF on new pieces of writing over time. While studies in category (1) are of obvious relevance to L2 writing teachers, they do not shed any light on whether written CF facilitates L2 acquisition. As Sheen (2007a) and Truscott (2007) pointed out, the fact that students are able to edit their papers when revising does not constitute evidence that they will be able to transfer this skill to a new piece of writing. Nor do studies in category (2) demonstrate that written CF affects acquisition unless they included a control group.

Much of the earlier research that responded to the Truscott/Ferris debate sought to compare the effects of different types of error feedback. In particular, they examined different ways in which direct feedback (where errors are indicated and corrected) and indirect feedback (where errors are just indicated) are provided to L2 writers (e.g., Chandler, 2003; Ferris & Roberts, 2001; Robb, Ross, & Shortreed, 1986; Semke, 1984). These studies produced mixed and inconclusive findings. They were dismissed by Truscott (2004) because they did not include a control group, making it impossible to say whether any gains in accuracy were the result of the feedback or simply of practice in writing and general exposure to the L2. The studies all had another feature in common—they all examined unfocused written CF (i.e., CF that was directed broadly at many types of linguistic errors) and in this respect differed from oral CF research, which as we have seen typically examined focused CF.

A number of recent studies (e.g., Bitchener, 2008; Sheen, 2007a) have set out to investigate focused CF and to address the methodological problems evident in the earlier written CF research by including a control group in a pre-test/post-test design. These studies have shown that focused CF does lead to gains in linguistic accuracy and also that the more explicit the feedback is, the bigger the benefit for the students. Sheen (2007a), for example, measured students' progress over time (in post-tests and delayed post-tests) and also included a control group (which received no feedback at all) and reported that both direct CF and direct + metalinguistic CF led to significant gains in accuracy, with the latter having a stronger effect than the former. However, these studies of focused CF have all investigated the same grammatical feature—English articles—so it is not clear whether focused CF will prove generally effective in improving learners' linguistic accuracy. What they do suggest is that written CF, when focused on a single feature, can be effective and thus this constitutes evidence to refute Truscott's (1996, 2004) claims.

From a pedagogic standpoint, given that the practice of written CF is generally unfocused in nature, it is important to examine the *relative* efficacy of unfocused and focused CF. Only two studies to date have addressed this, both using English definite and indefinite articles as the target feature. Ellis, Sheen, Murakami, and Takashima (2008) failed to find any difference between unfocused and focused CF, both proving to be equally effective. However, as they admitted, this may have been because the distinction between the two types of CF in this study was not made sufficiently clear. Sheen, Wright, and Moldawa (2009) overcame this problem by carefully distinguishing unfocused and focused CF. They also, importantly, investigated the effects of CF not just on a single grammatical feature (articles) but also on a broader range of features. Their results led to the conclusion that unfocused CF is of limited pedagogical value and that much can be gained by focused CF where grammatical accuracy in L2 writing is concerned.

It is likely that the debate concerning the value of written CF will continue. One or two studies showing that focused written CF can lead to acquisition are unlikely to convince the skeptics. So, clearly, more research is needed. Also, it will be necessary to show that written CF does not have some of the negative effects that Truscott (1996, 2007) has considered likely—for example, on students' fluency in writing.

Conclusion

Recently a number of meta-analyses of empirical CF studies have been published (Lyster & Saito, 2010; Mackey & Goo, 2007; Norris & Ortega, 2000; Russell & Spada, 2006; Li, 2010). By and large, these meta-analyses point to the importance of taking into account various moderating factors, such as feedback type, error type, interaction type, mode (oral/written/computer-mediated), L2 instructional contexts, age, gender, proficiency, L1 transfer, schema, anxiety and cognitive abilities, which in turn influence the extent to which CF can be beneficial to L2 learners. In other words, they support the position we have adopted in our review—namely that CF constitutes a highly complex *social* activity.

We conclude with some general statements about what is currently known about CF that can inform pedagogic practice:

1. Learners almost invariably express a wish to be corrected.
2. CF—both oral and written—is effective in assisting learners to improve their linguistic accuracy over time; in other words, CF promotes acquisition.

3. The positive effect of CF is evident not just in careful, planned language use where learners are able to make use of their explicit knowledge of L2 features, but also in meaning-centered, unplanned language use, which calls for implicit knowledge.

4. There is no clear evidence that CF needs to be provided on-line—in a "window of opportunity"—in order to impact on interlanguage development. The clearest evidence for this comes from the fact that written CF (which is invariably delayed) has shown to be effective. Both on-line/immediate and off-line/delayed CF can promote linguistic development.

5. In general, the types of CF that have the greatest impact on L2 development in a classroom context are those that are explicit and output-prompting rather than implicit and input-providing. For example, explicit feedback in conjunction with metalinguistic clues is more likely to result in learning than recasts.

6. For CF to work for acquisition, learners must be conscious that they are being corrected. CF that is conducted in the guise of some other speech act (for example, a confirmation check or a discourse-supporting move) may not be seen as corrective and, as a result, be ineffective.

7. One function of CF is to assist the learner to self-correct (i.e., to uptake the correction by repairing the error). While the role of self-correction in oral language use and of revision in writing remains to be clearly established, there is increasing evidence to suggest that when learners do self-correct, learning is more likely to occur.

8. If learner self-correction is the goal of CF, then this might be best achieved by means of CF that is fine-tuned to individual learners' level of L2 development and their capacity to benefit from CF. One way in which this might be achieved is by teachers systematically probing for the most implicit form of CF that will enable the learner to self-correct.

Corrective feedback constitutes an area where the discourses of theory and practice can comfortably rub shoulders. It affords an ideal area for researchers and teachers to engage in collaborative enquiry.

Notes

1. The distinction between implicit and explicit oral CF strategies is less clear when the CF is off-line (delayed). Arguably, delayed oral CF is invariably explicit as it will be clear to the students that the focus is on correcting errors.

2. Hedging strategies teachers use include: (1) lexical hedges (e.g., *maybe, please*); (2) syntactic hedges (e.g., "Can you add an example here?"); and (3) positive softeners (e.g., "You've raised some good points, but ...").

References

Aljaafreh, A., & Lantolf, J. (1994). Negative feedback as regulation and second language learning in the zone of proximal development. *Modern Language Journal, 78*, 465–483.

Allwright, R. (1975). Problems in the study of the language teacher's treatment of learner error. In M. Burt & H. Dulay (Eds.), *On TESOL '75: New directions in language learning, teaching, and bilingual education* (pp. 96–109). Washington, DC: TESOL.

Ammar, A., & Spada, N. (2006). One size fits all? Recasts, prompts, and L2 learning. *Studies in Second Language Acquisition, 28*, 543–574.

Bartram, M., & Walt, R. (1991). *Correction: Mistake management: A positive approach for language teachers.* Hove: Language Teaching Publications.

Basturkmen, H., Loewen, S. & Ellis, R. (2004). Teachers' stated beliefs about incidental focus on form and their classroom practices. *Applied Linguistics, 25*, 243–272.

Bitchener, J. (2008). Evidence in support of written corrective feedback. *Journal of Second Language Writing, 17*, 102–118.

Burt, M. (1975). Error analysis in the adult EFL classroom. *TESOL Quarterly, 9*, 53–63.

Byrne, D. (1988). *Teaching writing skills.* London: Longman.

Chandler, J. (2003). The efficacy of various kinds of error feedback for improvement in the accuracy and fluency of L2 student writing. *Journal of Second Language Writing, 12*, 267–296.

Chaudron, C. (1977). A descriptive model of discourse in the corrective treatment of learners' errors. *Language Learning, 27*, 29–46.

Chaudron, C. (1988). *Second language classrooms: Research on teaching and learning.* Cambridge: Cambridge University Press.

Cohen, A., & Cavalcanti, M. (1990). Feedback on written compositions: Teacher and student verbal reports. In B. Kroll (Ed.), *Second language writing: Research insights for the classroom* (pp. 155–177). Cambridge: Cambridge University Press.

Connors, R., & Lunsford, A. (1993). Teachers' rhetorical comments on student papers. *College Composition and Communication, 44*, 200–223.

Conrad, S., & Goldstein, L. (1999). ESL student revision after teacher-written comments: Text, contexts, and individuals. *Journal of Second Language Writing, 8*, 147–179.

Corder, P. (1967). The significance of learners' errors. *International Review of Applied Linguistics, 5*, 161–170.

Doughty, C. (2001). Cognitive underpinnings of focus on form. In P. Robinson (Ed.), *Cognition and second language instruction* (pp. 206–257). Cambridge: Cambridge University Press.

Edge, J. (1989). *Mistakes and correction.* New York: Longman.

Ellis, R. (2010). Cognitive, social, and psychological dimensions of corrective feedback. In R. Batstone (Ed.), *Sociocognitive perspectives on language use and language learning* (pp. 151–165). Oxford: Oxford University Press.

Ellis, R., Loewen, S. & Erlam, R. (2006). Implicit and explicit corrective feedback and the acquisition of L2 grammar. *Studies in Second Language Acquisition*, 28, 339–368.

Ellis, R., & Sheen, Y. (2006). Re-examining the role of recasts in L2 acquisition. *Studies in Second Language Acquisition*, 28, 575–600.

Ellis, R., Sheen, Y., Murakami, M. & Takashima, H. (2008). The effects of focused and unfocused written corrective feedback in an English as a foreign language context. *System*, 36, 353–371.

Ferris, D. (1995). Teaching ESL composition students to become independent self-editors. *TESOL Journal*, 4(4), 18–22.

Ferris, D. (1997). The influence of teacher commentary on student revision. *TESOL Quarterly*, 31, 315–339.

Ferris, D. (1999). The case for grammar correction in L2 writing classes: A response to Truscott (1996). *Journal of Second language Writing*, 8, 1–10.

Ferris, D. (2003a). Responding to writing. In B. Kroll (Ed.), *Exploring the dynamics of second language writing* (pp. 119–140). Cambridge: Cambridge University Press.

Ferris, D. (2003b). *Response to student writing: Implications for second language students*. Mahwah, NJ: Lawrence Erlbaum.

Ferris, D. (2004). The "grammar correction" debate in L2 writing: Where are we and where do we go from here. *Journal of Second Language Writing*, 13, 49–62.

Ferris, D., & Hedgcock, J. (2005). *Teaching ESL composition: Purpose, process, and practice*. Mahwah, NJ: Erlbaum.

Ferris, D., & Roberts, B. (2001). Error feedback in L2 writing classes: How explicit does it need to be? *Journal of Second Language Writing*, 10, 161–184.

Harmer, J. (1983). *The practice of English language teaching*. London: Longman.

Hedgcock, J., & Lefkowitz, N. (1994). Feedback on feedback: Assessing learner receptivity to teacher response in L2 composing. *Journal of Second Language Writing*, 3, 141–163.

Hedgcock, J., & Lefkowitz, N. (1996). Some input on input: Two analyses of student response to expert feedback on L2 writing. *Modern Language Journal*, 80, 287–308.

Hedge, T. (2000). *Teaching and learning in the language classroom*. Oxford: Oxford University Press.

Hendrickson, J. (1978). Error correction in foreign language teaching: Recent theory, research and practice. *Modern Language Journal*, 62, 387–398.

Hyland, F. (2000). ESL writers and feedback: Giving more autonomy to students. *Language Teaching Research*, 4, 33–54.

Hyland, F., & Hyland, K. (2001). Sugaring the pill: Praise and criticism in written feedback, *Journal of Second Language Writing*, 10(3), 185–212.

Hyland, K., & Hyland, F. (2006). Contexts and issues in feedback on L2 writing: An introduction. In K. Hyland & F. Hyland (Eds.), *Feedback in second language writing: Contexts and issues* (pp. 1–19). Cambridge: Cambridge University Press.

Johnson, K. (1996). *Language teaching and skill learning*. Oxford: Blackwell.

Knoblauch, C., & Brannon, L. (1981). Teacher commentary on student writing: The state of the art. *Freshman English News*, 10, 1–4.

Krashen, S. (1982). *Principles and practice in second language acquisition*. Oxford: Pergamon.

Lee, I. (2009). Ten mismatches between teachers' beliefs and written feedback practice. *ELT Journal*, 63(1), 13–22.

Leki, I. (1991). The preferences of ESL students for error correction in college-level writing classes. *Foreign Language Annals*, 24, 203–218.

Li, S. (2010). The effectiveness of corrective feedback in SLA: A meta-analysis. *Language Learning*, 60, 309–365.

Loewen, S. (2005). Incidental focus on form and second language learning. *Studies in Second Language Acquisition*, 27, 361–386.

Loewen, S., & Erlam, R. (2006). Corrective feedback in the chatroom: An experimental study. *Computer Assisted Language Learning*, 19(1), 1–14.

Loewen, S., & Philp, J. (2006). Recasts in the adult English L2 classroom: Characteristics, explicitness, and effectiveness. *Modern Language Journal*, 90, 536–556.

Long, M. (1977). Teacher feedback on learner error: Mapping cognitions. In H. D. Brown, C. A. Yorio & R. H. Crymes (Eds.), *On TESOL '77* (pp. 278–293). Washington, DC: TESOL.

Long, M. (1983). Native speaker/non-native speaker conversation in the second language classroom. In M. Clarke & J. Handscombe (Eds.), *On TESOL '82* (pp. 207–225). Washington, DC: TESOL.

Long, M. (1991). Focus on form: A design feature in language teaching methodology. In K. de Bot, R. Ginsberg & C. Kramsch (Eds.), *Foreign language research in cross-cultural perspective* (pp. 39–52). Amsterdam: John Benjamins.

Long, M. (1996). The role of the linguistic environment in second language acquisition. In W. Ritchie & T. Bhatia (Eds.), *Handbook of second language acquisition* (pp. 413–468). San Diego, CA: Academic Press.

Long, M. (2007). Recasts in SLA: The story so far. In M. H. Long (Ed.), *Problems in SLA* (pp. 75–116). Mahwah, NJ: Laurence Erlbaum.

Lyster, R. (1998a). Recasts, repetition, and ambiguity in L2 classroom discourse. *Studies in Second Language Acquisition*, 20, 51–81.

Lyster, R. (1998b). Negotiation of form, recasts, and explicit correction in relation to error types and learner repair in immersion classrooms. *Language Learning*, 48, 183–218.

Lyster, R. (2004). Differential effects of prompts and recasts in form-focused instruction. *Studies in Second Language Acquisition*, 19, 37–66.

Lyster, R., & Mori, H. (2006). Interactional feedback and instructional counterbalance. *Studies in Second Language Acquisition*, 28, 269–300.

Lyster, R., & Ranta, L. (1997). Corrective feedback and learner uptake. *Studies in Second Language Acquisition*, 19, 37–66.

Lyster, R., & Saito, K. (2010). Effects of oral feedback in SLA classroom research: A meta-analysis. *Studies in Second Language Acquisition, 32,* 265–302.

McDonough, K., & Mackey, A. (2006). Responses to recasts: Repetitions, primed production, and linguistic development. *Language Learning, 56,* 693–720.

McGarrell, H., & Verbeen, J. (2007). Motivating revision of drafts through formative feedback. *ELT Journal, 61,* 228–236.

Mackey, A., & Goo, J. (2007). Interaction research in SLA: A meta-analysis and research synthesis. In A. Mackey (Ed.), *Conversational interaction in second language acquisition: A collection of empirical studies* (pp. 407–452). Oxford: Oxford University Press.

Norris, J., & Ortega, L. (2000). Effectiveness of L2 instruction: A research synthesis and qualitative meta-anaylsis. *Language Learning, 50,* 417–528.

Oliver, R., & Mackey, A. (2003). Interactional context and feedback in child ESL classrooms. *Modern Language Journal, 87,* 519–533.

Poehner, M. E. (2008). *Dynamic assessment: A Vygotskian approach to understanding and promoting second language development.* Berlin: Springer Publishing.

Poehner, M., & Lantolf, J. (2005). Dynamic assessment in the language classroom. *Language Teaching Research, 9,* 233–265.

Raimes, A. (1983). *Techniques in teaching writing.* New York: Oxford University Press.

Robb, T., Ross, S. & Shortreed, I. (1986). Salience of feedback on error and its effect on EFL writing quality. *TESOL Quarterly, 20,* 83–93.

Rolin-Ianziti, J. (2010). The organization of delayed second language correction. *Language Teaching Research, 14,* 183–206.

Russell, J., & Spada, N. (2006). The effectiveness of corrective feedback for the acquisition of L2 grammar: A meta-analysis of the research. In J. Norris and L. Ortega (Eds.), *Synthesizing research on language learning teaching* (pp. 133–164). Amsterdam: John Benjamins.

Sachs, R., & Suh, B. (2007). Textually enhanced recasts, learner awareness, and L2 outcomes in synchronous computer-mediated interaction. In A. Mackey (Ed.), *Conversational interaction in second language acquisition: A collection of empirical studies* (pp. 197–227). Oxford: Oxford University Press.

Sauro, S. (2009). Computer-mediated corrective feedback and the development of L2 grammar. *Language Learning & Technology, 13*(1), 96–120.

Schmidt, R. (1994). Deconstructing consciousness in search of useful definitions for applied linguistics. *AILA Review, 11,* 11–26.

Schmidt, R. (2001). Attention. In P. Robinson (Ed.), *Cognition and second language instruction* (pp. 3–32). Cambridge: Cambridge University Press.

Seedhouse, P. (1997). The case of the missing "no": The relationship between pedagogy and interaction. *Language Learning, 47,* 547–583.

Seedhouse, P. (2004). *The interactional architecture of the language classroom: A conversation analysis perspective*. Malden, MA: Blackwell.

Semke, H. (1984). The effects of the red pen. *Foreign Language Annals, 17*, 195–202.

Sheen, Y. (2004). Corrective feedback and learner uptake in communicative classrooms across instructional settings. *Language Teaching Research, 8*, 263–300.

Sheen, Y. (2006). Exploring the relationship between characteristics of recasts and learner uptake. *Language Teaching Research, 11*(4), 361–392.

Sheen, Y. (2007a). The effect of focused written corrective feedback and language aptitude on ESL learners' acquisition of articles. *TESOL Quarterly, 41*(2), 255–283.

Sheen, Y. (2007b). The effect of corrective feedback, language aptitude and learner attitudes on the acquisition of English articles. In A. Mackey (Ed.), *Conversational interaction in second language acquisition* (pp. 301–322). Oxford: Oxford University Press.

Sheen, Y. (2008). Recasts, language anxiety, modified output and L2 learning. *Language Learning, 58*(4), 835–874.

Sheen, Y. (2010). Differential effects of oral and written corrective feedback in the ESL classroom. *Studies in Second Language Acquisition, 32*, 203–234.

Sheen, Y., Wright, D. & Moldawa, A. (2009). Differential effects of focused and unfocused written correction on the accurate use of grammatical forms by adult ESL learners. *System, 37*(4), 556–569.

Smith, B. (2005). The relationship between negotiated interaction, learner uptake and lexical acquisition in task-based computer-mediated communication. *TESOL Quarterly, 39*, 33–58.

Sommers, N. (1982). Responding to student writing. *College Composition and Communication, 33*, 148–156.

Swain, M. (1985). Communicative competence: Some roles of comprehensible input and comprehensible output in its development. In S. M. Gass & C. Madden (Eds.), *Input and second language acquisition* (pp. 91–103). Rowley, MA: Newbury House.

Swain, M. (1995). Three functions of output in second language learning. In G. Cook & B. Seidlhofer (Eds.), *Principle and practice in applied linguistics: Studies in honor of H. G. Widdowson* (pp. 125–144). Oxford: Oxford University Press.

Truscott, J. (1996). The case against grammar correction in L2 writing classes. *Language Learning, 46*, 327–369.

Truscott, J. (1999). The case for "the case for grammar correction in L2 writing classes": A response to Ferris. *Journal of Second Language Writing, 8*, 111–122.

Truscott, J. (2004). Evidence and conjecture on the effects of correction: A response to Chandler. *Journal of Second Language Writing, 13*, 337–343

Truscott, J. (2007). The effect of error correction on learners' ability to write accurately. *Journal of Second Language Writing, 16*, 255–272.

Ur, P. (1996). *A course in language teaching*. Cambridge: Cambridge University Press.

Van Lier, L. (1988). *The classroom and the language learner*. London: Longman.

Williams, J. (2001). The effectiveness of spontaneous attention to form. *System, 29*, 325–340.

Yoshida, R. (2008). Teachers' choice and learners' preference of corrective feedback types. *Language Awareness, 17*(1), 78–93.

Zamel, V. (1985). Responding to student writing. *TESOL Quarterly, 19*, 79–102.

Chapter 4

Computerized Technology for Teaching ELLs

Christina Kitson

Glossary

Term	Meaning	Usage
Active stylus	A pen-like device used to work on touchscreen technology that actively communicates with the technology	Has a fine point and its own power and computer parts, such as an Apple pen or Galaxy stylus
Asynchronous communication	Communication done with a delay	This would be communication where you expect a wait before a response is received, such as e-mail, letters, and blog posts
CALL	Computer-assisted language learning	Using a computer to help teach or train students in a language
LMS	Learning management system	A digital location where a teacher can post materials and grades as well as have students upload materials and view content
Passive or capacitive stylus	A pen-like device with a blunt tip used to work on touchscreen technology that does not actively communicate with the technology	Has a blunt point and no power or computer parts, your finger is a passive stylus
PLN	Personal learning network	Informal network of people that the user puts together to interact with and gain wisdom from
TELL	Technology enhanced language learning	A broader term than CALL that looks at digital technology in general being used to enhance language learning

(Continued)

Term	Meaning	Usage
SMART Boards	Interactive whiteboard done with computer technology (SMART Board is a brand)	This device allows you to project an image directly from your computer to the screen and interact with it (no projector needed).
Synchronous communication	Communication done in real time	This would be communication where you are able to immediately interact with your communication partner, such as phone, chatting, messaging, and interactive editing.
VLN	Virtual learning network	Informal group of people connected by a common theme or idea to interact with and gain wisdom from

Background

Technology has always been a part of classroom instruction. That technology started out in a very different manner than what we might think of today. Blackboards and chalk used to be innovative classroom technology. We used to use ink and typewriters and have now transitioned into using computers, iPads, and mobile devices. People react strongly to new technology, both positively and negatively (Bax, 2011). What starts out as new and potentially exciting and terrifying becomes normal over time and takes a back seat to what we are

FIGURE 4.1 Children in a classroom.

Source: https://commons.wikimedia.org/wiki/File:Children_in_a_classroom.jpg.

doing (Bax, 2011). Technology can expose language learners to language in a positive manner and allow for their own development (Parvin & Salam, 2015). A description of technology for use in teaching English as a second language (TESL) can be found in the *TESOL Technology Standards Framework* (Teachers of English to Speakers of Other Languages, 2008):

> The term technology ... refers to the use of systems that rely on computer chips, digital applications, and networks in all of their forms. These systems are not limited to the commonly recognized desktop and laptop computers: Almost all electronic devices these days include an embedded computer chip of some sort (DVD players, data projectors, interactive whiteboards, etc.). Mobile devices that employ a computer at their core (cell phones, personal digital assistants [PDAs], MP3 players, etc.) will undoubtedly occupy a more central role in language teaching and learning in the years to come. (p. 4)

In this chapter, the term "computerized technology" will be used to refer to anything that runs or uses a computer chip that is used in the classroom. This is somewhat an extension of **computer-assisted language learning** (**CALL**) where computers are used to assist in language learning. Rather than limit the idea to computers, I am suggesting that all technology that uses or contains a computer chip be included as part of computerized technology. Defining computerized technology this way is a more inclusive description and would include anything from standard computers, phones and mobile devices, interactive whiteboards, websites, and apps.

In the early years of CALL, the idea was that teachers could use computers to help teach aspects of language. CALL research started with the PLATO project at the University of Illinois in 1960 (Marty, 1982). This project was used for drills, grammar, and translation tests (Ahmad et al., 1985). This was part of what Warschauer and Healey (1998) referred to as the behaviorist period of CALL, which focused on the computer as a tutor. The computer was used for additional practice activities and nothing more. In the 1970s personal computers helped CALL reach a wider audience and allowed for the first wave of CALL research. This is part of what Warschauer and Healey (1998) referred to as communicative CALL, and it continued into the 1980s. This was a rejection of the behaviorist approach and moved to the idea that "CALL should focus more on using forms rather than on the forms themselves" (Lee, 2000, para. 5). This was a move away from the computer as tutor model. The last stage of CALL development according to Warschauer and Healey (1998) was integrative CALL. The main idea of this stage was to more fully incorporate technology into language teaching and integrate various more authentic skills into the classroom (Lee, 2000).

There has been a move away from the term CALL to something different by some researchers. They feel that computer-assisted language learning is no longer limited to computers, and thus the term should change to reflect modern practice. This new approach is referred to as **technology-enhanced language learning** (**TELL**). According to Walker and White (2013) in their book, *Technology Enhanced Language Learning: Connecting Theory and Practice*, this move illustrates a main difference between CALL and TELL, "technology not as assisting language learning, but as part of the environment in which language exists and is used" (p. 9). This is a shift in how we approach using technology in the classroom, it focuses on the idea that technology is part of the world around our students, and it should therefore be integrated into the classroom. According to Lee (2000) there are ways technology can significantly contribute to language learning, "experiential learning ..., motivation ..., enhanced student achievement ..., authentic materials for study ..., greater interaction ..., individualization ..., independence from a single source of information ..., and global understanding" (para. 7). Since there are positive benefits, it makes sense to learn a little about using technology in the language learning classroom.

No matter what we call it, CALL, TELL, or computerized technology, the main idea for this chapter is how to integrate it into the language learning classroom in meaningful ways.

For the Classroom Teacher

All teachers should know the basics of how to use computerized technology in their classrooms. Knowing how to use all the technology they have access to can help teachers better perform their jobs. If their school has whiteboards in the classrooms, then the teacher should know how to use them. If it is a one-to-one device school, then the teachers should be familiar with the devices. If a school expects the students to use computerized technology, then

FIGURE 4.2 STS modern classroom.

Source: Copyright © by Mnetka (CC BY-SA 4.0) at https://commons.wikimedia.org/wiki/File:STS_Modern_Classroom.jpg.

the teachers should also understand how to use it and be provided basic training when they are hired. This should also extend to training when technology is added to the classroom. I have seen schools try to improve their technology by adding **SMART Boards**, but not provide any training for the teachers. This can cause many issues, including teachers fearing the technology and avoiding it, teachers' inability to use the technology effectively, new technology taking more time to use than lower tech options, and teachers' inability to help their students learn and use the technology.

There are two major reasons for teachers to know how to use their classroom technology, the first is if the students struggle with the technology for any reason. Teachers can assist the students in figuring out how to use the technology or device. This is especially important when we look at standardized testing, which is being done on computers in many states. If a student does not understand how to use the technology, that could have an impact on their performance and anxiety levels on standardized tests administered using that technology. The second reason for teachers to understand computerized technology is to better use it to teach students. Teachers should have a complete understanding of technology for teaching language skills (Pourhosein Gilakjani, 2017; Solanki & Shyamleel, 2012). This helps make the students more familiar with the technology, so when they have to use it for something like standardized tests, anxiety is lower. Keeping up with technology is also an important life skill that will help ELLs as they move from school to jobs or higher education. Teacher modeling of technology can help learners use technology more for language learning (Costley, 2014). This might also allow for more interactive and engaging lessons and activities.

It is important to know what options there are for teachers to bring computerized technology into their classrooms as well as to use the existing technology that is already in their classrooms. It is also important that the teacher gets to choose how and what to use in their lessons. This helps the teacher fit their personal teaching style and work from their areas of strength. Teachers should not use technology just to use it; the technology needs to serve a purpose. This means picking appropriate technology for the activity, the classroom, the class, the students, and the teacher themselves. Technology is not an answer to every classroom issue, but it can be a tool to help in the classroom. Nemeth and Simon (2013) state, "Technology shouldn't replace the great things already happening in your classroom, but it can enhance, augment, and improve the teaching and learning experience when used for a specific purpose" (p. 52). According to Ahmadi (2018), "Technology resources cannot guarantee teachers' teaching and learners' learning" (p. 122). Technology is a tool for teaching language, and teachers need to be trained in the tool and how that tool can enhance their instruction.

This may seem unusual, but there are times when ELL students arrive in the United States and lack computer skills entirely. There are some general technology skills that teachers often expect their students to know when they arrive in class, but they may have to be taught how to use a mouse, type, and use applications and software. It is easy to assume that middle school students might know Microsoft products, or that high school students will be well versed in searching the internet and evaluating Web resources; but ELLs may need to be taught these much later than a teacher expects. They may also not have access to a mobile device or other computerized technology device in their home. This may also be true of non-ELL students. It is important to think about students' access and understanding of computerized technology when planning activities and their use in class. If each student has a mobile phone you can do activities that use their phones, but if you have students who do not have their own phones it is important to make sure your activities can be done by sharing, or by using a different type of device (like a computer or iPad).

General Language Skills

As we have seen in earlier chapters, ELLs must learn and be proficient in all domains of language, which include listening, speaking, reading, and writing. These domains can be addressed separately as well as merged together when needed during instruction. It is often very difficult to create a task for one domain that does not overlap with other domains. One area to think about if considering computerized technology for language teaching is if you want to have your students working in real time (**synchronous**) or working with a possible time delay (**asynchronous**). There are times when synchronous works best, for instance, if you are wanting them to work on their conversational skills. Having a long delay would be artificial and ineffective. However, if you want them to work on their academic note-taking skills and summarize a lecture, having them listen to a TED Talk and post their video response with notes would be appropriate.

TABLE 4.1 Examples of Synchronous and Asynchronous Communication

Type of communication	Example activity	Possible resource
Synchronous communication	Conference calls	Zoom, Skype, Facetime
	Chatting online	Facebook Messenger, WhatsApp, Viber, WeChat
	Document editing online	Google Documents, Microsoft Office Live, Etherpad
Asynchronous communication	Discussion board	BlackBoard, Canvas, Schoology, Edmodo, Google Classroom
	Video response	Flipgrid, Recap
	Blog and respond	WordPress, Wix
	E-mail correspondence	Google Gmail, school-provided e-mail account

TABLE 4.2 Dictionary Resources

	Dictionary	Website
Traditional dictionary	Collins English Dictionary	https://www.collinsdictionary.com/dictionary/english
Traditional dictionary	Oxford Learner's Dictionary	https://www.oxfordlearnersdictionaries.com/us/
Traditional dictionary	Longman Dictionary of Contemporary English	https://www.ldoceonline.com//
Visual dictionary	Visuwords	https://visuwords.com/
Video dictionary	Vidtionary	http://www.vidtionary.com/

An excellent resource for students is online dictionaries. Often in online dictionaries you can find not only definitions, but also pronunciations, with both written transcription and audio pronunciation. It is good to pick a dictionary that you like and have everyone use the same dictionary for projects and assignments. You can also compare different dictionary entries for the same words. If you are working with lower proficiency students there are online image and video dictionaries that might help them better understand the vocabulary items.

Using Games to Teach Language

One way to make lessons more engaging for ELLs as well as other students is to use games. Wright, Betteridge, and Buckby (2006) indicate that games are helpful for teaching and learning all skills at all levels. James Paul Gee (2008) in his book, *What Video Games Have to Teach Us About Learning and Literacy*, suggests that video games can help us better our pedagogical approach. Games work well for review of concepts before tests or after instruction. They also can be used to help build class rapport and better interaction. A great tool for this is Kahoot (https://kahoot.com/). Kahoot does not require that the students sign up or have any special device. It can be played on any device that can connect to the internet. The teacher needs a free account to create a quiz or survey but they are welcome to use materials created by other users if there are materials available that match their needs. This does require a way to project or share one screen with the students that will display the questions (there is sound that goes with the game but it is not necessary in order to play). Kahoot can support images in the questions and allows for up to four answers. Kahoot can be used to assess student understanding of spelling, vocabulary, basic concepts, surveying ideas, and much more. It is worth looking at to see if it might fit the needs of your classroom.

There are also many websites that will allow you to create your own version of Jeopardy with your content, crossword puzzles, as well as many other unique games. If you do a simple

Web search for ESL games you will find many online resources. *The Internet TESL Journal* maintains a website with games and activities for teachers (http://iteslj.org/games/) that has many valuable classroom resources. If your students have access to an **active stylus** and device you can even work on handwriting using your device. An active stylus has a point like a pen and has its own power and computer parts. This is like an Apple pen, or Galaxy stylus. The other type of stylus is a **passive or capacitive stylus**. With the passive stylus, you can interact and write on a touchscreen device, but it is larger and blunt. Your finger is a type of passive stylus. There is no communication between the device and the stylus so the product created is much less refined. To work on handwriting it is best to have an active stylus.

Another game-like approach to use computerized technology is through flashcards. Traditionally these were done on small pieces of paper or index cards that had content on both sides and were flipped to check understanding. Digital flashcards work in much the same way. Depending on the program or application used to create the flashcards they might be made by the teacher or the students, or they may allow for the teacher to create an original set and the students to add to and refine it. They can be used as a game where students work through their flashcards together in a timed environment or for individual study. Many applications for flashcards will also generate quizzes based on the entered information. Flashcards can be used to fill small amounts of time when a lesson is done early or when certain students finish their materials early. Two good sources for flashcards are Studyblue (https://www.studyblue.com/) and Quizlet (https://quizlet.com/); both offer many free services as well as their paid options.

Listening Skills

Listening involves immediate decoding of the message or translation in the listener's head, especially in conversations. Listening skills can be taught using computerized technology. Computerized technology choices depend on what aspects of listening you are trying to develop and improve. There are some basic skills and strategies that are usually taught to help improve listening based on the author's experience and on the materials from Helgesen and Brown (2007) and Walker and White (2013).

Listening serves somewhat separate functions as a tool for information processing and understanding and for conversational skills. Along with the basic skills, there are some strategies for teaching listening. These are not unique to listening and often overlap with the other language areas. As mentioned earlier, inference is a listening skill. Being able to take the information given and make an "educated guess" is vital to help fill in missing or unfamiliar information. The listener needs to be able to seek clarification if they did not understand something. This involves asking for the information again or

TABLE 4.3 Listening Skills

Listening skill	Description of listening skill
Sounds	Ability to perceive the sounds of the language. This involves being able to tell the different sounds apart based on if they make a difference in meaning. This also includes being able to identify when sounds are minimized (such as linked and blended speech) as well as stress patterns, intonation patterns, and the rhythm of the language.
Words	Focusing on the meaning behind the words. This includes being able to tell when one word starts and stops, as well as using knowledge of the rules of the language to see how words fit together and how that impacts meaning.
Meaning and intent	Decoding what the speaker means is a major part of listening. This might include being able to determine the speaker's attitudes or beliefs about what they are saying.
Inference and schemata	Inferring (using the context and prior knowledge to identify the meaning of a word or utterance) is a necessary listening skill. A listener may use their overall schemata to help them understand what is being said (like in a lecture or presentation).
Nonverbals	Being able to connect gestures, movements, facial expressions or other nonverbal cues to the intended message.
Gist	Working with information itself. This involves getting to the overall idea or gist of the message and understanding the main points, supporting details, and organization of the message.
Conversation	Interaction with the speaker. This requires understanding language variations (accents, dialects, individual differences) as well as the proper turn-taking strategies for conversation. Other elements of this skill might be related to understanding the speaker's mood and making some basic predictions of what they might say next, which helps the listener prepare their response.

perhaps to have it phrased differently. Listeners need to be able to predict, especially as they learn to be conversational listeners. This means they need to be able to rehearse in their heads what they think they might need to know, to be able to participate in a conversation. Another vital part of listening is learning to pay attention to the big picture. It is hard at the beginning of the language learning process to try not to understand each word individually. Trying to understand each word is hard to do and very time consuming. Learners need to learn to listen for the most important information and details rather than every word. There is not enough time to listen for each individual word, and the learner could get lost.

Using technology to teach listening may seem more difficult than a language aspect like grammar. The first part is to decide what specific listening element you are trying to develop and then find the appropriate computerized technology tool for that element.

TABLE 4.4 Listening Activities

Listening as lecture/ notetaking	Use an online lecture to have students listen and take notes to identify main ideas and details to infer speakers' intentions, etc.	TED Talks; YouTube; Khan Academy; vlogs; podcasts; TV shows and news programs
Listening as an exercise	Use lectures with a dictation activity; create your own or use an existing online opportunity, or music (create a dictation based on the lyrics).	Search for dictation exercises or use music; use word-processing program to develop worksheet
Listening as phoneme isolation	Work on individual sounds through use of minimal pairs, tongue twisters, and individual sound work.	Search for minimal pair, tongue twisters, or IPA sounds for audio to help with practice
Listening for response	This could involve students listening to a lecture/podcast/vlog and creating their own response (could be a paper or their own video) or carrying on a conversation (which could be done with teleconferencing software).	TED Talks; YouTube; Khan Academy; vlogs; podcasts; or Zoom, Skype, Facetime, etc.

One additional thought about using some of the websites mentioned in this section is learner autonomy. Students can choose an area that they are interested in for their listening task depending on the assignment, and that can help them be more engaged in the content and improve their listening skills. This is true whenever a student is given a choice in their content and allowed to focus on their own interests.

Speaking Skills

Speaking skills can be thought of very similarly to listening, but with the roles reversed. Rather than being the recipient of the message and decoding (or trying to understand the message), they are creating and encoding the message for the intended recipient. Similar to listening, what activities students work on and the computerized technology that is used is dependent on the students' proficiency level and the specific skill or strategy that you are teaching. There are a few major skills needed to be a good speaker based on the author's experience and on the materials from Bailey (2012), Folse (2014), Lane (2010), and Walker and White (2013).

Just as with listening, there are some basic strategies that can benefit those learning to speak English. The first is learning to paraphrase, summarize, or substitute in order to avoid unfamiliar concepts and vocabulary. Teaching how to work around unfamiliar information can be very beneficial in working on speaking. Another strategy involves being aware of what you are saying and planning what you are going to say: actively thinking

TABLE 4.5 Speaking Skills

Speaking skill	Description of speaking skill
Pronunciation	A student needs to be able to command the sounds of the language effectively to be properly understood. This also includes elements of intonation, stress, and rhythm.
Conversation and convention	Learning how to make requests and give opinions or other specific speech acts. Conversation and conversational skills including turn taking; starting, maintaining, and ending a conversation; as well as clarification requests when something is not initially understood. Some of the cues in English for conversation involve word stress, sentence stress, and intonation, which need to be taught.
Message	Construction of the message; making sure that your conversation is something that can be followed by the listener. Including transitions, signposts, and logical sequencing can make a difference in the listener's ability to understand and decode your message.
General skills	Being able to speak fluently, which means not including a lot of unnecessary breaks, pauses, or disfluencies (uh, um, err, etc.) as well as basic use of understandable English grammar and rules.

about the process and the message or rehearsing rather than speaking without thinking. The final strategy involves learning how to better interact and clarify: knowing how to ask for clarification, understanding when you are being asked for clarification so you can try to improve your message, and checking with your listener(s) along the way to ensure understanding.

Computerized technology offers a means to work on many of these skills and strategies in a less formal non-classroom setting. This can help reduce learner anxiety and increase their engagement. Much like listening this can seem like an ill fit for using technology. There is a certain ease to having students work with others in the classroom and using that as part of their speaking instruction. It is important to think about the specific aspects of speaking you want to work on and then find computerized technology that is appropriate for that aspect.

One reason for allowing students the option to record their presentations rather than having them present in class is that it allows for more practice and time to perfect their performance. They can record and listen to their performance, evaluating themselves and selecting areas they want to improve on before the final submission. Students who are shy or reticent to speak in class may also find recording their performance to be less anxiety provoking. Voki (www.voki.com/) can help lower anxiety even more by allowing students to create a representation of themselves or use a cartoon character rather than recording themselves physically.

TABLE 4.6 Speaking Activities

Speaking as a presentation	Speaking practice on presentation skills and all aspects needed for more formal speaking activities	Voki; video and audio recording on mobile device or computer
Speaking as a pronunciation exercise/ phoneme work	Speech practice with specific sounds to improve pronunciation and comprehensibility	Speech-to-text software (to see if speech can be properly understood); working with artificial intelligence (Alexa, Cortana, Siri) to see if speech can be properly understood
Speaking as conversation	Speaking with others to have a conversation. This may be on a specific topic or general conversation skills.	Use teleconferencing software (Skype, Zoom, Facetime) to interact with people not in your classroom; create a WebPal program where they get a Web-based speaking partner
Speaking for clarification/ speech acts	Speaking done to help gain information or practice a specific speech act	Use teleconferencing software (Skype, Zoom, Facetime) to interact with people for specific information

Reading Skills

Teaching reading is in some ways like teaching listening. One major goal of reading is to be able to decode a written message and make meaning from it. Many people will see a logical connection between teaching reading and using computerized technology tools in the classroom. Many teachers probably already use their phones and tablets to read content or e-mail daily. Just like listening and speaking, it is important to think about the skill that you are teaching and what computerized technology tool will be most beneficial for teaching it.

TABLE 4.7 Speaking Skills

Reading skill	Description of reading skill
Alphabet	Understanding of the letters and their representative sounds. For English this means being able to recognize letter combinations that might make different sounds in different contexts.
Context	Being able to use context clues to help with unfamiliar word meaning.
Sight words	Being able to identify simple words on sight rather than having to sound them out. This can greatly aid reading speed.
Inference	Inferring is also very important in reading and is often referred to as reading between the lines or looking past what the author wrote to what they meant.
Organization and genre	Having an understanding of how writing is organized. Understanding how an academic paper is organized can help a reader understand the paper. The same is true of children's stories and fairy tales, which tend to follow a specific pattern.

There are a few major skills that are needed in reading, based on the author's experience and on the materials from Farrell (2009), Nation (2009), Walker and White (2013), and Watkins (2018).

Understanding the alphabet is both a skill and a strategy. It often needs to be taught explicitly. As English is not a phonetic language we have to work on teaching sound combinations and variations as well. Think of the classic example of "ghoti," which if sounded out using the right pronunciation patterns sounds like the word "fish." The "gh" is like that found in rough, the "o" is like that found in "women," and the "ti" is like that found in "patient" (a video explanation of this concept can be found at www.youtube.com/watch?v=j9Q1cM7_ai4). Obviously, this is not how we would normally pronounce this word if we saw it and followed the rules of English pronunciation, so it is important to be able to know variations and find the right one for your context.

Context clues are important in learning to read. One way of working on this skill would be to circle unfamiliar words in a reading. Then have the students go back and look at everything around the circled words for clues to the unknown words' meanings. This goes along with being able to look words up in a dictionary or use a hyperlink (a clickable link to more information about the word) if one is available. Context clues are for those students who are starting to read, but those who are still working at the word level need to focus some time on sight words. Part of understanding sight words is gaining an understanding of basic grammar, and that understanding can help students with unfamiliar words in the future. Knowing that nouns might have an article in front of them (a, an, the) will help students identify that it is a noun, even if the meaning is not clear.

A strategy that is important for reading is to know what kind of information you are looking for and what reading skills are needed to acquire it. If you are looking to just get the main idea, you might just skim, versus if you are wanting a piece of specific information you might scan for that specific piece of information. The final strategy that will be discussed is appreciation and evaluating usefulness of reading passages and stories. The first part is based on personal preference. It might be easiest to pick stories that you know fit into a genre, or type of story, that you already enjoy. If you know you enjoy crime thrillers you might try reading the new crime novel that comes out because you think you will enjoy it. The other part of this strategy is to be able to evaluate reading materials. This might be evaluating the quality of the writing, but it could also be evaluating the source, the content, the message, or any number of other details. Evaluation can be done for any number of reasons and in any number of ways, but it is a crucial skill for a reader once they reach academic texts.

TABLE 4.8   Reading Activities

Reading simplified to level	Readings picked based on the level of the learner; can be done with the same main text but provided at different reading levels	Newsela has several versions of the same newspaper article; Breaking News English (https://breakingnewsenglish.com/) does something similar; Embedded Reading (https://embeddedreading.com/) provides scaffolded versions of one text; CommonLit has leveled readings at different levels on the same themes; Books that Grow offers adaptive reading based on level and needs.
Reading for speed	Reading for speed or reaching a specific reading speed. Partially making ELLs more aware of their reading speed since speed is important for testing and classroom function	There are many speed reading programs and apps out there; Spreeder (www.spreeder.com/) allows you to copy and paste text and look at reading speed.
Reading for enjoyment	Reading for fun or to get students reading something they are interested in learning more about	E-books from the local library; creating a reading group based on interests (perhaps global reading group); using the Web to find readings related to specific topic
Reading for academic content	Reading for academic purposes where you might have to take notes and refer to materials	Adobe PDF; Scrible (www.scrible.com/) a browser plug-in that lets you annotate and share
Organization	Reading can benefit from having a better understanding of how the materials are organized. Use of a graphic organizer can help the reader understand and remember the content.	Graphic organizers can be found online for free or created using Microsoft Word, Google Docs, or other similar word-processing programs.

Writing Skills

Teaching writing can be similar to teaching speaking. Both ask students to try to create language using their new language system and rules. Like speaking, writing is about encoding messages for someone else to decode and make meaning from. As mentioned with all the previous skills, it is important to pick the computerized technology tool based on the specific language features as well as the specific purpose for using technology. There are a few major skills involved in writing in the second language (L2) based on the author's experience and on the materials from Harmer (2013), Nation (2009), and Walker and White (2013).

Writing skills and strategies are very interconnected since writing is a more formal and explicit process. This can be said at all levels of writing. In college, students usually have to

TABLE 4.9 Writing Skills

Writing skills	Description of writing skills
Script/ characters	English uses the Latin or Roman alphabet (as do German, Swedish, French, Italian, Portuguese, Turkish, Vietnamese, Somali, Malay, and Tagalog to name a few). Each language uses a unique version of the alphabet, which may contain unique characters or sounds.
Sounds and spelling	Understanding the link between the sounds of English and their spelling. This can be very difficult in English as our spelling system and sound system are not an exact match.
Accuracy	Being able to use the written system to express ideas and thoughts correctly is also important. This means that the message can be accurately decoded by the reader.
Grammar	Being able to use appropriate words and structures to convey the desired meaning of the writing. The more correct the structure of the writing and word choices the easier it usually is to understand the message.

refer to a style manual to know how to properly write academic-style papers. The first writing strategy relates to how to organize thoughts and ideas in a meaningful way. This means using an appropriate structure, using markers and signals to indicate topic changes and meaningful information, and linking appropriate ideas. This might also involve including a pattern of organization meant to convey a specific type of text, such as problem-solution or compare and contrast. The organization and structure should match the genre or type of writing style. Another writing strategy is the writing process in general. Writing is not done in one try and never looked at again. It is important to develop a writing process. That process might include some or all of the following steps: brainstorming (generating ideas), drafting, editing and revising, and creating a final version. This process might have more or

TABLE 4.10 Writing Activities

Writing for academic purposes	Writing that is done for a specific academic purpose, like a report	Word-processing software like Microsoft Word or Google Docs
Writing for fun	Writing that might be done for class but allows for more freedom or is done for one's personal benefit	Word-processing software like Microsoft Word or Google Docs; blogs; wikis; online journals
Writing for communication	Writing that might be done to communicate with others on a topic or just to communicate and discuss ideas and thoughts	E-mailing; tweeting; chatting through instant messenger–type applications; chatbots (for writing practice)
Writing for information distribution	Writing to distribute information to others	Tweeting, e-mailing; Google document pair or group writing

less drafts, may involve peer- and self-evaluation, and may have teacher feedback at various points. The goal is to create a version that is as close to the meaning that the writer wants and free of grammatical and structural errors. A writing strategy that relates closely to the previous two is considering your audience. This may be part of the drafting process where you draft different versions of the same content based on your prospective audience or it may be that you start writing knowing who the audience is for your text. With all writing it is important to follow the rules for the style that you are writing and still use your own unique voice in some way.

Grammar Skills

Grammar is slightly different from the previously described domains of language. Grammar is a component of all of the other language domains, most specifically writing and speaking. Grammar is also unique in that most teachers are very used to using grammar checkers that are included in word-processing software. Grammar checkers are in fact excellent computerized technology tools for all writers. Grammar skills overlap a great deal with writing and speaking skills. There are a few major skills involved in learning grammar based on the author's experience and on the materials from Thornbury (2012), Ur (2009), and Walker and White (2013).

A major skill is to know the rules of the language and follow them. This involves knowing how to properly form sentences and clauses for both meaning and grammar. This occurs in both writing and speaking, but the rules are more strongly enforced in the written language. Grammar can also involve a number of mechanics. These mechanics might be things like capitalization, punctuation, spacing, spelling, and formatting (though this could be its own category). These categories could all be addressed separately or grouped together for evaluation. Another grammar skill is understanding how words work and function. This involves knowing the part of speech of each word and how that word can be modified and used. It is possible to create sentences in English that are grammatically correct but convey no actual meaning. Noam Chomsky did this with his famous sentence, "Colorless green ideas sleep furiously" (Chomsky & Lightfoot, 2009 p. 15). This indicates the importance of focusing on both meaning and structure. It is not enough to simply learn the rules and apply them, but to create meaning through the use of the rules.

Project Ideas and Application

One thing to think about with all the resources and ideas presented is that language does not usually occur in isolation. Learning language could be part of bigger project. There are many project ideas that would connect to multiple language domains and specific skills and

TABLE 4.11 Grammar Activities

Grammar for writing	Grammar used while writing. Activities that help the learner use grammar correctly in English	Word-processing programs like Microsoft Word and Google Docs
Grammar for structure	Grammar for the sake of learning grammar. This is a starting place before the students are ready to apply the rules or for additional practice of the rules	Online grammar tasks and instruction (many free resources are available); grammar games; Corpora and concordances of written grammar, the Michigan Corpora (https://lsa.umich.edu/eli/language-resources/micase-micusp.html)
Grammar for speaking	Grammar specifically focused on the spoken language; this may include presentation	Corpora and concordances of spoken English
Grammar rules	Places for help with grammar rules and usage	OWL at Purdue is an excellent resource for grammar and citation questions (https://owl.purdue.edu/owl/purdue_owl.html)

strategies. There are two major advantages to using computerized technology in language learning and with projects. The first is that it allows for more creativity. This might be in the construction of the lesson itself or in the product that the students are able to produce. The other is that there are chances for students to make choices, which might allow them to be more invested in their own learning.

One way to allow students to express their creativity is to allow them to create animated videos. Creating videos helps students form a message and share that message with their classmates in a low anxiety way (rather than having to stand up and present a speech, for instance). One tool for this is Moovly (www.moovly.com/blog/make-your-own-cartoon-video-for-free), which is available free to create animated videos. Another resource is Powtoon (www.powtoon.com/home/?), which also allows you to create animated videos. Both of these are free, but have premium paid versions. There are many other resources available with a quick search if you have more specific needs. The goal is for the student to create the story or message based on the parameters provided. If the class is discussing a famous piece of literature, the assignment might ask them to provide an alternative ending. If they are studying a math concept, the video might explain that math concept.

A similar concept to creating animated videos might be to create a comic strip or a digital story. This is using still images rather than video to convey meaning. They have to be able to tell the story of the pictures (the pictures could be provided for the students or ones they find themselves). You might have them choose a traditional story to tell (one from their culture) or maybe retell a movie they really enjoy. They have to think about how to retell the story with the pictures using the bubbles provided. One resource for digital storytelling is Storybird (https://storybird.com/), which focuses on creative writing using art and images.

One of the best overall projects to show growth and improvement is a portfolio. A great way to add computerized technology to this is to create a digital portfolio. The benefit of this is it allows for all types of input: audio, video, written, and artistic (visual). The easiest way to create a digital portfolio is using either a website or a blog. A great free website platform is Wix (www.wix.com/). Another website builder is Weebly (www.weebly.com/). They are both very user friendly, and there are many tutorials online already for these platforms. If a blog is preferred, then WordPress (https://wordpress.org/) or Tumblr (www.tumblr.com/) might be best. They do not have all the functions of a website but work well for blogs. A blog can be created on a website as well. Some students may prefer to do a video blog, or vlog, rather than a written version. The easiest way to start a vlog is through YouTube (www.youtube.com/). A student can create their own channel and then start their own vlog, which they can share with the teacher and/or the class.

Another assignment idea is to have students analyze a website or multiple Web resources. This can be looking to see if the site is credible, if it expresses opinions or facts, if it is trying to persuade, or any number of other elements that fit the context of the assignment. Each assignment could be very different, as the elements you are asking the student to look for could change. It might start by looking for a simple grammatical feature. You might ask your students to peruse three news websites and see how often the passive voice is used. You might ask students to look at three different news websites and see if they think the resources are biased, and if they are in what way. You might ask them to find information about a cultural activity they know something about and see if the information presented is accurate. There are many variations of this assignment.

Future Thoughts

The future of computerized technology in the classroom is linked to how this technology continues to grow and be part of our daily lives. The more we use computerized technology the more we need to include it into our classrooms. Mobile devices are becoming more and more common, and many children are growing up with access to multiple computerized technologies in their homes. They may have Alexa-, Siri-, or Cortana-enabled devices that they use to help search or find information. They may also have stored pictures and content in the cloud. These are all where computerized technology is going in the near future.

There are some things to think about as we move to this computerized future. As we focus more on virtual teaching tools we need to make sure that we keep as much real activity as possible. Using virtual tools is a way to simulate the real world that allows us to bring it into our classrooms in an efficient way. Computerized technology should not be a substitute for real activities or activities in real life. It is important not to assume that students will have knowledge of new computerized technology, and to always plan to have a step where the new tool is taught for those who might not know. The students could also take a survey to determine if they need additional training. As computerized technology allows us to interact more globally it is important to keep in mind the objectives and goals of the lessons. This global contact can actually require a lot of local and global work. Projects need to be planned and contacts made well ahead of time to ensure as much ease as possible.

TIPS FOR TEACHERS!

As mentioned at the beginning of the chapter, it is important for teachers to know the computerized technology that is available in their classrooms. They also need to know any technology and devices that the students are required to use in the classroom. Some computerized technology tools can help a teacher with their teaching responsibilities as well as their assignment and activity creation. There are also skills that a teacher should have. One skill is being able to identify if a website is a good resource. The first thing is to look at the author of the website. If it is a person, is that person an authority on the subject? If it is an organization, is this a reputable organization? Doing searches of the author or organization can help to identify their quality. Is the information biased or trying to endorse a product? If it is, then it might be more commercial than informative. There are many educational websites available; once you find reputable sources use those in your classes. Teachers who want to use computerized technology may at times have to create materials. This is an important skill. There are many resources online for tool creation as well as tutorials on how to use existing materials and resources.

Recorded lectures can also help ELLs with additional supports. If you have lectured and the students are still struggling you might consider creating additional help lectures that the students can access through the computer. You might use a screencast software to do this. There are a number of free options: Screencast-o-matic (https://screencast-o-matic.com/), Screencastify (www.screencastify.com/), or Jing (www.techsmith.com/jing-tool.html). They each offer different features and would need to be explored to determine how they would fit with the desired lesson. Creating lectures or short video tutorials this way would also allow students to work through content at their own pace.

Rubrics are a common tool for teachers to use for grading in a consistent and unbiased manner. There are many different online rubric creators that can help you create or find a rubric for your class. Most offer existing rubrics that can be modified and have a generator to create your own unique rubrics. Two of the more common rubric websites are Rubistar (http://rubistar.4teachers.org/index.php) and iRubric (www.rcampus.com/indexrubric.cfm). Both websites allow you to create or modify an existing rubric for free. They also allow you to save your rubric and share them with other teachers.

When working on listening or other audio-based projects, Audacity (www.audacityteam.org/) is a free computerized technology tool that allows you to record and edit your own audio files. If you use the Lame encoder (https://lame.sourceforge.io/) with Audacity you can download your work as MP3 audio files. You can use this to create a lecture for your students and post it online for them to listen to. One problem sometimes with having students listen to online lectures to help their listening skills is that they will find a transcript of the audio and read it rather than listen. The nice thing about a lecture you create with Audacity is that you have the transcript or script of what you read. You can choose to share that or not, depending on what your goal is with the project. Audacity is very user friendly and has a lot of free tutorials and help available online. The nicest part is that you can edit out background noise and unnecessary pauses and fumbles to create a clearer audio track. This is also a computerized technology tool that the students could use to create their own audio recordings.

Computerized tests and quizzes are part of most teachers lives. For many the state content and/or language assessments are delivered via the computer. Many teachers themselves had to pass computerized tests to get their licenses. There are two steps to this skill. One is having a basic understanding of how the tests work and what they mean. That is more of an assessment idea. The other is to be able to use computerized tests in the classroom. This could involve creating online quizzes and tests. The design of the test should follow testing practices, but the delivery could use computerized technology. One tool for this is Quizlet (https://quizlet.com/). If the school has a **learning management system (LMS)** the tests could also be created on that system. Some examples of LMS's are Schoology, Edmodo, Blackboard, Canvas, and Google Classroom. If your school has access to an LMS, it could give a teacher the ability to create and deliver quizzes and tests. Some of the advantages of computerized tests are ease of grading (depending on question type), randomization, security (if you have a concern), and the ability to provide instant feedback.

Professional development is critical for using computerized technology. It can often be overwhelming and intimidating to try to use in the classroom. It is important to keep up to date on what computerized technology exists and how it can help in the language learning classroom. Schools can bring in technology experts to help teachers learn about and learn to use the new tools. Schools can also encourage teachers to attend local and national conferences where computerized technology is discussed and presented. Another option open to teachers is to join a **virtual learning network (VLN)** dedicated to computerized technology or technology in the classroom. There are many different networks available online that a teacher can join. You could also consider forming a **personal learning network (PLN)** with other educators that you interact with regularly. This is a way to share ideas, questions, and resources. LinkedIn is an example of a platform that would work as a PLN or a VLN if you connected with the right groups. Locally, a lot can be done by working with local colleges and universities and having professional development days to teach new ideas.

It is important for a teacher to think about why they want to use technology in the classroom. If it is just to have technology there or because the students already have the devices, those might not be the best reasons. For instance, I can have my students create flashcards in class using paper and markers or pens. What is the benefit of using technology to create flashcards? There might not be one in your situation. If there is not a clear benefit, then using technology is not necessary. If, however, you would like the students to be able to all be using the same definitions and do not want to take the class time to check each student's self-created flashcards, having them use online cards you have created might make sense. If you would like them to be able to take practice quizzes on their own using the content from the flashcards, again it makes sense to use technology. If the students have no way to use their digital flashcards outside of school and that is when you want them to use the flashcards, paper cards would make more sense. The teacher needs to always think about why they are using technology and make sure the reasons justify the use. Computerized technology needs to let you do something better or something more than traditional methods allow.

Recommended Websites

Group	Resource	URL
Parents	Scrible: Helps to organize and use Web content. Allows for annotation in articles and comments on webpages.	https://www.scrible.com/
	Books That Grow: Provides texts at a variety of levels and for ELLs specifically. Good for helping kids with their reading.	http://www.booksthatgrow.com/
	Reading Rockets: Reading resources to help parents work with their children on reading skills.	https://www.readingrockets.org/audience/parents

(Continued)

Group	Resource	URL
Teachers	Kahoot: Allows teachers to create and use interactive and competitive quiz games using computers or mobile devices.	https://kahoot.com/
	Screencast-O-Matic: Allows users to create videos of their screen. This would allow a teacher to create lessons that students could view on their own.	https://screencast-o-matic.com/
	RubiStar: Allows users to create (or modify an existing stored) rubric. Allows you to save and download your rubric.	http://rubistar.4teachers.org/index.php
	Remind: Allows teachers to communicate with students and parents via texts that do not originate on their phone.	https://www.remind.com/
Students	Voki: Allows students to create talking characters. They can record and upload audio for the created character.	https://www.voki.com/
	OWL at Purdue: This resource is for more advanced learners and those working on their writing using popular style conventions. There are also grammar rules and examples.	https://owl.purdue.edu/owl/purdue_owl.htm
	EWE (Easy World of English): Has activities that students can work on independently to improve their English skills.	http://easyworldofenglish.com/Default.aspx
Students and teachers	CommonLit: A reading program that allows for customization to student level. Has materials for students and teachers.	https://www.commonlit.org/
	Wix: Allows users to create their own website or blog.	https://www.wix.com/
	WordPress: Allows users to create their own blog.	https://wordpress.org/
All	Colorín Colorado: Has information for teachers, parents, and students, as well as resources for all, to help improve English skills as well as Spanish/English bilingual students.	https://www.colorincolorado.org/

Questions to Consider

1. Were any of the computerized technology tools discussed in the chapter present in your language education (either English or additional languages you have learned)? If so, how and what technology was used? In what ways was the technology helpful in your language learning experience?
2. As more and more students are equipped with smart phones, are there ways you can make them a tool rather than a distraction in the classroom based on the chapter reading? What ideas do you have that were not discussed in the chapter?
3. Is there a way to safely and effectively use social media with your students? Can you require that students use social media for their classes? How would you deal with concerns of privacy?
4. Plagiarism is seen very differently in other cultures. Think about how you would teach your students about this concept. Would you use plagiarism-detection software? How would you discuss this with your students?

References

Ahmad, K., Corbett, G., Rogers, M. & Sussex, R. (1985). *Computers, language learning, and language teaching*. Cambridge University Press.

Ahmadi, M. (2018). The use of technology in English language learning: A literature review. *International Journal of Research in Education (IJREE)*, 3(2), 115–125. http://ijreeonline.com/article-1-120-en.pdf

Bailey, K. M. (2012). *Practical English language teaching: Speaking*. McGraw-Hill.

Bax, S. (2011). Normalisation revisited: The effective use of technology in language education. *International Journal of Computer-Assisted Language Learning and Teaching*, 1(2), 1–15. https://doi.org/10.4018/ijcallt.2011040101

Chomsky, N., Lightfoot, D. W. (2009). *Syntactic Structures*. Germany: De Gruyter.

Costley, K. C. (2014). *The positive effects of technology on teaching and student learning.* Arkansas Tech University.

Farrell, T. S. C. (2009). *Teaching reading to English language learners: A reflective guide.* Corwin.

Folse, K. S. (2014). *The art of teaching speaking: Research and pedagogy for the ESL/EFL classroom.* University of Michigan Press.

Gee, J. P. (2008). *What video games have to teach us about learning and literacy.* Palgrave Macmillan.

Harmer, J. (2013). *How to teach writing.* Pearson/Longman.

Helgesen, M., & Brown, S. (2007). *Practical English language teaching: Listening.* McGraw-Hill.

Lane, L. (2010). *Tips for teaching pronunciation: A practical approach.* Pearson Longman.

Lee, K-W. (2000). English teachers' barriers to the use of computer-assisted language learning. *Internet TESOL Journal, 6*(12). http://iteslj.org/Articles/Lee-CALLbarriers.html

Marty, F. (1982). Reflections on the use of computers in second language acquisition—II. *System, 10*(1), 1–11. https://doi.org/10.1016/0346-251x(81)90062-2

Nation, I. S. P. (2009). *Teaching ESL/EFL reading and writing.* Routledge.

Nemeth, K., & Simon, F. S. (2013). Using technology as a teaching tool for dual language learners in preschool through grade 3. *National Association for the Education of Young Children, 68*(1), 48–52.

Parvin, R. H., & Salam, S. F. (2015). The effectiveness of using technology in English language classrooms in government primary schools in Bangladesh. *FIRE: Forum for International Research in Education, 2*(1), 47–59. http://preserve.lehigh.edu/fire/vol2/iss1/5

Pourhossein Gilakjani, A. (2017). A review of the literature on the integration of technology into the learning and teaching of English language skills. *International Journal of English Linguistics, 7*(5), 95–106.

Shyamlee, S. D., & Phil, M. (2012). Use of technology in English language teaching and learning: An analysis. *International Conference on Language, Medias and Culture IPEDR. 33.* (pp. 150–156). Retrieved from http://www.ipedr.com/vol33/030-ICLMC2012-L10042.pdf

Teachers of English to Speakers of Other Languages. (2008). *TESOL technology standards framework.* Author. https://www.tesol.org/docs/default-source/books/bk_technologystandards_framework_721.pdf?sfvrsn=2&sfvrsn=2

Thornbury, S. (2012). *How to teach grammar.* Pearson Education.

Ur, P. (2009). *Grammar practice activities: A practical guide for teachers.* (M. Swan, Ed.). Cambridge University Press.

Walker, A., & White, G. (2013). *Technology enhanced language learning: Connecting theory and practice.* Oxford University Press.

Warschauer, M., & Healey, D. (1998). Computers and language learning: An overview. *Language Teaching, 31*(2), 57–71.

Watkins, P. (2018). *Teaching and developing reading skills: Cambridge handbooks for language teachers.* Cambridge University Press.

Wright, A., Betteridge, D., & Buckby, M. (2006). *Games for language learning* (3rd ed.). Cambridge University Press.

Chapter 5

Assessing English Learners
What Does It Look Like and Why Is It Important?

Lynn David Tarvin

Glossary

Term	Meaning	Usage
Academic English proficiency	Ability to use school English successfully	Can require several years to acquire, but needed for successful participation in class work without accommodations
Academic language	Specific language used to discuss and display academic knowledge and skills	Can vary by content area; often follows typical, repeated patterns and includes discourse, sentence, and word levels
Content knowledge and skills	Topics of information and actions that the curriculum states students should be able to know and do	Informs the content to be assessed and instructed during a lesson or unit
Cultural bias	Favoring the practices and knowledge of one culture over others	In assessment, often refers to assumed background knowledge or ways of thinking that students from other cultures may not know, even if they are fluent English speakers
English proficiency test	Test covering English skills in listening, reading, speaking, and writing	In most states, given annually to any student currently receiving ELD services to determine if a student can exit from services or needs to continue

(Continued)

Term	Meaning	Usage
ESSA	Every Student Succeeds Act	Current version of the Elementary and Secondary Education act that outlines federal guidelines for schools
Formative assessment	Assessment given during instruction as a check for understanding	Data from formative assessment used to guide further instruction in the lesson or unit
LUS	Language use survey	Questions completed by families at enrollment indicating students' language use; if answers indicate a student speaks or understands a language other than English, they must take an ELP screener to determine if they qualify for ELD services
Portfolio	Collection of student work	Can be used to demonstrate student's content and language skills, including development over time
Rubric	A table showing desired criteria of success	Often columns may indicate level of success for each criterion
Screener	Shorter language proficiency test	Given when a student first enters a district to determine if the student qualifies for ELD services
Summative assessment	Assessment given after instruction, guided practice, and independent work are completed	Data from summative assessment indicates students' final level of mastery on a skill or topic

ASSESSMENT IMPACTS ENGLISH LEARNERS (ELS) FROM the day they enroll in a school district until even after they exit from English language development (ELD) services. Educators must consider many purposes, pitfalls, and procedures of assessment for ELs, as the scores obtained from these assessments can greatly affect the choices and opportunities available to these students. This chapter will address how students are assessed (at classroom, district, state, and national levels), how schools use the scores from assessments and those school choices' long-term effects on student opportunities, and how ELs may experience difficulties in various assessment settings.

A Year of Assessment for English Learners

To help understand how ELs are involved with assessment throughout the school year, this chapter will look at several snapshots of days from the school calendar where ELs are assessed, with important related information. Stories of six ELs from three families will help clarify how assessment affects these students' day-to-day lives.

Following this calendar of EL assessment snapshots, the chapter will discuss overarching reasons for assessment of ELs, including **ESSA's** effect on assessment for ELs, and tips for classroom teachers to implement effective assessment for ELs.

Day 1: Is This Student an English Learner?

Imagine different families arriving to enroll their children in school districts across the United States. Parents have to answer many questions during the enrollment process, including key questions about the children's ability to use English and/or other languages. These questions about the children's language use form the **Language use survey** (LUS) and are the gateway for determining if the children need ELD services. If parents mark on enrollment forms that their children speak or understand a language other than English, the school district must determine if children qualify for ELD services.

Figure 5.1 demonstrates the possible methods of determining if students qualify for ELD services and their effects on students being able to start classes. Each state sets a cut score on its **English language proficiency** (**ELP**) test to determine who qualifies for ELD services. Any student scoring below the cut score qualifies and will participate in the ELD program. Students' ELP scores are obtained either from the students' prior school districts, or students must take a shorter version of the ELP test called a **screener**. Once schools obtain these scores, parents are notified to say whether their children qualify for ELD services and the type of services their children will receive.

In smaller districts with fewer ELs, there may not be an ELD coordinator or even an ELD teacher. If no formal teachers or district leaders are named to work with ELs, teachers should ask their principals who to contact if they have a concern about a student possibly qualifying for services.

TABLE 5.1 Methods for Determining if a Student Qualifies for ELD Services

If student comes from ...	Elementary	Secondary
• Another country • A school/state that uses a different English language proficiency test	Students can start classes but must take a "screener" to determine ELP level within 10–30 days.	Students must take a "screener" to determine ELP before a class schedule can be developed so that student can start classes.
• A school/state that uses the same English language proficiency test	Students can start classes, but the school district must obtain ELP scores from prior district in order to determine ELD service/supports.	School districts must obtain ELP scores from prior district before a schedule can be developed so that students can start classes.

Case Scenario

Bilingual families in the United States are often very mobile. They may be migrant families following crops available to harvest. They may work in a variety of jobs that require frequent travel. They may move to be closer to different family members or to find better housing prices, more bilingual resources, or better ELD programs for their children.

This case scenario will consider three families who are moving to Missouri from Kansas, Iowa, and New Mexico.

Julia Guijarro Perez (pronounced "HOO-lee-uh g-ee-HA-ro PEH-res"), a seventh grader, and her brother, Marco, a second grader, have moved across the state line from Kansas to Missouri. Julia and Marcos's parents already know their children likely need ELD support, but because the two states use different English screening assessments, their children will have to be screened again by their new school district.

The Nguyen (pronounced similar to "win") brothers, Thao (pronounced "t-ow" and rhymes with "now") in ninth grade and and Phu (pronounced "foo") in fourth grade, have also crossed the state line from Iowa to Missouri. In Iowa, the Nguyen children were screened and did not qualify for services, but parents and children are both surprised to find out the children do qualify for services based on Missouri's ELP screener test.

The Chen children, Wei (pronounced "way") in 11th grade and Li (pronounced "Lee") in third grade, have come from New Mexico. Wei and Li were already identified as English learners in New Mexico. Because New Mexico and Missouri use the same ELP screener, the Chens' new district does not have to screen them again and can provide ELD services right away.

Districts provide ELD services in many different ways, and ELs' English proficiency scores often determine how the ELs are placed in those services. Often, district ELD coordinators and ELD teachers will work with counselors and principals to identify the best supports available. In smaller districts, different people, such as curriculum directors, Spanish teachers, special education directors, or building principals, might be in charge of figuring out how to support ELs who enroll in their districts.

The Chen children can start classes right away because their new district has English proficiency scores and can make ELD services placements right away. Wei's high school and Li's elementary school have ELD-certified teachers in almost all classes, so they will not be placed in separate ELD classes or programs.

Marco Guijarro Perez can start classes in second grade right away. After Marco is screened, he will see an ELD teacher at his elementary school for three 30-minute pull-out sessions to support the language he is learning in his class. However, his sister Julia has to wait to start classes until after she completes her ELP screener test. Julia's middle school has separate classes to provide ELD services, so the ELD teacher and counselor need her ELP scores to develop her seventh-grade schedule.

> *Like Julia, Thao has to take his ELP screener test before he can have a ninth-grade schedule made. He scores almost proficient, so an ELD teacher will check in with him occasionally and coach his teachers to provide ELD supports. Phu can start classes right away, and after he is screened Phu will attend a 3-hour intensive English program once a week along with all the other fourth-grade ELs in his district.*

Colorado, Illinois, Missouri, New Mexico, Oklahoma, and Wisconsin are 6 of the 35 states who form the WIDA Consortium, a group of states using the same ELP screener test (WIDA Screener) and annual **English proficiency test** (ACCESS for ELLs). Scores ranging from 1.0–6.0 on the screener and annual English proficiency test are used for identifying English learners (ELs) and determining how long ELD services continue to be needed (see Table 5.2). Another seven states, including Nebraska, Iowa, and Arkansas, belong to the ELPA21 consortium, which offers similar assessments on a scale of 1 to 5. The remaining states, including Kansas, either use Las Links assessments or their own state-developed assessments (Villegas & Pompa, 2020). Because 35 of the 50 states are members of the WIDA Consortium, this chapter will often reference materials related to the WIDA assessments and instructional support materials. (More information about these items can be found at wida.wisc.edu.)

When ELs are assessed for their English proficiency level, the assessments go beyond the ability to speak about day-to-day social topics. For example, the WIDA Screener (initial entry ELP screener test) and the ACCESS for ELLs (annual ELP test) assess the domains of listening, reading, writing, and speaking across the standards of social and instructional language, language of language arts, language of mathematics, language of science, and language of social studies (Board of Regents of the University of Wisconsin System, 2019b). While the WIDA Screener and ACCESS for ELLs do address social language, the majority of the assessments address academic language. ELs may be able to talk about daily social activities within a couple years and appear to be fluent, but they will often need several years to acquire **academic English proficiency** to be able to participate successfully in their coursework.

As soon as ELs enter a school district, their ELP scores from the screener test or prior district will determine many things: (a) the number of available elective options, (b) the

TABLE 5.2 WIDA English Language Proficiency Levels

ELP Score	1.0–1.9	2.0–2.9	3.0–3.9	4.0–4.9	5.0–5.9	6.0
Descriptor	Entering	Emerging	Developing	Expanding	Bridging	Reaching

time they may be pulled out of class to work on their English, and even (c) access to more challenging coursework. It is an expectation that teachers provide **accommodations** so that ELs can access the skills and knowledge being taught in every course, and ELs should be allowed to take the same rigorous coursework their peers do. However, it can be challenging for ELs to go into coursework where they cannot understand instruction. Teachers may have especially strong concerns about danger to ELs and other students in high school classes where power machinery is used. Teachers, counselors, ELD specialists, and ELs must work together to identify the courses where they will most likely have the greatest success.

Days 2 Through 20: How Do Teachers Know the Prior Knowledge ELs Bring to Their Classes and What ELs Have Actually Learned From Class Instruction During the First Few Weeks of Class?

Once ELs start their classes, they participate in classroom assessments just like every other student. Teachers must think very carefully about the purposes of their assessments. Why are the students being assessed, and how will teachers and students use the information gathered from the assessment? Students can be assessed on different skills found in the curriculum, and they can also be assessed on specific knowledge identified in the curriculum. Students might be assessed before a unit of instruction so teachers can understand the background knowledge students bring to the lessons. They might be assessed informally during a lesson so that the teacher can identify any misconceptions and areas needed for re-teaching or further explanation. This is called **formative assessment.** Students might be assessed after a lesson or unit of instruction to determine the skills and knowledge they have learned. This is called **summative assessment.**

For example, students learning about the life cycle of a butterfly might read some books and watch short videos learn about the cycle. During the lesson, the teacher may make notes of ideas students discuss with each other about what they have learned, and the teacher may also ask students some informal questions to discover what they understand and any misconceptions they might have. This checking for understanding is a formative assessment. The teacher will use what they learn from the formative assessment to make decisions for planning the next day's lesson. When the unit is complete, the students may write a story or answer questions on a formal test to display their learning. This end of unit test would be a summative assessment.

Cultural Bias and Assessment

As teachers implement these before, during, and after instruction assessments, they must reflect on their ELs' English proficiency levels and cultural backgrounds. Something that may seem straightforward, such as directions on a map, may be communicated in a very different way in other cultures. Students in the United States have different cultural experiences, regardless of the languages they speak, and this affects the background knowledge they bring to an assessment.

FIGURE 5.1   Reflect on how these homes are similar and different. How might your idea of a home be different from your students' ideas?

Source: (a) Copyright © by Johan Wallhammar (CC BY-SA 4.0) at https://commons.wikimedia.org/wiki/File:Brunnberg_%26_Forshed_Arkitektkontor_-_Enzymet,_Hagastaden.jpg. (b) Copyright © by audioselect (CC BY-SA 3.0) at https://commons.wikimedia.org/wiki/File:Bamboo_Hut_at_Bananas_Bungalows_-_panoramio.jpg.

A simple example is found in the terms "home" and "neighbors." A student from a major city might think of home as an apartment in a skyrise building, surrounded by many other apartments, with neighbors being people who share a common wall, ceiling, or floor with you and live beside, above, and below. A student from a suburb might think of a home as a house on a street that looks similar to most of the other houses on the same block, with neighbors being people who live on the same street, or perhaps a block or two away. A student from a rural area might think of a home as a house that is a mile or more from the next house, with neighbors being people that form a community within a several mile radius.

Students from other countries may have even more different ideas of a "home" and who lives there. The word "home" is difficult to translate into many languages. It is not exactly the same thing as a "house"; the English word has connotations that go beyond the physical structure, and helping a student to understand those nuances can be important when "home" and "neighbor" are essential concepts to an assessment.

A specific example demonstrating **cultural bias** among native English-speaking students is displayed in a clip of Season 2, Episode 4 of *Good Times* (Milligan, 2016). Michael, the younger son of an African American family, is frustrated by doing poorly on an IQ test given by the school. Michael discusses questions that assume background knowledge such as "cup and saucer" or "guest rooms." These questions reflect the culture of upper middle-class families, so students from poorer families might not have the assumed background knowledge to perform well. Later in the episode, the parents meet with the counselor who is adamant that Michael will not be successful in college based on the results of this test. Educators must be careful to ensure that the data gathered from assessments is valid because recommendations and decisions based on that data can open or close doors to future opportunities for students.

If words such as "home" and "neighbor" have nuanced, slightly different meanings for native English speakers, words such as "left," "right," "in front of," and "behind" can be even more challenging for speakers of languages that do not even have these concepts. Kuuk Thaarorre is a language spoken by an Aboriginal community in Australia. In Kuuk Thaarorre, any discussion of location is always based on cardinal directions. Here are a couple of examples: "Oh, there's an ant on your southwest leg" and "Move your cup to the north-northeast a little bit" (Boroditsky, 2017). A student from this culture might do poorly on a test that asks for which item is on the left, but they can always tell you which direction is north. They bring a skill set to class that students growing up in American culture may not have. For them to be successful on U.S. school assessments, they have to learn not only the word "left" but also the cultural ideas surrounding it.

These descriptions of "home" and "neighbor," "cup and saucer" and "guest rooms," and "left" and "right" are examples of cultural bias. Cultural bias assumes that others have grown up with the same experiences, beliefs, and customs as you have, so you assume that the other person has a shared background knowledge with you. Educators must work to ensure that assessments have as little cultural bias as possible, so that all students can demonstrate what they truly know and can do.

Day 40: How Successfully Are ELs Learning During Class Instruction?

Li (third grade), Phu (fourth grade), and Marco (second grade) appear to be participating well in class. They are respectful, quiet, and give their teachers good eye contact. When teachers ask if they understand, they want to be polite, so they always nod and say yes. Marco has been in the United States the least amount of time; he only arrived 8 months ago. He does not say much, so his teacher is not sure what he comprehends. Li and Phu want to be respectful and not draw much attention to themselves, so they do not ask questions if they do not understand. Each of their teachers has good intentions, but some strategies to support ELs' language learning would lead to greater understanding of curricular skills and knowledge. Teachers need to be strategic when assessing ELs, looking for ways to help ELs demonstrate their learning based on their available English skills. Simply asking students to say if they understand is rarely effective.

Teachers must provide scaffolding, or extra instructional supports, to ELs as they navigate learning both content knowledge and academic English. ELs who have recently arrived to the United States may still be in the silent period; they are likely taking everything in and learning a lot, but they are not ready to produce language to demonstrate their learning. Even ELs with more academic English proficiency still need supports to access lessons.

As teachers design their lessons, they need to have both content objectives (drawn from their curriculum) and language objectives. Teachers must teach the language ELs need to understand the instruction and to display the knowledge and skills they have learned. As teachers and students work together through class activities, teachers need to be assessing ELs to see if they are using the new language needed to participate successfully in the lesson. Teachers need to give ELs a variety of methods to display their learning. See Table 5.3 for just a few specific ideas to implement.

Teachers need to review ELs' English proficiency levels (for example from their WIDA Screener or ACCESS for ELLs scores) to determine which scaffolding supports and alternate methods of assessment are most appropriate. WIDA provides a great deal of instructional support materials based on these scores, including the WIDA Can Do Descriptors, Key Uses edition (Board of Regents of the University of Wisconsin System, 2019c). Teachers can use these Key Uses documents to identify what ELs are able to do based on their English proficiency levels, across the four language domains in the genres of recounting (storytelling and procedures), explanation (how or why something occurs), argument (claim with supporting evidence and explanation), and oral discussion (in-class listening and speaking interaction with peers).

TABLE 5.3 Scaffolding Supports and Alternate Methods of Assessment

Scaffolding Supports	Alternate Methods of Assessment
• Provide simpler texts about the same content. • Provide pictures and video to develop understanding and background knowledge. • Allow ELs to work with a partner. • Allow ELs to use their L1 to process ideas from the lesson. • Provide graphic organizers. • Provide notes that have just a few missing words. • Provide sentence frames.	• Provide word banks on tests. • Reduce number of choices on multiple choice or matching question items. • Reduce overall length of assessment. • Allow individual or small-group testing to reduce anxiety. • Allow ELs to draw or speak their answers if they are not ready to write. • Allow ELs to point at pictures to indicate their answers. • Use a portfolio of multiple artifacts created by ELs demonstrating the skills or content knowledge. • Assess for ability to use the content knowledge/skills or language features in interactions with others during class.

When teachers provide ELs with these scaffolding supports and alternate methods of assessment, they are leveling the playing field. ELs experience a higher cognitive load because they are learning both content knowledge and skills and academic English for their classes. These supports and alternate methods take away barriers that might prevent them from showing their teachers what they actually are able to know and do.

Day 85: What Have ELs Learned During First Semester?

Julia (seventh grade), Thao (ninth grade), and Wei (11th grade) are facing semester final examinations. They are supposed to show their teachers that they have remembered everything they have learned throughout the first semester. In all of their classes, they have been exposed to so much information. They have each worked hard, taking good notes in class from what they have understood of teachers' lectures, comparing notes with classmates to catch the things they did not understand because the teachers spoke so fast, reading and re-reading, and even translating, portions of their textbooks to grasp concepts that just have not made a lot of sense.

While each student wants to perform their best on these examinations, they know they will face some challenges. First, questions on tests are often worded in slightly different ways than the topics were discussed during class instruction. ELs may understand the content knowledge, but the different vocabulary of the question keeps them from understanding how to answer the questions correctly. Second, ELs may have internalized the content knowledge, reflecting and developing connections between ideas in their L1s, but they may not have the complex language skills in English to display what they have learned. Third, ELs sometimes become overwhelmed by having to process so much academic language so quickly during the week of semester final examinations. When they feel anxious or exhausted or likely to fail, ELs may struggle to produce English that they do know.

Teachers need to identify what students have learned to know (a) what instructional strategies have been effective and (b) what gaps of knowledge will need to be addressed in order for students to make progress with their learning. While having students take an examination at the end of the semester to see what knowledge they have retained is a common practice, there might be other methods of assessment that actually show what students know and can do.

Problem- or Project-Based Learning Experiences

Seeing students able to implement the content knowledge, skills, and academic language of the curriculum is the most authentic form of assessing their learning. This can occur through carefully designed problem- or project-based learning experiences. When teachers see this learning displayed in action, they have greater assurance that students have acquired skills and knowledge than if ELs are guessing on a multiple-choice test. When designing a problem- or

TABLE 5.4 Identifying Content Knowledge, Content Skills, and Language Needed to Participate in a Project- or Problem-Based Learning Experience.

Content Knowledge Identified in Curriculum	Content Skills Identified in Curriculum	Language Needed to Participate in the Learning Experience
• Geographical land and water forms of southern United States • Leading forms of pollution in waters surrounding North America • Mechanical and chemical methods of containing and cleaning oil from ocean water	• Using the steps of the engineering design process • Making hypotheses based on data gathered through research • Creating and revising small-scale prototypes • Reporting processes and decisions made during the experience	• Academic vocabulary related to land and water forms and pollution • Academic vocabulary related to engineering design process • Language for making predictions based on data: "I think that this will work because …" • Sequence language: first, then, next, finally.

project-based learning experience, teachers must be very intentional to focus on the desired learning outcomes.

Students may enjoy creating a papier-mâché globe to learn about the earth's continents and oceans, but the time spent learning the curricular material might be much less than the time spent on creating the papier-mâché. To target the learning and make the best use of class time, teachers should create **rubrics**, sometimes with students' input, that clearly define what a successful outcome of the project will look like. See Table 5.4 for an example from a STEM class where students must design a product to clean up an oil spill just off the coast of Louisiana. While the student-specific outcomes may be unknown, teachers need to identify the skills and knowledge from the curriculum, along with the needed academic language, that students should be able to use successfully by the end of the learning experience.

Student Portfolio Development

ELs can also demonstrate the content knowledge and skills and academic language they have developed by creating a portfolio of their work. With platforms such as Microsoft 365 and Google Drive available, students can now create portfolios that include both written and spoken artifacts. An EL with stronger speaking skills who is still developing writing skills might record their answers orally instead of writing them down. ELs can use drawing tools to communicate their thinking if they are not ready to speak or write their thoughts.

Teachers must think creatively: What are the essential skills necessary to show mastery for this unit of curriculum, and what are a variety of ways that any student, including ELs, could demonstrate their learning in the best manner possible? Again, teachers can use WIDA materials, such as the Can Do Descriptors, Key Uses documents, to identify the level of language to expect students to produce and shape the kinds of outputs or products students might create to demonstrate unit mastery.

Traditional Assessments

Sometimes, students do have to take more traditional assessments. There may be common district end-of-unit or end-of-semester summative assessments, or class time may not allow for a more authentic problem-solving experience. These more traditional assessments often involve question types such as multiple choice, true/false, fill-in-the-blank, short answer, and essay questions. Students are often asked to explain their reasoning or critique the reasoning of others. These types of questions require a great deal of complex language to understand and to respond.

When possible, students should be provided the same supports on summative assessments as they have received throughout the unit(s) of instruction. While scaffolding supports are gradually taken away over time, teachers should not expect students to perform well on a summative assessment without supports if they have never practiced without supports on formative assessments.

Day 100: How Much Academic English Have ELs Learned This Year?

Each year, every student identified as an English learner must take an annual English proficiency test. As described, different states use different tests, but the 35 states of the WIDA Consortium use ACCESS for ELLs 2.0.

WIDA ACCESS for ELLs Annual English Proficiency Test

There are four versions of ACCESS for ELLs 2.0 (Board of Regents of the University of Wisconsin System, 2019a). The kindergarten test is given as a one-on-one interview with a test administrator and takes about an hour. ACCESS for ELLs Online, for grades 1–12, is given individually or in small groups in three to four sessions and can take up to 4 hours. Grades 1–3 complete their writing tests by hand in booklets, but all other grades type their written responses. ACCESS for ELLs Paper, for grades 1–12 may be appropriate for students with limited experience using technology and also takes up to 4 hours. Alternate ACCESS for ELLs, for grades 1–12, is paper based and available for students with significant cognitive disabilities. It is given individually and can take up to 2 or 3 hours, depending on a student's need for a scribe to write answers that are orally given. All versions of ACCESS for ELLs address the four language domains (listening, reading, speaking, writing) across WIDA's five standards of social and instructional language, language of language arts, language of mathematics, language of science, and language of social studies.

The majority of ELs take ACCESS for ELLs Online. ELs are fairly comfortable taking online listening and reading assessments, as these occur frequently as part of ongoing instruction and state assessments. Students work on learning to type even in upper elementary grades, so writing online does not seem to be a barrier to demonstrating ELs' writing skills. It is important for classroom teachers to provide ELs with many opportunities to type extended writing so that ELs have practice before they take ACCESS.

ELs do struggle with the speaking test platform. In WIDA's former version of ACCESS, the speaking domain test was given as an oral interview with the test administrator. While ELs might have felt nervous about speaking to an adult, they often did quite well. In the online version, ELs must record themselves on the computer as they respond to prompts from the screen. This is not an activity that commonly occurs in the classroom, and ELs often feel very anxious, especially if other students nearby might be able to hear them. This is a challenge that teachers must help ELs overcome in order to demonstrate their true academic English-speaking abilities.

After taking the test, ELs must wait 2 or 3 months to receive their scores. Scores range from 1.0, indicating a new beginner ready to start learning English, to 6.0, indicating a student with academic English proficiency similar or even surpassing monolingual English-speaking peers. Because ELs do not receive their scores for several months after taking the test, they and their teachers never truly know a standardized current English proficiency level score. For this reason, it is important for classroom teachers to work closely with ELD specialists to curate **portfolios** demonstrating ELs' linguistic strengths. WIDA provides performance definitions, indicating linguistic complexity at the discourse, sentence, and word level for both writing and speaking. Teachers should conference frequently with ELs to discuss the language ELs are able to display and suggest specific areas to improve in order for ELs to increase their proficiency scores over time.

Wide Range of Uses for ELs' Annual ELP Scores

It is very important for ELs to take the annual English proficiency test seriously. Many decisions are based on the scores they earn on this test. Teachers use the scores to identify supports and accommodations to provide, along with the level of language they require for ELs to demonstrate mastery. ELD specialists and coordinators will use the scores to determine the level of ELD services students will need the following year, including if students are ready to exit the ELD program. Counselors may use the scores to make guidance suggestions about courses to take that could affect college entrance and career opportunities in the future, including whether students are allowed to take more choice electives or must take more intervention courses. In the United States, students' standardized test scores are given more weight than any other form of data that teachers might collect. While teachers must remember that these scores reflect a snapshot of 3 or 4 days of a student's year, in reality an EL's English proficiency scores can shape much of his or her future.

Classroom teachers can help ELs do their best on annual ELP tests by providing encouragement to do well, by sharing specific examples with ELs of how their English has improved, and by placing an appropriate weight on the importance of the test. When students know that their teachers feel like they have improved, they are more likely to feel confident and display the language skills they have developed. For secondary students in particular, it is helpful to discuss the benefits of having higher scores, including access to more interesting elective classes and not having to pay for college-level ELD classes that are required before students are allowed to take degree coursework.

Day 150: How Will ELs Perform on State and National Assessments?

Marco has now been in the United States for 13 months. In Missouri, second graders do not have to take state achievement assessments, so Marco has another year before he will take these intensive tests. However, all Missouri students in third through eighth grade and many students in high school do take state achievement tests. Therefore, the other five students in third grade and beyond will have to participate in state achievement testing this year.

Thao feels prepared to do well on his ninth-grade Algebra I and General Biology state achievement tests. His English has continued to develop this year, and he fully expects his English proficiency score will allow him to exit ELD services at the end of the year. Thao has worked on his English for a long time, and he is looking forward to his goal of exiting ELD services.

The other students are less confident about how they will perform. Wei will take the 11th grade American Government test. Julia (seventh grade), Li (third grade), and Phu (fourth grade) will take their grade-level ELA and math tests. All the students have made progress this year, but they are not looking forward to almost 2 weeks of testing. Their parents encourage them to do their best; their teachers tell them not to worry if they do not do as well as they would like. The children are not sure what to think; they just know there are a lot of words they do not know and that they will have to sit there without a break from this intensive academic language for hours at a time.

Annual State Achievement Tests

Most students have to participate in annual state assessments, especially in the areas of English language arts (ELA) and math. ELs with less than 1 year in the United States may be exempted from the ELA test that first year, but moving forward they have to participate in the same state assessments as their peers. States may provide guidance regarding the possible accommodations allowed on state assessments, including the use of an interpreter or a bilingual dictionary. States may only allow certain accommodations for ELs who have been in the country less than a certain number of years or have an English proficiency level below

FIGURE 5.2 Bilingual dictionaries may be an accommodation allowed on state achievement testing.

Source: Copyright © by LinguistAtLarge (CC BY-SA 3.0) at https://commons.wikimedia.org/wiki/File:BilingualDictionaries.jpg.

a certain threshold score. States may also suggest that certain accommodations—such as interpreting, translating, or use of a bilingual dictionary—are inappropriate if students have not experienced schooling in their L1. A 5-year-old may be quite fluent in his L1, but that does not mean he has learned the names of all the planets in his L1. **If a student has not studied the content in his or her L1, providing L1 language support will not be helpful.** Likewise, ELs are not likely to perform better on state assessments with accommodations if they have not been practicing the use of those accommodations throughout the school year.

EL Supports on College Entrance Tests

Recently, ELs have been allowed to have English learner supports when taking the ACT, a college entrance test used by many universities. "The goal of providing English learner supports is to ensure that the test scores earned by English learners accurately reflect what they have learned in school" (ACT, Inc., 2018, p. 1). The allowed supports include the following:

- Extended time testing (50% time extension, single session)
- Use of an approved word-to-word bilingual dictionary
- Use of test directions in the native language

- Testing in a familiar environment or small group

Again, students should be encouraged to practice testing using a bilingual dictionary before attempting to use one during an actual test administration. Students have to learn the skill of identifying which words are most important to look up because there may not be enough time to translate everything. Also, while extended time does give the opportunity for time to use the bilingual dictionary and to process the concepts in both the student's L1 and English, extended time will not help if the student has not had enough background knowledge about a topic to be able to understand it.

Day 180: What Happens Next for These ELs?

At the end of the school year, the students receive their WIDA ACCESS scores. Thao is excited! He earned an overall composite score of 4.9, so he will get to exit ELD services. This means he will not have to take ACCESS next year in 10th grade. However, the school district will continue to monitor Thao for 2 years to see how successful he is in his classes. Wei earned a 4.3, below the required Missouri cut score of 4.7, so he will have to continue ELD services in 12th grade. Marco scored a 2.2; this is significant growth for him from last year. Julie earned a 3.7, up only from 3.5 the year before. It is common for students in middle school to struggle to score well, and they often do not make expected progress. Phu and Li both score a 3.5. They both made some growth from last year and need to keep pressing on toward that 4.7.

When students earn the state-defined exit cut scores on the ELP test, such as ACCESS, they are able to exit ELD services. Earning a qualifying exit score allows secondary ELs to choose more elective courses for their schedules and elementary students to remain in their classes instead of being pulled out by their ELD teachers. Districts will check in with exited students' teachers for 2 years after exit. This monitoring period allows the district to ensure that students really have academic language they need to be successful in the classroom without additional ELD supports.

Why Do Schools Assess ELs?

Reflect on the assessment experiences of the six English learners described in this chapter. What are ways they are able to show their strengths? What are barriers that limit their ability to show their understanding? Why is it so important to assess these students on their content knowledge, content skills, and language development?

First, teachers assess ELs so that they know what students understand and where they still need help. This is the most essential reason. Effective educators will identify creative ways to draw out of students what they know and can do. They will use appropriate scaffolding supports and accommodations, they will find alternative methods of assessment that are more appropriate, and they will help students identify their strengths—what they can do—as they develop and learn even more.

Second, teachers assess ELs to identify which teaching strategies are most effective. Different approaches will reach students in different ways, and effective teachers are always reflecting on how they can lead their students to learn most successfully. This reflection often may come through data team discussions or peer collaboration, where teachers discuss openly and honestly what they have tried, what was successful, and what needed improvement.

These first two reasons are important and are within teachers' control, but there is a third reason that drives much of the decision-making processes for schools: compliance with state and federal statutes.

Every Student Succeeds Act

The Every Student Succeeds Act (ESSA) of 2015 is the most recent update to the Elementary and Secondary Education Act and addresses EL assessment specifically in the following ways (U.S. Department of Education, n.d.):

1. Each state must identify and standardize entry and exit procedures for English learner services. All districts within a state must use the same criteria for identifying ELs and the ELP score necessary for exiting ELD services. Within the WIDA Consortium, different states have identified different ACCESS for ELLs scores needed for exit (ranging from 4.2–5.0), and some states require additional data from other assessments as well.

2. ELs must show growth on both annual English proficiency tests and state achievement tests. When ELs do not demonstrate appropriate growth, state education departments may increase oversight of Title I schools. ELs typically have greater ELP growth at younger grades and soon after they arrive in the United States. This rate of growth decreases as students spend more time in U.S. schools. Schools with ELs who have been here longer and have not exited from ELD services are more likely to be identified for concern.

3. Former ELs are now counted as part of the EL subgroup for 4 years after exiting ELD services. This is extremely important, as it recognizes the efforts ELD specialists and classroom teachers have made to help students reach academic English proficiency. In the past, only current ELs were counted in this subgroup. By definition, if ELs were receiving ELD services, they were very unlikely to score proficient on state achievement tests.

4. ESSA states that ELs should be exiting from EL services within 6 years. If ELs are not able to exit within that time frame, there is a question about the effectiveness of the ELD program. School districts must use their resources to help ELD specialists and

classroom teachers together support ELs so that they can make appropriate progress with their English language development.

Schools assess ELs to help these students be more successful in school and in life. However, if schools do not meet the obligations set forward in ESSA, other regulations, and case law established by important court cases, they are out of compliance and can be sued or investigated by the U.S. Office of Civil Rights.

TIPS FOR TEACHERS!

1. Make sure you know if any of your students are English learners. If you have a question, be sure to ask your ELD specialists, coordinator, or principal.

2. Know your English learners. Find out where they are from and research a little to find out about some of their typical cultural ways of thinking and doing. Incorporate some of these ideas into your instruction and classroom assessments.

3. Review the questions of your classroom assessments for cultural bias. Is there any cultural background knowledge that is assumed? How can you either help students develop this knowledge or rephrase questions so the curricular standards are addressed without relying on that assumed prior knowledge?

4. Be sure to identify and assess language objectives that students need to support the curriculum skills and knowledge you teach.

5. Base your expectations on your ELs' English language proficiency levels. Use the WIDA documents (or similar for your state) to help you know what students can do.

   a. Know your students' most recent ELP scores (from the prior year) or screener scores (from this year when they entered the district).

   b. Keep a portfolio of student work to determine if ELs are progressing in their academic language development; confer with your ELD specialists, if available, about progress or concerns they notice.

   c. Check in with ELD specialists, principals, or counselors if you have concerns about ELs not making progress with their academic language development.

6. Consider appropriate scaffolding supports and alternative methods of assessment that will allow you to know what ELs really know and are able to do.

---

7. Work closely with your ELs' ELD specialist teachers to support annual ELP assessments such as ACCESS.

8. Find out about any allowable accommodations on state testing as early as possible and provide students opportunities to practice using those accommodations.

9. Carefully consider any high-stakes decisions made based on ELs' ELP scores. Try to consider other data points, such as artifacts found in ELs' portfolios, that give you a more up-to-date reference of ELs' ELP levels. Stress the importance of multiple data points with other teachers, counselors, and principals, so ELs are not excluded from more rigorous, challenging opportunities.

10. Balance the importance of ELs' strong performance on district and state assessments with the recognition of ELs' ongoing English language development. They might not be proficient yet, but they are still developing their skills every day.

Questions to Consider

1. How does a student's grade level/age and prior experience with English proficiency testing affect his or her ability to get started in classes?

2. What are some creative ways you might identify students' prior knowledge about topics in a unit of instruction?

3. What is the difference between formative assessment and summative assessment, and how would you use each during a unit of instruction?

4. The chapter provides several examples of how cultural bias might affect assessment of ELs. Think of tests you have taken yourself or ones you have seen provided for courses you have taught. What is at least one example of assumed prior knowledge or an expected cultural pattern of thinking that could cause ELs to perform poorly on those tests? Why would this example prove difficult for some ELs?

5. When students are in the silent period, what are some ways you might have them demonstrate their understanding without speaking or writing?

6. Describe at least two examples of nontraditional assessment that you think might better demonstrate what ELs are able to know and do than traditional multiple choice, true/false, fill-in-the blank, short answer, and essay tests. Why would these nontraditional assessments be better?

7. Why are ELs tested annually on an English proficiency test? What are some effective uses of the scores obtained from that test?

References

ACT, Inc. (2018). *English learner supports guide.* https://www.act.org/content/act/en/products-and-services/the-act/registration/accommodations/policy-for-el-supports-documentation.html

Board of Regents of the University of Wisconsin System. (2019a). *ACCESS tests.* https://wida.wisc.edu/assess/access/tests

Board of Regents of the University of Wisconsin System. (2019b). *ACCESS for ELLs.* https://wida.wisc.edu/assess/access

Board of Regents of the University of Wisconsin System. (2019c). *Can do descriptors key uses edition, grades 9–12.* https://wida.wisc.edu/sites/default/files/resource/CanDo-KeyUses-Gr-9-12.pdf

Boroditsky, L. (2017). *How language shapes the way we think* [TED Talk]. https://www.ted.com/talks/lera_boroditsky_how_language_shapes_the_way_we_think/transcript

Milligan, N. (2016, April 16). *"Good Times"—The IQ test (1974) Culturally biased questions on test* [Video file]. https://www.youtube.com/watch?v=hoP-4J_J4-I

U.S. Department of Education. (n.d.). Every Student Succeeds Act (ESSA). https://www.ed.gov/essa?src=rn

Villegas, L. & Pompa, D. (2020). *The patchy landscape of state English learner policies under ESSA.* Migration Policy Institute. https://www.migrationpolicy.org/sites/default/files/publications/ESSA-Compendium-Final.pdf

Chapter 6

Latino Migrant

Velma D. Menchaca

Glossary

Term/acronym	Meaning	Usage
Asylum seeker	Someone who fled their native country and seeks protection/asylum in another country	Many central Americans and other facing persecution, threats, and other dangers seek asylum in the United States.
Illegal immigrant	Someone who does not possess the required legal documentation to reside in a country	While many associate illegal migrants with illegal border crossers, many illegal immigrants had legal visas to be in the United States but overstayed their visas.
Immigrant	Someone who crosses borders to live in a new country either lawfully or unlawfully	Generic term referring to those people coming to the United States from other countries
Latino/a	A person of Latin American heritage or descent	In the United States, the term most frequently applies to people of Mexican, Cuban, Puerto Ricans, or other Latin American countries.
Latin/x	A gender-neutral or nonbinary alternative to Latino or Latina	A term that is becoming more widely used for its inclusivity.
Migrant	Someone who changes residence within a country, usually for economic reasons	In the United States, the term often refers to agricultural migrants. For example, someone who moves from California to Missouri is a migrant.
Prescriptive measures	Measures that are dictated by the establishment of rules and punitive measures	These measures are often used to describe the way schools address issues through rules and regulations.

Introduction

Each year, approximately 3 to 5 million migrant farmworkers and their families leave their homes to *follow the crops,* hoping to improve their financial situations (National Center for Farmworker Health, 2001). They "move for the purposes of obtaining seasonal or temporary work in agriculture or fishing" (U.S. Department of Education, 1994, p. 4). Approximately 92% of all migrants are culturally and linguistically diverse, of whom 85% are Latinos. The largest Latino subgroup is Mexican Americans (60%), followed by Puerto Ricans, Cubans, and Central and South Americans (Kissam, 1993). Migrants who have immigrated to the United States from Mexico and parts of Central America primarily harvest fruits and vegetables. In the summers, they may harvest tomatoes or broccoli in Texas or possibly apricots, peaches, or grapes in California. They tend to migrate along three known geographic routes: the East Coast Stream, the Mid-Continent Stream, and the West Coast Stream following seasonal crops.

This chapter addresses the educational experiences of Latino migrant students, culturally relevant teaching, migrant parental involvement, and the challenges of secondary schools. The chapter also provides an array of information on the lives of Latino migrant children and hardships they encounter in the fields. Also discussed are the challenges they encounter in schools because of their mobile lifestyles, the obstacles that keep them from graduating from high school, and the hurdles they must successfully negotiate to enter college.

Profile of the Migrant Family

Over 80% of migrants and seasonal farmworkers are U.S. citizens or are legally in the United States (Fix & Passel, 1994). The average annual income for these families is less than $7,500 per year, far below the federal poverty level (Oliveira, Effland, & Hamm, 1993). Because the work of migrant farmworkers tends to be seasonal, it is often extremely inconsistent. The number of farmworkers needing housing exceeds the number of available substandard housing units, which are usually barracks-like structures, run-down farmhouses, trailer homes, or small shacks (National Center for Farmworker Health, 2001). Some migrants may be forced to sleep in tents, cars, or even ditches when housing is unavailable. Many migrant families live without adequate rest-room facilities and clean drinking water. Although agricultural employers recognize that lack of adequate housing is a serious challenge, they often resort to temporary housing such as labor camps, of which the construction and maintenance can be expensive, especially since the camps are occupied only during harvest season. In addition, the housing that is readily available for most migrant families may not meet even the minimum inspection standards, consequently contributing to serious health problems.

Many migrant families suffer occupation-related health problems such as risk of injury from farm machinery and equipment and also from pesticide poisoning (Menchaca & Ruiz-Escalante, 1995). Respiratory problems caused by pesticide poisoning, natural fungi, and dusts are common. Lack of safe drinking water contributes to dehydration, heat stroke, and heat exhaustion. Dermatitis is often intensified by overexposure to the sun, by sweat, and by lack of sanitary facilities. Some commonly reported health problems among migrant children include lower height and weight, respiratory diseases, parasitic conditions, chronic diarrhea, and congenital and developmental problems, among others. Poverty, hunger, fear, and uncertainty fill the lives of migrant children. Thus, the intensity of health problems for migrant farmworkers is far more frequent than for the general population (National Center for Farmworker Health, 2001).

Migrant Parental Involvement in Education

Historically, school districts have lacked coherent policies and practices that attend to the needs of migrant parents. Because their lives revolve around moving from workplace to workplace, the hardships migrant parents confront are much greater than what most other parents encounter. Migrant parents tend to be intimidated by and unresponsive to schools, particularly if they did not enjoy positive experiences as students. Many are unsure about how best to be involved in schools and the degree of involvement that is appropriate. Language barriers also play a major role in their lack of participation. In addition, some Latino migrant parents believe it is the school's responsibility to educate their children; therefore, parental participation is sometimes non-existent (Chavkin, 1991). Thus, it is critical for educators to understand how migrant parents define schooling and education and their perceptions of how schools operate (Martínez & Velásquez, 2000). Often schools limit parental involvement to open houses, parent-teacher conferences, monitoring children's homework, and reinforcing school discipline policies. These approaches are one-way communications from school to home, rather than respecting the home situation and recognizing that parents have something valuable to contribute. A directed, authority-based form of communication that lacks a sense of closeness and mutual interest intensifies feelings that lead to a lack of parental participation.

Parent involvement strategies should be adopted and incorporated to develop strong relationships between the school and community (Ruiz-Escalante & Menchaca, 1999); however, many current intervention programs tend to be *prescriptive* instead of inclusive (Valdes, 1996). A strong partnership between the family and the school can support and empower Latino migrant parents to become more involved in schools. Thus, educators should begin to rethink their communicative approach, include Latino migrant parents in schools, and respond to their specific needs.

Educational Experiences of Migrant Students

Children of Latino migrants tend to be academically unsuccessful. Their mobility interrupts their education several times throughout the school year and puts enormous stress on them and their schools. The particular educational needs of Latino migrant students vary considerably; some lack the literary skills in Spanish, while English language abilities are limited for others. The quality of instruction for Latino migrant students could also be hampered if the curriculum does not adequately address their needs or provide supplemental instructional services to overcome academic difficulties that result from frequent disruptions in schooling. Most school personnel are not well prepared to adequately serve the academic needs of Latino students in general and Latino migrant students in particular (Menchaca, 1996).

Migrant students have the lowest graduation rate of any other population in the United States (Johnson, Levy, Morales, Morse, & Prokop, 1986); their dropout rate is almost twice that of children from non-migrant families. Approximately 50% of Latino migrant students are one or more years below grade level. Thus, half of all migrants could be at risk of leaving school early (Migrant Education Secondary Assistance Project, 1989). Poverty is another factor that leads to dropping out; the addition of another family member's income is welcomed. In addition, Latino migrant students tend to drop out of school if they are not proficient in English, and some teachers become disinterested in Latino migrant students due to their diverse academic, social, and economic needs.

In a study conducted by the Migrant Youth Program (1985) some students indicated that the school personnel did not meet their needs, although teachers and counselors believed the students' needs were met. Martínez (1994) reported that, according to principals and teachers, factors that influence the school performance of migrant children are: (a) social prejudice, (b) lack of communication, (c) mobility, (d) lack of educational continuity, (e) not valuing education, (f) inappropriate home environment, and (g) lack of knowledge of how educational systems operate. Yet, migrant advocates such as mentors, counselors, or advisers had a more holistic perspective on reasons migrant students leave school. Many indicated that poverty contributed to school absences because these students needed to work; and they often had to care for younger siblings or were absent due to illnesses (Martínez & Cranston-Gingras, 1996).

Because Latino migrant children can transfer schools as much as three times per year, schools must provide an environment for them to adjust as quickly as possible. The Jackson County Migrant Education Program (1981) in Medford, Oregon, produced a handbook titled *Migrant Education—Harvest of Hope*. This handbook covers several topics including knowledge of children for whom English is a second language (ESL) and how migrant students relate with teachers and provides suggestions for meeting the needs of ESL students. Most important is the message that the migrant students need teachers' care, respect, understanding, and encouragement. Another site that provides migrant children with rich learning experiences is Waitz Elementary in Mission, Texas; approximately 30% of its students are from migrant families and live in tar-paper shacks or in trailer homes along dirt roads. With a 99% Mexican American student population, Waitz Elementary annually places among the top 10% of all Texas schools in reading and mathematics achievement. The school "defies predictions of low achievement by a sustained focus on multiple factors" (Cawelti, 1999, p. 1) that remarkably improve student performance. The principal and teachers are committed to high expectations and make every effort to ensure high student achievement. For example, teachers use bilingual education approaches with students who enter with limited English skills, making sure that all students pass the state-mandated assessment. These two programs are good examples of how schools, with motivation and effort, can effectively serve the unique needs of Latino migrant students.

Culturally Relevant Teaching

Culturally relevant teaching is a pedagogy that empowers students intellectually, socially, emotionally, and politically (Ladson-Billings, 1990, 1995). It rests on three criteria: (a) academic success, (b) cultural competence, and (c) cultural consciousness (Ladson-Billings, 1995). It also utilizes students' home culture to help create meaning and understanding of their world. Thus, the culturally relevant teacher emphasizes academic, social, and cultural success and believes that academic success is possible for all students.

Making the connection between home culture and school allows migrant students to learn from a familiar cultural base that acknowledges their ancestors and develops understanding in their culture, thus empowering them to build on their personal backgrounds (Banks, 1994; Barba, 1995). Culturally relevant teachers believe that Latino migrant students have special strengths that need to be explored and utilized in the classroom. When needed, teachers encourage students to use their home language while acquiring English as a second language. Latino migrant students must have opportunities to make decisions and to take actions related to the topic, issue, or problem they are studying. In other words, when students identify a problem and are given the liberty to make decisions on what actions need to be taken to remedy the problem, they will have a sense of pride and satisfaction. It is important for teachers to communicate to students that they are being successful.

Teachers must direct, reinforce, and cultivate academic success and excellence in their migrant students. Culturally relevant teachers validate students' cultures by integrating culturally relevant content into the curriculum (Menchaca, 2000). Teachers legitimate Latino migrant students' real-life experiences as part of the formal curriculum. In a science lesson, for example, the use of culturally familiar plants, flowers, and fruits prevalent to the Latino culture could be presented along with the content in the textbook. Studying the production of plants, fruits, and vegetables gives teachers an excellent opportunity to introduce the mobile lifestyle of migrant students. In addition, when studying the food pyramid in a health lesson, the use of culturally familiar foods and examples enhances concept acquisition. Also, examples of foods and diseases that are prevalent in migrant family households should be presented along with the examples in the textbook.

In a language arts lesson, teachers can incorporate a variety of Latino children's books. Much of the Latino literature focuses on the life and experiences of migrant students. Nurturing ethnic affiliation helps migrant students learn about and respect cultural groups' heritage and histories while keeping their own culture instilled in their hearts and minds. Adolescent novels can be used at the middle or high schools with migrant students (e.g., *White Bread Competition*, Hernández, 1997; *Spirits of the High Mesa*, Martínez, 1997; and *Trino's Time*, Bertrand, 2001). These novels explore conflict, friendships, loyalties, romances, racial identities, death, and Latino traditions. With humor and sensitivity, the authors shed light on the lives of middle school and high school Latino adolescents. Migrant students can read about their own life experiences as they read about the mysteries, challenges, dreams, and conflicts of other young Latino adolescents. It is also important for White students to read about the successes, challenges, and dreams of Latino students to view different perspectives and to understand the ways in which the histories and cultures of our nation are inextricably bound.

Instructional Strategies for Migrant Students

Cooperative learning, metacognitive skills, positive educational environments, and extracurricular activities can help build on Latino migrant students' strengths and foster self-esteem. Cooperative learning lowers anxiety levels and strengthens motivation, self-esteem, and empowerment by using students as instructional agents for migrant students (Platt, Cranston-Gingras, & Scott, 1991). Students take responsibility for both their own learning and the learning of their peers. By becoming active group participants, they gain equal access to learning opportunities.

Metacognitive skills assist students in becoming independent learners by helping them comprehend concepts, monitor their success, and make the necessary adjustments when meaning is elusive. Students learn to recognize when they are approaching an obstacle, make necessary corrections, and proceed. Teachers instruct students to employ alternative strategies once they have recognized and determined a lack of comprehension. Because migrant students often find themselves in new and unfamiliar classrooms, the challenges of adjusting to strange, new learning and home environments often contribute to feelings of isolation and loneliness. Teachers can help students overcome these feelings by modeling respect and eliminating any form of threat or ridicule. A sense of safety and trust can be fostered by allowing students to share some of their own experiences and by assigning older students to act as mentors or buddies to new students.

Since schooling for migrant students is interrupted with each move, most are not involved in any form of extracurricular activity. Many of them do not participate in after-school activities because they lack transportation or have after-school responsibilities or because their parents are unaware of the extracurricular activities available. Yet, participating in these types of activities can provide enriched learning experiences to develop social skills and talents and promote positive attitudes. Some of these challenges can be overcome by providing after-school transportation. Parents should be informed of all before- and after-school activities. In some communities, after-school programs are sponsored by clubs, organizations, or local park and recreation departments. In Florida, for example, the Dade County Park and Recreation Department has activities specifically designed for migrant students, since the enrollment of these students has increased dramatically in that area. The facility, located close to a migrant camp, offers adult supervision and activities in which games and activities are planned in both English and Spanish. The goal of this facility is to contribute to the total well-being of children regardless of language or ethnicity.

The Challenges of Secondary Schools

High dropout rates, low achievement test scores, poor attendance, mobility, cultural differences, and limited proficiency in English are among the challenges that many Latino migrant students encounter in secondary schools. These challenges are overwhelming for public schools and present difficult instructional problems to educators. Secondary schools have begun to seek assistance from external entities to respond to the needs of Latino migrant students by establishing, for example, bilingual or dual-language programs in elementary schools and ESL programs in secondary schools. Flexible instructional and support programs are needed to facilitate schooling through reading, writing, and critical thinking skills. Such support programs include tutorial services, counseling services, enrichment activities, career awareness, health services, and medical referrals. Because intervention must be provided to highly mobile students, placement in small classrooms, in which instruction is more personalized, is important.

Migrants who are high school seniors have needs that are numerous in nature, and schools must provide solutions for their success. There are more Latino seniors in vocational or general education programs than in the college preparation programs. There are fewer numbers of Latino seniors in senior-level courses such as trigonometry, calculus, physics, chemistry, or English. Fewer Latinos take the Scholastic Aptitude Test (SAT) and

American College Test (ACT), examinations used for college admissions. These deficits exclude Latino migrant students from entering college. Schools should provide academic opportunities for making up credits, tutoring, taking appropriate courses, and developing test-taking skills. Also, school counselors should assist migrants in applying to and preparing for college. This type of involvement increases college attendance rates (Horn & Chen, 1998). Other more personal services that schools can provide migrant students are counseling, extended day/week/year programs, and special summer schools. Career awareness about work experiences and vocational education has also been successful for migrant students. Because even successful migrant students are at risk in high school, programs such as the College Assistance Migrant Program (CAMP) have been designed for continued support. CAMP is a *Title IV* program that provides tutoring, orientations, and counseling for migrants planning to enter college. Such programs are found on many university campuses and have been successful. They have lowered freshman dropout rates by offering academic support to students during their first year of college (National Commission on Migrant Education, 1992). In addition, College Bound is a summer program to assist seniors in the transition from high school to college. Students work, study, and receive assistance and counseling at a college campus. Approximately 90% of College Bound students enroll in colleges the following semester.

The U.S. Department of Education's Migrant Education Program has worked for more than 20 years with states to prepare migrant students for a successful transition to post-secondary education or employment (Morse & Hammer, 1998). To be admitted into college, migrant students need to have completed high school with the appropriate courses for postsecondary education and understand the application requirements and financial aid deadlines and strategies and skills to progress through a system that was not created for them. Factors that have contributed and facilitated migrant students' college attendance are (a) access to counseling centers that offer an array of options; (b) students' self-efficacy; (c) access to financial aid and scholarships, loans, and work-study programs; (d) support from family, friends, and educational personnel; and (e) parental involvement in decisions about their children's education. Thus, schools must take an active role in ensuring that migrant students receive assistance in preparing and applying for college.

Conclusion

This chapter has provided an array of information on the lives of migrant students in general and the condition of Latino migrant students in particular. These students encounter many hardships; the poverty and health aliments from which they suffer can be severe. These are among the many obstacles that prevent them from succeeding in school; thus, they require a supportive school environment. It is imperative that educators remember that migrant students dream of being successful and of transcending the lifestyles of their families. They understand what it means to work hard; they want to graduate and be successful. As educators, we must help them realize their dreams.

References

Banks, J. A. (1994). *Multicultural education: Theory and practice.* Boston: Allyn & Bacon.

Barba, R. H. (1995). *Science in the multicultural classroom: A guide to teaching and learning.* Boston: Allyn & Bacon.

Bertrand, D. G. (2001). *Trino's Time.* Houston, TX: Arte Público Press.

Cawelti, G. (1999). Improving achievement. *American School Board Journal, 186,* 34–37.

Chavkin, N. F. (1991). *Family lives and parental involvement in migrant students' education.* Washington, DC: U.S. Department of Education, Office of Educational Research and Improvement. (ERIC Document Reproduction Service No. ED 335174)

Fix, M., & Passel, J. S. (1994). *Immigration and immigrants: Setting the record straight.* Washington, DC: The Urban Institute.

Hernández, J. Y. (1997). *White bread competition.* Houston, TX: Arte Público Press.

Horn, L. J., & Chen, X. (1998). *Toward resiliency: At risk students who make it to college.* Washington, DC: U.S. Department of Education Office of Educational Research and Improvement.

Jackson County Migrant Education. (1981). *Migrant education—Harvest of hope.* Medford, OR: Jackson County Educational Service District. (ERIC Document Reproduction Service No. ED 212441)

Johnson, F. C., Levy, R. H., Morales, J. A., Morse, S. C., & Prokop, M. K. (1986). *Migrant students at the secondary level: Issues and opportunities for change.* Las Cruces, NM: ERIC Clearinghouse on Rural Education and Small Schools. (ERIC Document Reproduction Service No. ED 270242)

Kissam, E. (1993). Formal characteristics of the farm labor market: Implications for farm labor policy in the 1990s. In Briefing of the Commission on Security and Cooperation in Europe, *Migrant farmworkers in the United States.* Washington, DC: U.S. Government Printing Office.

Ladson-Billings, G. (1995). But that's just good teaching! The case for culturally relevant pedagogy. *Theory into Practice, 34*(3), 159–165.

Ladson-Billings, G. (1990). Like lightning in a bottle: Attempting to capture the pedagogical excellence of successful teachers of Black students. *International Journal of Qualitative Studies in Education, 3*(4), 335–344.

Martínez, F. (1997). *Spirits of the high mesa.* Houston, TX: Arte Público Press.

Martínez, Y. G. (1994). Narratives of survival: Life histories of Mexican American youth from migrant and seasonal farm workers who have graduated from high school equivalency program. Unpublished. University of South Florida.

Martínez, Y. G., & Cranston-Gingras, A. (1996). Migrant farmworker students and the educational process: Barriers to high school completion. *The High School Journal*, 28–38.

Martínez, Y. G., & Velázquez, J. A. (2000). *Involving migrant families in education.* Charleston, WV: ERIC Clearinghouse on Rural Education and Small Schools. (ERIC Document Reproduction Service No. ED 448010)

Menchaca, V. D. (2000). Culturally relevant curriculum for Limited English-Proficient students. *The Journal of the Texas Association for Bilingual Education, 5*(1), 55–59.

Menchaca, V. D. (1996). The missing link in teacher preparation programs. *Journal of Educational Issues of Language Minority Students, 17,* 1–9.

Menchaca, V. D., & Ruiz-Escalante, J. A. (1995). *Instructional strategies for migrant students.* Charleston, WV: ERIC Clearinghouse on Rural Education and Small Schools. (ERIC Document Reproduction Service No. ED 388491)

Migrant Education Secondary Assistance Project. (1989). *MESA national MSRTS executive summary.* Geneseo, NY: BOCES Geneseo Migrant Center.

Migrant Youth Program. (1985). *Perceptions of why migrant students drop out of school and what can be done to encourage them to graduate.* Albany, NY: Upstate Regional Offices and Migrant Unit, State Education Department.

Morse, S., & Hammer, P. C. (1998). Migrant students attending college: Facilitating their success. Charleston, WV: ERIC Clearinghouse on Rural Education and Small Schools. (ERIC Document Reproduction Service No. ED 423097)

National Center for Farmworker Health. (2001). *About America's farmworkers.* Available: http://www.ncth.org/abouttws.htm.

National Commission on Migrant Education. (1992). *Invisible children: A portrait of migrant children in the United States.* Washington, DC: Author. (ERIC Document Reproduction Service No. ED 348206)

Oliveira, V., Effland, J. R., & Hamm, S. (1993). *Hired farm labor use of fruit, vegetable, and horticultural specialty farms.* Washington, DC: U.S. Department of Agriculture.

Platt, J. S., Cranston-Gingras, A., & Scott, J. (1991). Understanding and educating migrant students. *Preventing School Failure, 36*(1), 41–46.

Ruiz-Escalante, J. A., & Menchaca, V. D. (1999). Creating school-community partnerships for minority parents. *Texas Teacher Education Forum, 24,* 45–49.

U.S. Department of Education. (1994). *Improving America's schools act, 103–382 statute, Title 1, part C, (Migrant Education) Program purpose, Section 1301-(4).*

Valdes, G. (1996). *Con respeto: Bridging the distance between culturally diverse families and schools: An ethnographic portrait.* New York: Teachers College Press.

Chapter 7

Culturally Responsive

Kathryn H. Au*

Glossary

Term/acronym	Meaning	Usage
Asylum seeker	Someone who crosses into another country out of fear of persecution in their home country	Often used to refer to refugees and others fleeing from persecution, violence, or war
CAMP	College Assistance Migrant Program	One of many programs designed to support migrant students who aspire to attend college
Collectivism	A term used to describe cultural values that focus on the family/group over the individual	Often used to describe cultural groups or ethnicities that focus on the family/group over the individual
CRI	Culturally responsive instruction	Teaching that values students' home culture, learning styles, and knowledge and integrates them into instruction. It also is predicated on the belief that all children can succeed and that teachers have an obligation to support students' academic, social, emotional, and psychological development.
CRP	Culturally responsive pedagogy *Sometimes referred to as culturally relevant teaching	
Diverse worldview	A worldview that acknowledges the variety of diverse beliefs, values, and perspectives	Often used to describe educators who recognize and value other cultural ways of being

(Continued)

* **Kathryn H. Au,** formerly of the University of Hawaii, is Chief Executive Officer, SchoolRise, LLC.

Term/acronym	Meaning	Usage
Individualism	A term used to describe the cultural value of independence and places greater importance on the individual rather than the group	Often used to describe Western/American value systems that focus on the individual's rights
Multicultural approaches	Approaches that include a variety of different cultural groups featured in instruction to make education more diverse	Often used in contrast to culturally responsive teaching where the cultural knowledge, values, and learning styles are incorporated into instruction

I'M STANDING JUST INSIDE THE DOOR of the third-grade classroom where I'm scheduled to conduct observations. In this elementary school on the Wai'anae Coast of the island of O'ahu, about 60 percent of the students in this school are of Native Hawaiian ancestry, while about 20 percent are Filipino, about 5 percent White, and another 5 percent Samoan. Almost all speak Hawai'i Creole English (a nonmainstream variety of English) as their home language. About two-thirds come from families living in poverty, including homeless families camping on the nearby beaches. The school day hasn't officially begun, but students are entering the room, signing in by flipping their name cards, and going quickly to their seats. They look at the whiteboard to read the teacher's message, make sure their homework is ready to be checked, and get out a book to read. By the time the bell rings, the students are settled at their desks, ready to begin the day.

The teacher walks to the front of the room, makes a few announcements, and launches into her first lesson, which requires the students to work in small groups to comprehend, summarize, and generate questions about a newspaper article. At the same time, students assigned to take attendance and the lunch count and to collect homework carry out their tasks independently. I'm impressed by how quickly the students have become engaged in challenging academic work, by how self-directed they seem, and by the teacher's calm yet business-like manner.

This smoothly running classroom, in which the teacher and students are obviously in tune with one another, shows many features of culturally responsive instruction. I sensed that the classroom belonged as much to students as it did to the teacher, that the students felt "at home" in school. I saw that both students and teacher were focused on academic learning, another hallmark of culturally responsive instruction. I noticed that the teacher had built in time for students to work in small groups, that there was a place for collaboration and cooperation in the classroom.

Culturally responsive instruction appears to offer the potential to improve students' academic achievement and chances for success in school. However, it is not easy to see how culturally responsive instruction can be applied, especially in classrooms with students of many different cultural and linguistic backgrounds. In the first section of this article I discuss the key characteristics of culturally responsive instruction. In the second section I respond to three frequently asked questions about culturally responsive instruction. In the final section I discuss practical implications in terms of classroom structures for participation.

Culturally Responsive Instruction: What Is It?

Culturally responsive instruction resides firmly within a pluralist vision of society,[1] which recognizes that the cultures of different ethnic groups provide content worthy of inclusion in the curriculum. Culturally responsive instruction aims at school success for students of diverse cultural and linguistic backgrounds, acknowledging that a disproportionate number of these students typically experience failure in school. To close the achievement gap between students of diverse backgrounds and their mainstream peers, we use culturally responsive instruction—teaching that allows students to succeed academically by building on background knowledge and experiences gained in the home and community.

Three Key Questions

I teach in an urban school, and my students come from a dozen or more different cultural and linguistic backgrounds. Can teachers in a multiethnic setting like mine still use culturally responsive instruction?

Yes, you certainly can, although you will need to think carefully about how you will implement culturally responsive instruction. This question grows from the fact that much of the research on culturally responsive instruction has been conducted in classrooms in which the majority of students are from one particular ethnic group. For example, my research linked the classroom use of talk story, a speech event observed among Native Hawaiians, to improved reading performance in Hawaiian children.[2] These and similar studies seem to highlight a precise match between instructional practices and students' cultural backgrounds. Many teachers feel that they cannot achieve such a match, because they teach in settings in which students come from many different cultural and linguistic backgrounds.

There is, however, another way of applying research on culturally responsive instruction to multiethnic, multilingual settings. This approach involves identifying patterns of instruction consistent with a *diverse worldview* that resonates with the cultural values of many nonmainstream groups.[3]

TABLE 7.1 Mainstream and Diverse Values

Mainstream	Diverse
Individual effort	Working with others
Competition	Cooperation
Personal achievement	Well-being of the group
Success measured in material terms	Success measured in spiritual terms
Independence	Interdependence
People control nature	People live in harmony with nature

Gollnick and Chinn[4] identified individualism and freedom as paramount values of the dominant group, a conclusion supported in research by Spindler and Spindler.[5] These and related mainstream values, shown in the first column of Table 7.1, underlie dominant society beliefs about how schooling should be conducted.

In contrast, consider a diverse worldview based on beliefs in the importance of working with others and cooperation, as shown in the second column of Table 7.1. In the diverse worldview, cooperation allows challenges to be met more easily, as members of the group all bring their thoughts and efforts to bear. What is important is the well-being of the group, especially the family, extended family, or kinship network. These values are shared by many students of diverse backgrounds and their families.

As you can see, both the mainstream and diverse worldviews have positive features, and it is not a matter of having to choose between the two. In the classroom, students are likely to benefit from a classroom environment in which they have experiences with both kinds of values. The challenge is to make sure that values reflected in the diverse worldview find a place in the classroom because patterns typically observed in classrooms tend to reflect primarily mainstream values.

Classroom and home settings should remain distinct and different from one another, so that teachers can carry out classroom activities in a manner that promotes academic achievement, and families can carry out their lives in a manner consistent with their own goals. In other words, culturally responsive instruction does not involve duplicating home and community settings in the classroom. Instead of duplication, think of culturally responsive instruction in terms of hybridity.[6] Hybridity refers to the creative blending of elements from students' home cultures with elements typical of the classroom and academic learning. In culturally responsive instruction, the teacher is creating hybrid settings that (1) have a focus on academic goals that students of diverse backgrounds, like all other students, should meet to do well in school and in later life and (2) provide students with a comfortable, understandable environment that enables them to meet these goals.

Can mainstream teachers who are outsiders to the students' cultures still implement culturally responsive instruction?

Again, the answer is yes. A finding common to all the research reviews is that teachers of mainstream backgrounds, as well as teachers of diverse backgrounds, can successfully use culturally responsive instruction and teach students of diverse backgrounds. For example, in my study of talk story-like reading lessons,[7] one of the teachers, Teacher LC, was a mainstream teacher. Although initially unsuccessful in conducting reading lessons with young Hawaiian students, Teacher LC learned after a year to use talk story-like participation structures and to link her lessons to students' interests. Ladson-Billings' study[8] of teachers effective in promoting the literacy of African American students included five African Americans and three European Americans. Although teachers who share their students' cultural backgrounds may have an advantage in establishing positive relationships and providing students with effective instruction, other teachers can definitely learn to adjust their teaching to become more effective.

Isn't culturally responsive instruction just good teaching, and shouldn't good teaching be the same in every setting?

This time the answer is no. To understand why, consider this statement from Geneva Gay:

> Many educators still believe that good teaching transcends place, people, time, and context. They contend it has nothing to do with the class, race, gender, ethnicity, or culture of students and teachers. This attitude is manifested in the expression "Good teachers anywhere are good teachers everywhere." Individuals who subscribe to this belief fail to realize that their standards of "goodness" in teaching and learning are culturally determined and are not the same for all ethnic groups. The structures, assumptions, substance, and operations of conventional educational enterprises are European American cultural icons ... .[9]

In other words, to advocate a universal concept of good teaching may actually amount to advocating teaching from a European American or mainstream perspective.

It remains true that certain general principles of good teaching appear widely applicable. An example of such a principle is establishing positive relationships with students. However, the way these principles are instantiated may well differ depending on the cultural backgrounds of the students. For example, a teacher may seek to establish positive relationships with students by praising them by name: "Noah is doing a great job of organizing his ideas in a web." In the eyes of some students, however, the teacher may inadvertently have violated the cultural value of working for the good of the group rather than calling attention to one's individual accomplishments. The teacher's well-intentioned comment may cause the student to feel uncomfortable and to be looked down upon by his peers.[10] Instead, this teacher could try to establish positive relationships with students by praising a small group of students or referring to the students' good work indirectly: "Team B, you're doing a wonderful job of organizing your ideas in webs."

As this example implies, the way we usually "do school" is itself a form of culturally responsive instruction, in this case, instruction responsive to the cultural backgrounds of mainstream students. From this perspective, it becomes apparent that the concept of culturally responsive instruction is applicable to *all* students, those of mainstream as well as diverse backgrounds. In both cases, the idea is that students have a better chance of experiencing academic success and of reaching high levels of literacy when instruction is responsive to their cultural backgrounds.

Classroom Structures for Participation

How can teachers adjust classroom structures for participation so that instruction becomes culturally responsive? Teachers can make these adjustments by using a variety of different groupings and interactional patterns in their classrooms. Some of these structures for participation will be consistent with a mainstream worldview oriented toward individual achievement, while others will be consistent with a diverse worldview oriented toward the well-being of the group. Both are important, because culturally responsive instruction is never intended to limit students' learning only to structures for participation that they already find comfortable.

Whole Class Lessons

Whole class lessons usually require students to learn at the same pace and to conform to the same expectations for behavior. These expectations for conformity mean that teachers tend to rely on classroom recitation to keep the students under tight control. In classroom recitation, the teacher singles out individual students to answer questions.[11] In classrooms with many African American or Native Hawaiian students, to give two examples, use of individual recitation during whole class lessons often leads to difficulty, because teachers make themselves visible targets for students' disruptive behavior.[12] Rather than being the most easily managed arrangement, whole class lessons may actually turn out to be the most difficult to manage, especially for novice teachers.

The solution is to use whole class instruction judiciously, such as for mini-lessons lasting about 10 to 15 minutes.[13] During this time, teachers provide instruction in new content, strategies, and skills, and set the tone and focus for the small group and independent work to follow.

Teachers who use whole-class instruction effectively in classrooms with many African American students, Native Hawaiian students, and others consider the pace of interaction. Teachers in some classrooms—notably, with many African American students—find that a brisk, rhythmic pace, including choral responding, works well.[14] Teachers in other classrooms, such as those with many Native American students, may find it effective to speak in a slower, measured manner.[15]

Another factor is the means by which students obtain turns at speaking. Students from some cultural backgrounds are very comfortable with raising their hands and eager to be chosen. Students from other cultural backgrounds are reluctant to volunteer to speak, even when they have many ideas to share.[16] These students may believe that responding in front of the whole class is a form of showing off, bragging, or putting oneself above others. In these situations, in order to involve all students, teachers may want to vary the participation structure. Specifically, instead of relying on students to volunteer, the teacher may have each student in turn give a brief response.

Another factor relates to whether or not students have had time to prepare their responses to teachers' questions. Students from some cultural groups are taught at home to rehearse, practice, and otherwise prepare themselves before displaying their knowledge.[17] Students from some cultural groups may be especially hesitant about sharing their responses when questions require interpretation or speculation rather than factual answers, because they have been taught to provide the answers expected by the teacher.[18] To get around this problem, teachers can pose a question and have students discuss their ideas with a partner or a small group of three or four. A representative of each pair or small group then shares a key idea or answer with the whole class.

Teacher-led Small Group Lessons

Teacher-led small group lessons provide students with many opportunities to respond and to receive recognition for their efforts from both the teacher and peers. When the small group includes no more than six students, everyone usually feels obliged to make a contribution, and a student's lack of participation is readily noticed. Small group lessons often provide teachers with the most valuable instructional time, both to engage students actively with academic concepts and vocabulary and to establish positive relationships with students.

As in whole class lessons, teachers must continue to attend to issues of turn-taking and pacing. If the teacher allows students to speak when they have something to say, instead of tightly controlling turntaking, small group lessons become consistent with a worldview oriented toward the well-being of the group and cooperation. To establish a collaborative tone to the lessons, teachers must avoid calling on students and instead allow students to determine when they will speak. Some students have ideas to offer but do not know how to enter the conversation on their own, particularly if it is fast-paced. If the teacher sees that a student wants to speak but has not been able to do so, the teacher can make a space by quieting the group. For example, the teacher might say, "Excuse me, let's stop for a moment to see if Sarah has anything to add. Sarah, do you have an idea to share?"

Small group discussions may proceed at a brisk pace, as in talk story-like reading lessons, or the pace may need to be more leisurely. Teachers should watch students for clues about their comfort with the pace of the lesson and make adjustments accordingly. For example, research suggests that teachers in classrooms with Native American students may need to wait an extra moment to be sure students have finished speaking and do not feel interrupted.[19]

Student-led Small Groups

To make sure that student-led small groups are organized in a manner consistent with a diverse worldview, the teacher can guide students to set the ground rules to be followed during these small group discussions. These ground rules can reinforce values of cooperation. For example, the fourth graders in Torry Montes' class agreed that everyone should participate and that shy students would be invited to join the conversation.[20] Rules such as these promote collaboration rather than competition among students within the group.

Student-led small groups in the form of book clubs[21] can be used to promote higher level thinking about text. Teachers can take a number of steps to enhance students' ability to engage in thoughtful discussions about biographies, historical fiction, and other texts and so make good use of the time in book clubs. Teachers should make sure all students have access to the text, for example, by having struggling readers engage in partner reading or giving them access to a listening center where they can hear the book on audiotape or CD. In general, teachers should model the kinds of comments students might make about the text, such as offering interpretations or making personal connections, as well as giving students help with learning how to ask open-ended questions. Teachers can have students observe and comment upon live or videotaped book club discussions, so that students see the difference between productive and unproductive conversations. Some groups of students, such as the African American students observed by Florio-Ruane,[22] may have the skills to engage in discussions of literature with little or no teacher guidance.

Another valuable use of student-led small groups involves having students work together to complete a project. For example, in a thematic unit on civil rights, one small group might choose to conduct research on Rosa Parks and the Montgomery bus boycott. Students in the group pull together information from a number of different sources, and summarize their information in a written report. They can devise other ways to share their information with the class, such as through web pages or dramatization.

In some cases, as in classrooms with many Native Hawaiian students, teachers should not assign roles for members of the student-led groups but let students work out these roles on their own. Native Hawaiian students, for example, often have considerable experience working with their siblings and cousins to accomplish tasks, and so know how to organize a small group to reach a common goal. In other cases, small groups may function more smoothly if the teacher assigns students roles, such as recorder or reporter. This approach may be necessary if students prefer to work on their own, are not accustomed to working with their peers, or come from cultural backgrounds with an orientation toward individual accomplishment.

Individual or Independent Work Time

Obviously, if students of diverse backgrounds are to be successful in school, they need to learn to work on their own. The ability to complete academic tasks independently is valued in school settings oriented toward individual achievement and competition and that emphasize standardized or state tests. As with the previous three structures for participation, teachers should discuss the expectations and rules for participating appropriately with students. For example, in a primary grade classroom, the teacher might explain the situation to students in the following way:

> Today you're going to be reading a section in your social studies textbook. Your job is to read this section on your own and then write the answers to the three questions. We're going to be doing this work in a different way. Usually, if you need help, you can ask someone at your table. With this work, you cannot ask anyone at your table. If you need help, you will raise your hand and wait for me to come over to you. The reason we're doing things this way is so that I can see the kind of social studies reading you can do on your own. This information will help me know what I need to teach you. Do you have any questions about what we're going to be doing now?

In this explanation, the teacher has made the rules for participation explicit for the students. This new structure for participation has been contrasted to the structure with which students are familiar. The teacher has given the students the reason that this structure for participation is being used.

However, despite the teacher's clear explanation, it may not be easy for students to engage successfully in this new participation structure on the first few tries. In order to support students' learning of these new rules for participation, the teacher should take a few minutes at the end of the lesson for a whole-class discussion. During this discussion, the teacher has the students evaluate their performance during the activity and provide suggestions about how they might improve their performance the next time. It takes time for students of diverse backgrounds to learn to participate appropriately in new structures, particularly if those structures reflect an individualistic, competitive worldview.

A final insight about individual work time is provided by Philips, who observed that Native American students used this time to approach the teacher for help with their work.[23] These students preferred to receive assistance from the teacher individually and in private, rather than during whole-class or small-group lessons. This study suggests that teachers in multiethnic classrooms may want to make themselves available for individual conferences with students at some time during the school day. The teacher may have students sign up for these conferences in advance, as during the writers' workshop, or students may simply come over to the teacher's desk when no other student is there.

Conclusion

Yes, culturally responsive instruction is good teaching. But I hope it has become clear that what constitutes good teaching—teaching that helps all students to learn and prosper in school—may vary from setting to setting. This means that teachers cannot follow a simple formula for implementing culturally responsive instruction but must creatively experiment and make adjustments until they find the right combination of structures for participation. Teachers who wish to use culturally responsive instruction in multiethnic classrooms have the challenge of organizing to create a place for different structures for participation over the course of a week, if not a day. This variety of structures for participation is necessary if students of diverse cultural backgrounds are to engage successfully in academic learning, at least part of the time, from the beginning of the school year. As the year goes on, teachers enable students to participate effectively in structures that may initially have been unfamiliar or uncomfortable. The opportunities for academic learning available to students of diverse backgrounds increase as they begin to engage successfully in all the structures for participation commonly found in school, those consistent with a worldview oriented toward competition as well as with a worldview oriented toward cooperation. In this way, culturally responsive instruction offers the potential for closing the achievement gap so often seen between students of diverse backgrounds and their mainstream peers.

Notes

1. Gollnick, D. M., & Chinn, P. C. (2002). *Multicultural education in a pluralistic society* (sixth ed.). Upper Saddle River NJ: Merrill Prentice-Hall.
2. Au, K., & Mason, J. M. (1981). Social organizational factors in learning to read: The balance of rights hypothesis. *Reading Research Quarterly*, 17(1), 115–152.

3. Spindler, G., & Spindler, L. (1990). *The American cultural dialogue and its transmission*. London: Falmer Press.

4. Gollnick & Chinn, op cit.

5. Spindler & Spindler, op cit.

6. Au, K. (2006). *Multicultural issues and literacy achievement*. Mahwah NJ: Erlbaum.

7. Au & Mason, op cit.

8. Ladson-Billings, G. (1994). *The dreamkeepers: Successful teachers of African American children*. San Francisco: Jossey-Bass.

9. Gay, 9. G. (2000). *Culturally responsive teaching*. New York: Teachers College Press, p. 22.

10. See Philips, S. U. (1983). *The invisible culture: Communication in classroom and community on the Warm Springs Indian Reservation*. New York: Longman.

11. Au, op cit; and Mehan, H. (1979). *Learning lessons: Social organization in the classroom*. Cambridge MA: Harvard University Press.

12. D'Amato, J. (1988). "Acting": Hawaiian children's resistance to teachers. *Elementary School Journal*, 88(5), 529–544.

13. Routman, R. (2000). *Conversations: Strategies for teaching, learning, and evaluating*. Portsmouth NH: Heinemann.

14. Hollins, E. R. (1982). The Marva Collins story revisited. *Journal of Teacher Education*, 33(1), 37–40.

15. Erickson, F., & Mohatt, G. (1982). Cultural organization of participation structures in two classrooms of Indian students. In G. B. Spindler (Ed.), *Doing the ethnography of schooling: Educational anthropology in action* (pp. 132–174). New York: Holt, Rinehart & Winston.

16. Boggs, S. T. (1972). The meaning of questions and narratives to Hawaiian children. In C. Cazden, V. John & D. Hymes (Eds.), *Functions of language in the classroom* (pp. 299–327). New York: Teachers College Press.

17. Philips, op cit.

18. Wong-Fillmore, L., Ammon, P., McLaughlin, B., & Ammon, M. (1985). *Learning English through bilingual education (final report)*. Washington DC: National Institute of Education.

19. Vogt, L. A., Jordan, C., & Tharp, R. G. (1987). Explaining school failure, producing school success: Two cases. *Anthropology & Education Quarterly*, 18(4), 276–286.

20. Montes, T. H., & Au, K. H. (2003). Book Club in a fourth-grade classroom: Issues of ownership and response. In R. L. McCormack & J. R. Paratore (Eds.), *After early intervention, then what? Teaching struggling readers in grade 3 and beyond* (pp. 70–93). Newark DE: International Reading Association.

21. Raphael, T. E., & McMahon, S. I. (1994). Book Club: An alternative framework for reading instruction. *The Reading Teacher*, 48(2), 102–116.

22. Florio-Ruane, S. (2004, October). Personal communication (email message).

23. Philips, op cit.

Chapter 8

Teaching ELLs in Classrooms

Nan Li

Glossary

Term/acronym	Meaning	Usage
Bloom's taxonomy	A list of educational objectives ranging in level of cognitive difficulty	Used as a general tool to establish learning goals
Comprehensible input	Speech or written language that is level appropriate for target students.	Often used to describe how teachers need to modify communication both verbally and nonverbally to ensure student understanding
Content objectives	Clearly established content area objectives for a particular lesson topic	Objectives often established by state standards related to specific content areas
Explicit instruction	Instruction that directly addresses a particular topic	Often used to describe language instruction that specifically targets a language feature (i.e., verb tense, capitalization, etc.)
Idiom	A word or phrase that has meaning different from the meanings of the individual words used	Common idioms in English: hand in, hit the light, blow me away, heads up, what's up?
K-W-L	Know-Want to Know-Learned	Often used to guide teachers on what students already know before instruction and what they need to know and then gauging what they have learned

(Continued)

Term/acronym	Meaning	Usage
Language objectives	Specific language targets students' need to accomplish the content objective	Refers to the language the instructor identifies that students need to know in order to understand content presented. This can be grammar related, new vocabulary, punctuation, idioms, etc.
Modeling	Instructional technique that teaches via demonstration	Often used to describe a technique in language instruction where the teacher models a process while also proving students' verbal input to support language acquisition
SIOP	Sheltered Instruction Observation Protocol	An approach to teaching that aims to address the unique needs of culturally and linguistically diverse students
TPR	Total physical response	A method used in various educational settings that uses physical activity to enhance learning/memory
Transitional words or phrases	Words or phrases used in written texts or speech that connect ideas in meaningful ways	Refers to words that link ideas and are often problematic for English language learners (i.e., words or phrases to describe cause and effect; sequencing words; comparisons; stating examples)

Case Scenario

Martina arrived in America a week after she celebrated her 14th birthday. Although she was nervous about going to a new country where she did not speak the language, she was excited to see her father, who had left Mexico 5 years before and was working on a small chicken farm. Martina boarded the bus to Arizona and left her mother, grandmother, a cousin, and her friends. The bus trip took 2 days before she finally arrived. Her father enrolled her in a public school, where the Guidance Counselor asked her father to complete a Home Language Survey in Spanish. The survey asked many questions. Martina could understand these questions. Yet, as to what the people in school were saying, she had no clue. Her father spoke a little English and was able to explain to Martina that she would be in the ninth grade. She completed the eighth grade and was a good student in Mexico. Here on her first day at school, she was paralyzed, and everything was in English. However, she was greeted by a smiling teacher, who told Martina that she was her ESOL teacher. The ESOL teacher told Martina that she was going to take a test to see how much she understood English. Of course, Martina did not know what the teacher was saying, but she understood the gesture of asking her to follow. When she looked at the test, everything was in English. Martina started crying and knew that school would be difficult. Soon she was attending an English class where the teacher was as nervous as Martina because she had never had a non-English-speaking student before. The lesson was on Macbeth. The teacher wondered how she was going to teach this ELL who did not speak, read, write, or comprehend a word of English.

The above scenario occurs daily in schools, from big cities to small towns of every state across the country. Schools in the United States are facing the ever-present challenge of providing effective instruction for a growing population of immigrant students, most of which are ELLs (Egbert & Ernst-Slavit, 2010; OELA, 2010; Zacarian & Haynes, 2012). From the school year 1997–1998 to 2008–2009, the number of English-language learners enrolled in U.S. public schools increased from 3.5 million to 5.3 million, an increase of 51%, according to a 2012 Report from the National Clearinghouse for English Language Acquisition (NCELA, 2012). During the same period, the general population of students grew by only 7.2% (OELA, 2010). As the number of immigrants from many countries continues to grow, teachers are faced with the challenge of how to best help children who come to school with little or no English.

In the above case scenario, we can see that the frustration is on both sides on the first day at school between the teacher and the ELL. The teacher is frustrated not knowing what to do. She knew that she could not just watch Martina sit quietly in the corner of her classroom without taking any action. Yet should she give this ELL the same materials but speak a little slower so that the ELL could understand? What will happen when the ELL needs to take the standardized test in the spring? To help teachers deal with this challenge as described in the scenario and faced by many teachers daily, this chapter provides specific lesson plan models and useful instructional strategies to help them prepare lessons. Most of these teaching strategies, such as using visual aids, relating previous knowledge, and presenting contextual information, have been proven to work in classrooms.

Planning to Teach

Due to the challenge that confronts teachers daily on how to work with ELLs, researchers have been in search for answers. Data reveals that teachers' lack of preparation has made the situation worse in meeting the needs of the English language learners. The official report from the Office of English Language Acquisition in the U.S. Department of Education indicates that the national ratio of ESL-certified teachers to ELL students is 1 to 44, with many states with even higher numbers (OELA, 2010). The OELA data also indicates that professional development needs attention because a growing number of teachers who have English learners in their classrooms have little or no preparation. The National Center for

Education Statistics survey data also reveals that 42% of teachers reported having ELLs in their classrooms; yet only 12.5% had received more than 8 hours of training geared toward educating ELLs (Jong & Harper, 2005). However, since the Supreme Court ruling in the *Lau v. Nichols* case in 1974 (U.S. Department of Education, n.d.), teachers and schools have to ensure that the students whose first language is not English receive equal services when it comes to the delivery of instruction. For instance, here is an excerpt from this ruling as the guidelines for teachers:

> The failure of the San Francisco school system to provide English language instruction to approximately 1,800 students of Chinese ancestry who do not speak English, or to provide them with other adequate instructional procedures, denies them a meaningful opportunity to participate in the public educational program and thus violates § 601 of the Civil Rights Act of 1964. ... Where inability to speak and understand the English language excludes national origin-minority group children from effective participation in the educational program offered by a school district, the district must take affirmative steps to rectify the language deficiency in order to open its instructional program to these students ... designed to meet such language skill needs as soon as possible and must not operate as an educational dead end or permanent track.

With this ruling, school districts and educational experts have sought various ways to deliver adequate educational services to ELL students. Many approaches and philosophies on teaching English language learners have been created and implemented. Among them, the SIOP model is among the most successful and widely accepted models.

SIOP Lesson Model

The term SIOP stands for *Sheltered Instruction Observation Protocol*. It is considered as an empirically tested approach that helps teachers prepare all students, especially English language learners, to become college and career ready (Person, 2013). The SIOP model was developed by Dr. Jana Echevarria, Dr. Mary Ellen Vogt, and Dr. Deborah Short as a framework for mainstream teachers to effectively teach ELLs and give the students like Martina access to content areas. This model of teaching has been tested among mainstream teachers across the country, and now many schools with growing number of English language learners are implementing this teaching model with much success.

Teachers should know that, for school-age ELL students, academic language is crucially important for the students' school success (Francis, Rivera, Lesaux, Kieffer, & Rivera, 2006). The SIOP model helps ELL students like Martina, who would be graduating from school in a few years, to meet their linguistic and academic needs simultaneously. Teachers can also provide ELLs with access to content areas for a beginner English learner if they implement the SIOP model. In addition, research shows that English learners acquire English best when language forms are explicitly taught and when the students have many opportunities to practice the language in meaningful contexts (Goldenberg, 2008). In this chapter, the SIOP model will be introduced and explained in detail, with activities for implementation. Specifically, the SIOP model consists of these eight interrelated components:

- Lesson preparation
- Building background
- Comprehensible input
- Strategies
- Interaction
- Practice/Application
- Lesson delivery
- Review/Assessment

Component #1: Lesson Preparation

The SIOP model requires teachers to incorporate these components when planning and preparing a lesson: clearly define *content* and *language objectives* (i.e., write on the board and as well as state these objectives orally); choose age-appropriate *content concepts* (i.e., appropriate for the educational background of students); use *supplementary materials* to make lessons clear and meaningful; adapt content to all levels of student *proficiency* (i.e., using graphic organizers, study guides, taped texts, jigsaw reading); provide meaningful and authentic *activities* that integrate lesson concepts with language practice and opportunities (i.e., surveys, letter writing, making models, plays, games).

To clearly define the *content* and *language objectives* means that teachers need both to write and state these objectives and review them with students at the beginning and the end of the lesson to see whether the objectives have been met. *Content objectives* need to state the content that the students need to know. When writing the content objectives, teachers should make language student-friendly while not simplifying the content. *Language objectives* should specify the type of language that students need to learn in order to accomplish the lesson content objectives. Quality language objectives should complement the content knowledge and skills identified in content area standards and address the aspects of academic language that will be developed or reinforced during the teaching of grade-level content concepts. The

TABLE 8.1 Writing Content and Language Objectives

7th Grade Social Studies on Colonial Communities		
Content Area Standard	**Content Objective**	**Language Objective**
State Standard: Students will use a variety of intellectual skills to demonstrate their understanding of the geography of the interdependent world in which we live.	Students will be able to show how geographic features have affected colonial life by creating a map.	Students will be able to summarize in writing how geography impacted colonial life.

Note: For resources on the SIOP Lesson Plan Model tools, teachers can go to this website: http://siop.pearson. com/books-resources/index.html. The SIOP Lesson Plan Model template can be downloaded at http://www. gcu.edu/Documents/Education/Clinical-Practice-SIOP-Lesson-Plan-Template.pdf. There are also other modified SIOP lesson templates that can be downloaded for teaching with this website as an example: http://www. wl.k12.ia.us/Page/94.

language objectives should also cover the four aspects of the language skills (i.e., speaking, listening, reading, and writing), but they can also include the language functions related to the topic of the lesson (e.g., justify, hypothesize); vocabulary essential to a student being able to fully participate in the lesson (e.g., axis, locate, graph); and language-learning strategies to aid in comprehension (Echevarria, Vogt, & Short, 2010; Thrower, 2009). Table 8.1 is an example of how to write content and language objectives.

The SIOP lesson model requires teachers also to choose *content concepts* that are appropriate for the age and educational background of students. For example, teachers need to consider the ELL students' L1 literacy, L2 proficiency, and the reading level of the materials. It is also important that mainstream teachers collaborate with ESOL teachers and discuss ELL student information in order to plan well for instruction. In preparing a lesson, teachers must also select *supplementary materials* to be used to promote comprehension. These include charts, graphs, pictures, illustrations, realia, math manipulatives, multimedia, and demonstrations by teacher and other students. Teachers also need to adapt content to all levels of student *proficiency* by using appropriate graphic organizers, study guides, taped texts, and jigsaw reading. The use of these materials can promote higher critical thinking and engage students in interacting with various resources instead of listening to lectures that could be boring to children. Finally, teachers must also prepare to engage students in *meaningful activities* that integrate lesson concepts with language and also provide opportunities to practice listening, speaking, reading, and writing across content areas in the learning process.

Building background requires that teachers link concepts to students' backgrounds and experiences. These backgrounds and experiences can be personal, cultural, or academic. A reader's schema knowledge of the world provides a basis for understanding, learning, and remembering facts and ideas found in texts. Teachers must know that ELLs from culturally diverse backgrounds may struggle to comprehend texts and concepts due to a mismatch in schema. It is important for teachers to know their students' background, not assuming that the students understand the context of the lesson. For example, if the lesson is related to winter activities like sledding or skiing, many students from the Hispanic background may not have even seen a photo of a sled. If they have, they may not know how it is used unless a teacher can bring a real sample of a sled or show a video of people sledding. Now, they may have something similar that they use in their country for a race through the sand or in the desert. Most reading material, such as content area texts, relies on an assumption of common prior knowledge and experience.

In building background knowledge, it is also important to recognize the value of vocabulary development or vocabulary proficiency. Knowledge of vocabulary correlates strongly with academic achievement and reading comprehension. Students' limited vocabulary can hinder them in comprehending content texts, following instructions correctly, in directions for completing assignments, or overall academic achievement. In math, there are many words that students need to be taught explicitly, such as *addition, subtraction, continent, sentence, classify, summarize, identify, beaker, compare, paragraph*. Key vocabulary words must be emphasized (e.g., introduced, written, repeated, and highlighted for students to see). Do not just say it but show it; write it; give illustrations; give examples and be more powerful; discuss and ask students what they know. A great teacher must also explicitly link past learning to new concepts. After all, students are not just blank slates, even if they may have limited knowledge of English. By linking past knowledge to the lesson, a teacher is making learning relevant. One great way is to link student background knowledge is to use the graphic organizer, such as the K-W-L chart. Ask the students *what* they already know about the topic, what they *want* to know, and after the lesson has been completed, students should write or state what they have *learned*. This chart is a great way to activate students' background knowledge.

Component #3: Comprehensible Input

The SIOP model requires that teachers use speech that is appropriate for students' language proficiency level so that it is comprehensible to them. For example, students who are at the beginning levels of English proficiency benefit from teachers who slow down their rate of speech, use pauses, and enunciate clearly while speaking. As students become more comfortable with the language and acquire higher levels of proficiency, a slower rate becomes unnecessary. In fact, for advanced and transitional students, teachers should use a rate of speech that is normal for a regular classroom. Effective teachers adjust their rate of speech and enunciation to their students' levels of English proficiency. Students will respond according to their proficiency level. The following is an example of using appropriate speech for different levels of ELL students who have different English proficiency when asking them to describe the setting in a story related to the cold day:

- Level 1: (No response, not sure what setting is yet or in silent period)
- Level 2: "Cold day."
- Level 3: "The day is cold and there is snow."
- Level 4: "The day is very cold and heavy snow is falling."
- Level 5: "It is a cold, winter day, and it is snowing more heavily than usual."
- Level 6: "The unusually heavy snow on the day the story takes place causes a number of problems for the characters."

Paraphrasing and repetition enhance understanding for ELLs and all students. Brain research tells us that repetition strengthens connections in the brain (Jensen, 2005). ELLs benefit from repeated exposures to a word in order to hear it accurately because they often lack the auditory acuity to decipher sounds of English words. Teachers should also explain academic tasks clearly and use a variety of techniques to make content concepts clear; for example, modeling, visuals, hands-on activities, demonstrations, gestures, body language (Thrower, 2009). An example of a clear explanation of tasks is to write on the board for a reading selection which contains lots of words about people, places, and things in the community as follows:

- Read the story together.
- Read word cards with your partner.
- Place each card in a column: people, places, things.
- Tell your partner why the card goes in that column.
- The teacher goes over each step showing visuals with each step.

Use of a variety of techniques helps make content concepts clear. These techniques could include modeling, hands-on materials, visuals, demos, gestures, film or video clips. Yet teachers need to focus attention selectively on the most important information, introduce new learning in context, and help students learn strategies such as predicting, summarizing.

Component #4: Strategies

Teachers must provide many opportunities for students to use strategies such as problem solving, predicting, organizing, summarizing, categorizing, evaluating, and self-monitoring. These learning strategies should be taught through explicit instruction to help students develop independence for self-monitoring. Scaffolding techniques should be used consistently throughout the lesson with the right amount of support to move students from one level of understanding to a higher level. When introducing a new concept, teachers should use scaffolding but gradually decrease support as time goes on. The following are several strategies teachers can use to help students build strategies to learn productively:

- Use visual cues, such as pictures, objects, gestures, demonstrations, graphic organizers, and hands-on learning. These visuals increase comprehension by equating words with the objects and ideas they represent. Refraining from using idioms, speaking slowly and clearly, and finding ways to repeat the words, phrases, or sentences are useful strategies in increasing lesson comprehension (Allen & Franklin, 2002).

- Preparing thematic units that reuse or recycle vocabulary is a good strategy to help reinforce important concepts for ELLs and all students. For example, teachers can encourage the students to reuse vocabulary connected to the topic by putting pictures around the walls of the classroom and ask the students to walk around to look at the pictures/photos and stop next to one that they want to talk about.

- Utilize multicultural/bilingual texts that reflect the backgrounds of the students to help students respond better to texts (Drucker, 2003). These types of text capture their interest and encourage them to work harder to understand the content. Teachers can even further enhance the reading comprehension skills of ELLs by providing audiotapes corresponding to the text they are reading. This can be recorded by the teacher or another student. This gives ELLs more opportunities to hear the spoken word and equate it with its graphic representation on the page (Drucker, 2003).

- Building collaborative learning communities enhances ELLs' learning experiences. Teachers can pair ELLs with an English-speaking "buddy" to read text together, encouraging reading and pronunciation development. Students often feel less intimidated working in a one-on-one situation with no fear of being laughed at by the entire class. Teachers may also use the *Language Experience Approach* within the paired students. The ELL can orally describe a personal experience and the buddy can write the response and repeat it back to the ELL. This tactic helps ELLs learn how language is encoded and builds sight-word knowledge and fluency (Reed & Railsback, 2003).

- Making appropriate accommodations for ELL students is another important way, especially during state assessments. Teachers should offer ELLs extra time, bilingual dictionaries or glossaries, and clarify the meaning of words on tests when they do not relate to the test content (Echevarria et al., 2010). Teachers may also read the directions or even simplify the questions on the test without altering the difficulty of the content so that ELLs can understand the content being tested.

Component #5: Interaction

Teachers should provide opportunities for interaction and discussion between teacher and student and among students, and encourage elaborated responses. To fully connect with the content concepts and develop a deeper understanding of the content-specific vocabulary, ELLs must have opportunities to use the language in authentic situations. Opportunities to interact with others also create an environment for students to develop oral literacy. Thus, when designing a lesson, teachers must plan activities that give students opportunities to talk with their peers about the key concepts by using the key vocabulary terms. Corporative learning is a great way for ELLs to interact with peers, and teachers can use activities such as clock buddies, pair-shares, and cooperative groups.

Sometimes, ELLs may struggle to respond appropriately to teachers' prompts and questions because questions are not clearly understood. Teachers should provide clarity and give enough waiting time to promote higher-order thinking. ELLs may also come from cultures that do not expect students to ask or answer questions during class time. These students often perceive the teacher to have elevated status and think that, as students, they should respectfully listen rather than talk in the company of their teachers. In this case, teachers should be patient and encouraging. Technology can help engage students in the interactive world. Teachers can use technology resources to involve students in an active, dynamic, and interactive learning process instead of being a passive bystander. In all, benefits of interaction are many, such as increased comprehension, personalized input, feedback on output, opportunities for hypothesis testing, and identifying gaps in knowledge. To be proficient and productive learners, ELLs must have many opportunities to interact with peers and teachers.

Component #6: Practice and Application

Teachers should provide hands-on materials and manipulatives for students to have opportunities to practice when learning new knowledge. Teachers also need to provide activities for students to apply content and language knowledge in the classroom. These activities need to integrate all four language skills: reading, writing, listening, and speaking (Echevarria et al., 2010). Students have a greater chance of mastering content concepts and skills when they are given multiple opportunities to practice in relevant, meaningful ways. Reading, writing, listening, and speaking are complex, cognitive language processes that are interrelated and integrated. These four language processes are also mutually supportive. Although the relationships among these language processes are complex, practice in any one domain promotes the development in the others.

As mentioned, the purpose of practice is to increase the chances for students to remember what they have learned and transfer that learning to new situations. When planning hands-on activities to practice, teachers may want to know how long the practice should be. Hunter (1982) suggests that teachers keep these questions and answers in mind when practicing:

Questions	Answers
1. How much material should be practiced at one time?	It should be a short meaningful amount and always use meaning to divide content into parts.
2. How long should a practice period be?	It should be a short time so the student exerts intense effort and has intent to learn.
3. How often should students practice?	For new learning, practice should be massive; for older learning, practice should be distributed.
4. How should teachers give feedback?	It should be frequent, early, positive feedback that supports students' beliefs they can do well.

For ELL students acquiring a new language, the need to apply new information is critically important because discussing or *doing* makes abstract concepts concrete. Application can occur in a number of ways, such as clustering, using graphic organizers, solving problems in cooperative learning groups, writing a journal, engaging in discussion circles, or a variety of other meaningful activities (Peregoy & Boyle, 2005).

Component #7: Lesson Delivery

The SIOP lesson model requires teachers to effectively deliver each lesson by supporting the content and language objectives. To support content objectives in the lesson delivery, teachers should write these objectives in a student-friendly format, focusing on the lesson content, providing a structure for classroom procedures, allowing students to know the direction of the lesson, and helping students on task. To support lesson delivery, language objectives may be related to an ESL strand. For example, students will write to communicate with different audiences for different reasons. Language objectives may also be related to the teachers' scope and sequence of language skills that their own students need to develop. For example, students will make text-self and text-world connections. In addition, language objectives must be addressed explicitly during the lesson and reviewed at the end. Teachers should also pace the lesson appropriately to the students' ability level.

Generally, teachers should engage students approximately from 90% to 100% of the class period for lesson delivery. This means that students should take part in tasks throughout the lesson. This also requires that teachers be sure that students are able to follow the lesson, respond to teacher directions, and perform activities as expected. Teachers must also balance time by allocating class time appropriately and by engaging students in appropriate time. Effective teachers balance teacher presentation time and the time for students to practice and apply the information in meaningful ways. Students need to have time for active participation. The more actively students participate in the instructional process, the more they achieve (Hunter, 1982). Thus, it is important to create interesting and fun activities relevant to the lesson objectives and pace the lesson to students' ability so as to reduce boredom, inattention, or off-task behaviors in order to deliver each lesson that maximizes student engagement.

Component #8: Review and Assessment

The process of review and assessment is to gather and synthesize information concerning students' learning. In gathering this information about what students understand or do not understand, teachers can adjust their instructional plan accordingly. Basic features of review and assessment should include these components: comprehensive review of key vocabulary, comprehensive review of key content concepts, regular feedback provided to students on their output, assessment of student comprehension, and learning of all lesson objectives throughout the lesson.

Comprehensive review of *key vocabulary* and *key concepts* means that teachers take the time to review and summarize key vocabulary and concepts throughout the lesson and wrap up at the end of the lesson. There are several ways to review vocabulary words. For example, teachers can help students review words in nonprint ways, such as using the pictures in a picture dictionary or using games, for example, flyswatter and Jeopardy. An example of comprehensive review of key concepts in a lesson can be demonstrated by reviewing Egyptian mummification. Teachers might say something like, "Up to this point, we learned that little was known about Mummy No. 1770 until it was donated to the museum. After the scientists completed the autopsy, they discovered three important things. Who remembers what they were?"

It is important to link the review to content objectives so that the students stay focused on the basic content concepts. Students' responses to review should guide the decisions on what to do next, such as summative evaluation or additional reteaching if needed. A favorite wrap-up technique for many teachers is the use of outcome sentences. A teacher can post sentence starters on the board or on a transparency to review and wrap up the lesson:

- I have learned ...
- I wonder ...
- I still want to know ...

- I still have a question about ...

- I still don't know ...

- I discovered ...

It is also important to provide regular feedback. Periodic review of language, vocabulary, and content enables teachers to provide specific academic feedback that clarifies and corrects misconceptions and misunderstandings. Such feedback helps students' proficiency in English when it is supportive and validating. Teachers should also provide assessment of student comprehension and learning of all lesson objectives throughout the lesson. Such assessment, as evidenced in lesson plans and in periodic review, should be used to determine if students understand and are able to apply content concepts. The format of assessment should be multidimensional, with multiple indicators that reflect student learning. For example, portfolio assessment is an authentic way to gather information on student learning over the period.

Total Physical Response

Another popular approach in teaching ELLs is the Total Physical Response (TPR) method. This method was developed by James Asher in the 1960s and it is based on the theory that the memory is enhanced through association with physical movement (Byram, 2000). Thus, TPR incorporates physical movement to react on verbal input. It allows students to react to language without thinking too much and therefore reduces stress, lowers affective filter, and facilitates long-term retention. Asher developed this method based on his observation of interactions between parents and children: (a) language is learned primarily by listening, (b) language learning must engage the right hemisphere of the brain, and (c) learning language should not involve stress. TPR often used alongside other methods is popular with beginner ELLs and with other young learners, although it can be used with students of all levels.

The TPR approach is supported by theories. It is believed that the left brain is for logical function when analyzing, talking, or discussing is involved. Most classroom activities are aimed at the left brain. The right brain is used when moving, acting, using metaphor, drawing, pointing, and such. It is targeted by sports and extracurricular activities. When language is taught by lecturing or explaining, the left brain is targeted and the information is kept in the short-term memory. It will be soon forgotten if it never becomes *real* to the student. When language is taught actively through movement, the right brain retains the information, in the same way that skills such as swimming or riding a bicycle are remembered in the long term.

Teachers using TPR usually give commands to students in the target language, and students respond with whole-body actions. For example, teachers can use TPR to teach action words, such as words related to body movements. An example is to teach the movement of *stand up* and *sit down*. Teacher and students can sit in a circle. The teacher makes the movement by standing up while saying the words, "Stand up" and using a gesture to command all students to stand up. Then, the teacher can sit down while saying the words, "Sit down" and using the gesture to tell students to sit up. The teacher can repeat the movement a few times until the students understand these words through command and action. Similarly, the teacher can teach other action words, such as *touching shoulder, walking, stopping,* and *turning around*. TPR can also help introduce speaking. For example, the teacher can play a ball game by throwing a soft ball to one student when saying clearly, "Tom, catch the ball." Then ask the student, "Tom, throw the ball back to me" with a gesture and clue. Then repeat this action with the second and third students and among students and ask students to speak in action. The teacher can then ask, "Who has the ball?" TPR can be used along with other teaching strategies to enhance the ELLs' understanding and learning success. Other teaching strategies will be introduced in the following sections with the purpose of helping teachers to engage ELLs and learn productively.

Teaching Strategies

Teaching strategies refers to the combined instructional methods, learning activities, and materials that are used to help actively engage students and that reflect learning goals to improve student learning outcomes. An effective teacher chooses a strategy to fit a particular situation. It's important to consider what students already know and the learning goals for the specific situation. In this section, different teaching strategies are introduced to help teachers better work with the ELLs and all students. These strategies discussed in these categories are *using visual aids, relating to existing knowledge, presenting contextualized information, other teaching tips,* and *integrating technology*. Many of these strategies have been used by teachers and proven to help improve student learning outcomes and achieve their academic goals. Mainstream classroom teachers should be able to implement these teaching strategies easily and use them help their ELLs with access to the academic contents.

Using Visual Aids

Visual aids refers to a device (e.g., a picture, image, chart, map, gesture, or model) that students can look at and that is used to make learning easier to understand. Using visual aids can help students visualize information and convey an idea in a vivid way for ELLs and all students, especially for those ELLs who have language barriers to understanding the concepts. When using visual aids in classrooms, teachers not only provide supplementary information to students, but the visual aids show visual images that allow students to connect a topic to what it looks like and increase students' interest. There are many types of visual aids teachers can use and adapt creatively to make learning motivational and comprehensible.

Using Pictures and Images

Using pictures and images is a powerful way to build student engagement and interest. This is because pictures and images can help ELLs make the connection between what is presented to them and what it means in a visualized context. Teachers can use pictures, images, or even real objects to help ELLs understand the concepts. Technology also provides easy access to downloading many forms of pictures and images. For example, teachers can download any images easily by using the Google search engine to find pictures and images to help ELLs learn the concept. Earthquake is an abstract concept. Without an image, it is difficult to explain to ELLs. Yet, if the teacher types the words, "earthquake images" in the Google search, tons of images and pictures on earthquakes can help ELL students make an instinctive connection to the concept. Many cartoon pictures and images can also be found by a Google search to make learning more interesting.

Using Graphic Organizers

A graphic organizer is a communication tool through visual symbols to express knowledge, concepts, thoughts, ideas, and relationships. A graphic organizer is also seen as a knowledge map, concept map, cognitive organizer, advance organizer, or concept diagram. Graphic organizers make concepts and information more accessible to ELLs and all students and make complex information manageable because they help organize information in a meaningful way. There are many different graphic organizers, such as a K-W-L chart, semantic map, Venn Diagram, flow chart, and story map. Using the story map as an example, it helps students organize the story, that is, the main character, place and time, order of events, and the ending. A story map sample is provided in Table 8.2, and teachers can use it to help ELLs organize the story for better understanding. For more graphic organizers for ELLs, teachers can visit Judy Haynes' everythingESL.net, which provides many free graphic organizers for teaching ELLs: http://www.everythingesl.net/inservices/graphic_organizers.php.

Semantic Mapping

Semantic mapping is a visual strategy that graphically represents concepts and portrays schematic relations that compose the concept. Semantic mapping is introduced because this visual aid can help ELLs expand vocabulary. Based on prior knowledge, it helps display word categories and how they are related to one another. A unique feature of semantic mapping is that it recognizes important components and shows the relationships among the concepts. For example, when discussing food, teachers can create a semantic map to help students expand their vocabulary based on categories (see Figure 8.1). With modeling, the teacher can ask students to provide food categories they know and use the semantic map to confirm familiar words and learn new vocabulary. Teacher can encourage ELLs to also share

TABLE 8.2   Story Map

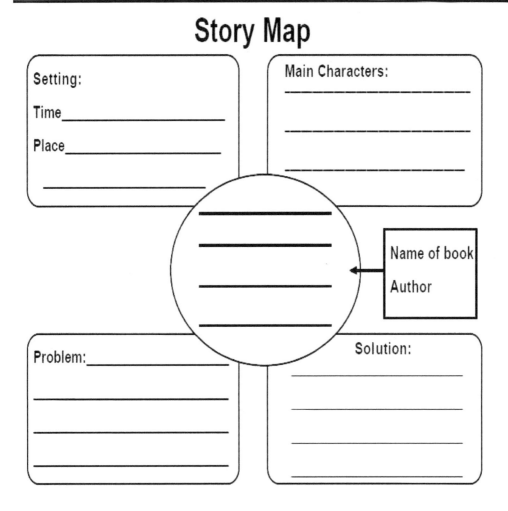

Story Map

Setting:

Time_____

Place_____

_____

Main Characters:

_____

_____

_____

Name of book

Author

Problem:_____

_____

_____

_____

Solution:

_____

_____

_____

_____

Source: http://www.everythingesl.net/downloads/story_map.pdf

food items that they consume in their cultures. This strategy can even be used for previewing and assessing how much knowledge students have about the concepts.

K-W-L Chart Strategy

The K-W-L chart is an instructional strategy that helps students better understand through reading a text. The teacher can guide students by starting with brainstorming about things they *know* about a topic and having an initial discussion with the students to ask what they already know about this topic in the text. This information is recorded in the *K* column of a

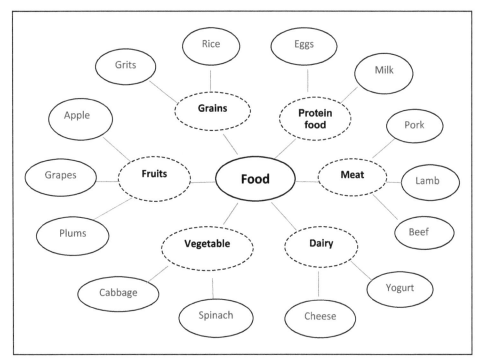

Example of the semantic map to teach food concepts. The orange color in the center is the main concept and green is for categories and blue is for specific food items.

K-W-L chart. The teacher can then ask students what they *want* to know and generate a list of questions about what they want to know about the topic. This information is listed in the W column of the chart. After reading, students answer the questions that are in the W column. Ask the students to write down what they have learned from the reading. This information that they have *learned* is recorded in the L column of the K-W-L chart. To use a K-W-L strategy, the teacher can create a chart easily on the smart-board or on an overhead transparency. In addition, students should have their own chart on which to record information. See the example of a K-W-L chart in Figure 8.2.

Many other visual aids, such as the Venn diagram, flow charts, flashcards, videos, or artworks, can be used making learning easier. When a graphic organizer is designed, teachers can expand its use or adapt it to teach other learning concepts. The following websites provide graphic organizer information in subject areas with interactive activities. Teachers can find and download a graphic organizer and print it out for learning.

1. Venn Diagram: a graphic organizer with a set of diagrams that shows all possible logical relations between concepts. Venn diagrams were created around 1880 by John Venn, an English logician and philosopher. Here is a useful link on Venn Diagrams: http://www.readingquest.org/strat/venn.html

K	W	L

FIGURE 8.2   Example of a K-W-L chart to help students.

2. K-W-L-S Chart: this is an extension of the KWL strategy and K-W-L-S stands for what I already *know*, what I *want* to know, what I have *learned*, and what I *still want* to know. Here is a link for the K-W-L-S chart: http://www.readwritethink.org/files/resources/lesson_images/lesson398/kwls2.pdf

3. More useful graphic organizers that teachers can download from these links:
   http://edhelper.com/teachers/graphic_organizers.htm
   http://www.eduplace.com/graphicorganizer/
   https://www.teachervision.com/graphic-organizers/printable/6293.html

Relating to Existing Knowledge

Prior knowledge affects how students perceive new information, and relating existing knowledge can help make learning easier. This is because students cannot be perceived as blank slates to passively inscribe. Even ELLs bring their interpretation associated with their existing knowledge and cultural background. Therefore, learning new information is often conditioned by what they already know about a concept, and it is closely related to their particular background knowledge or cultural information. When teachers link new information to their existing knowledge, it activates the students' interest and curiosity. Schema theory also indicates that personal previous experiences, knowledge, emotions, and understandings affect what and how people learn new information (Harvey & Goudvis, 2000).

Providing background information helps students make connection. Here is a scenario explaining why it is important. An ESOL teacher was decorating the classroom with ELLs for Easter. Colorful eggs and an Easter bunny were created. A new ELL suddenly pointed to the bunny and said that this was wrong. To this ELL growing up in a farm country, chickens should be associated with eggs instead of a bunny. The ELL student could not make the connection because of the lack of background information. Therefore, helping ELLs build background and make the connection is important. Egbert and Ernst-Slavit (2010) believe that language is vital to content access and thus to academic achievement. In their book, *Access to Academics: Planning Instruction for K–12 Classrooms with ELLs*, the authors suggest using three types of connection to improve student learning: personal, academic content, and instructional connection.

1. *Personal connection.* Teachers need to help students connect learning to their personal experiences. Making personal connections can make learning accessible by connecting students' personal experiences. For example, teachers can use students' familiar experiences such as exercises to make connections. ELLs may have some types of exercises that American students do not have, yet they may never have a chance to, for instance, learn to ski. Graphic organizers, for example, the chart of text-self and text-world connection, can be a useful tool to help students make personal connection (see Table 8.3).

TABLE 8.3   Text-Self Chart to Make Personal Connections

Text-to-Self Connections	
Student Name: _____ Date: _____	
Title of the Story: _____	
Author: _____	
Choose a book you have read. Think about parts of the book that are similar to your own life and write or draw about them in the boxes below.	
In the Story	**In My Life**

Note: This text-self chart can be adapted to the text-world chart to help ELLs make connections.

2. *Academic content connection.* Making academic connection means to connect learning content in a meaningful way and make it connected and accessible. For example, teachers can connect current learning to past learning by reviewing previous lessons or making connections across content areas. In a math lesson, the teacher can make language connections by asking students, "Sophia had five peaches. She gave Tom two. How many peaches are *left* in her basket?" The purpose of this math problem is to teach the concept of subtraction. Yet the teacher can also teach the language. After using the word, "left," the teacher can introduce new phrases and alternatives, such as *"What is the difference now in Sophia's basket?"* or *"How many peaches are still there in her basket?"* In doing so, teachers are making academic connections.

3. *Instructional connection.* Instructional connection means that teachers provide instructional support to help students make connections by using instructional strategies to make learning productive. For example, teachers can invite guest speakers to talk about experiences relevant to the lesson content and help students make connections; teachers can also assign students to work on a project through research to make connections related to students' needs, interests, learning styles, and cultural and linguistic backgrounds for instructional connections. In all, it is important that teachers build background by making connections through a variety of means and strategies.

Preteaching

Preteaching is a strategy of teaching students before an activity. For example, ELLs are going to hear a discussion on the topic of environmental issues. Before listening, the teacher can help the students match key environment words to definitions. Or teachers can also give students a list of words and look up any of the words on the list that they don't know. Then discuss the words and ask students to guess what the text will be about. Such preteaching helps ELLs develop confidence in mainstream classrooms. Preteaching also helps the teacher find out what the students already know and what might cause problems. Thus, teachers should take time to preteach and identify problem areas. It is also a better idea to work in a small group to avoid overwhelming ELLs when preteaching concepts.

Making Vocabulary Connections

Teachers can help ELLs make vocabulary connections by exploring new meanings from familiar words. This strategy helps ELLs expand their vocabulary based on existing words. For example, when teaching vocabulary, teachers can guide students to explore new meanings in the context of familiar words, such as finding *synonyms, antonyms, homophones,* or *homonyms* to expend their vocabulary. In this way, teachers are helping students enlarge their vocabulary words and make connections from familiar words to new meanings. Instead

TABLE 8.4 Making Vocabulary Connections: Connect Familiar Words With New Meanings

Familiar words	New meanings
I saw these words in the text:	I know the synonyms (or antonyms) are:

of presenting the students with those new words, teachers can encourage ELLs to be active learners and find new meanings by doing. Helping ELLs create a chart and listing the familiar words to compare with new meanings can be a helpful tool (see Table 8.4).

Preview Survey

The purpose of preview survey is to find out what students know and don't know. Although the K-W-L chart strategy is helpful, ELLs may struggle with writing down what they know or don't know. This is because they may have developed basic oral English skills but not cognitive academic language proficiency. Thus, they may not be able to write down the ideas or what they have known about the topic. Yet creating a brief survey that *connects to the students' existing scheme* can help ELLs overcome this barrier. For example, a "True" or "False" preview survey can help find out ELLs' knowledge level. The survey can be also used as the pre-assessment tool. The following is an example of such preview survey:

According to what you have known about hurricanes, please put either "T" for true or "F" for false in the blank.

- _____ Hurricanes are large storms with rotating winds.
- _____ Hurricanes usually happen in the summer.
- _____ A hurricane forms over oceans in tropical climate regions.
- _____ A hurricane is another name for tornados.
- _____ A hurricane can cause more damage than a tornado.
- _____ The wind speed of a hurricane is always over 100 kilometers per hour.
- _____ The eye of a hurricane can be up to 20 miles wide.
- _____ Hurricanes can cause severe flooding.

Presenting Contextual Information

Contextual information is relevant information that helps in understanding the text. Presenting contextual information requires the teacher to provide relevant contextual information about learning content. This strategy helps students understand the important concepts in the relevant context and helps with students' comprehension. For example, an arithmetic problem may be difficult to explain to students, but teachers can connect to the relevant real-life situation to *contextualize* the math problem and make it understandable for students. An example is that a teacher uses simple cooking ingredients that the students are familiar with to explain a math calculation concept, for example, a measuring cup with familiar ingredients.

Using Context and Modeling

Context refers to the circumstances that form the setting and environment for an event, statement, idea, or the background information that helps in understanding and accessing information. When providing the contextual information related to new content and providing modeling, the teacher helps students understand the meaning of a word more easily. For example, teachers can guide students to search for hints and clues. Modeling is an instructional strategy in which the teacher demonstrates a new concept or approach to learning, and students learn by observing. Theory of modeling as an instructional strategy indicates that it helps students' to better understand the content through modeling. Therefore, when teachers provide contextual information and also modeling, it helps unlock the meaning of an unfamiliar word by providing the context in which a new word appears. To provide modeling, the teacher can use a variety of contextual modalities, such as visual, auditory, or kinetics to help ELLs see, hear, and interact with the teacher and peers in the process for a better understanding of the new information and the concepts to be taught.

Using Idiomatic Expressions Related to Cultural Context

Teachers can find familiar idiomatic expressions that have similar meanings related to concepts and students' cultures. For example, the following sayings in English may be found in other cultures: "*Hit the nail on the head,*" "*Bite off more than you can chew,*" or "*Between a rock and a hard place.*" However, these idioms, proverbs, or expressions may have cultural connotations, so teachers need to explain them to ELLs. For example, a sent-home flyer with the invitation for an event may not be understood by ELLs and parents: "Come to join our tailgating party at 6:00 before the game starts." Tailgating is one American event that ELLs may not be familiar with. Therefore, teachers need to explain the words and their cultural connotation.

TABLE 8.5 English Idiom and Expression Dictionary

English Idioms/Expressions	Similar Idioms in My Culture
Costs an arm and a leg. Meaning: Something very costly	In my language:
Hit the nail on the head. Meaning: Do something preciously right	In my language:
Between a rock and a hard place. Meaning: In a very difficult position	In my language:
Let the cat out of the bag. Meaning: Disclose a secret	In my language:
Bite off more than you can chew Meaning: Take more than one can handle	In my language:
Rob Peter to pay Paul. Meaning: Solving a problem that makes another problem worse	In my language:

Writing down idiomatic words on the board is helpful. Encourage ELLs to see if they have similar sayings in their languages. Teachers can also help ELLs create an *Idiom & Expression Dictionary* (see Table 8.5) that connects English idioms and expressions with ones in the ELLs' culture, and encourage them to add a new expression each time when they learn a new idiomatic expression. The teacher should allow students to write idioms in their native languages. This strategy also offers the students an opportunity to share their own cultures and develop an ownership in learning. Teachers can also involve parents.

Other Useful Tips and Integrating Technology
Thinking Aloud

Thinking aloud is a reading strategy that allows the teacher to model how a good reader thinks about text while reading. This strategy can be taught through explicit modeling, and it benefits ELLs and all students as they strive for deeper understanding of what they read. The teacher can model this strategy by reading an appropriate selection, stopping periodically to make predictions, clarify meaning, decode words, make personal connections, question the author, and summarize what has been read. This strategy also helps students learn to monitor their thinking while reading the passage. It is relatively easy for teachers to use in the classroom. Teachers can discuss this strategy with students and show students how good readers often read, reread, read ahead to look for context clues and to make sense. Teachers can guide students to (a) connect what they are reading to their own life experience, (b) predict what is going to happen next, (c) agree or disagree with what the author talks about, and (d) give their own opinion about a statement. The teacher can model this strategy by reading any appropriate text. For example, when teaching the poem by Langston Hughes (1926) entitled, "Dream Variations," which was published in his first collection entitled, *The Weary Blues*, teachers can read the poem and pause to demonstrate thinking aloud by talking about thoughts as follows:

> To fling my arms wide
> In some place of the sun,
> To whirl and to dance
> Till the white day is done.
> Then rest at cool evening
> Beneath a tall tree
> While night comes on gently,
> Dark like me—
> That is my dream!

The teacher may stop several times during reading to say things like, "*I'm picturing a young girl with bare feet who is twirling with her arms outstretched.*" "*I can see a large willow tree where she's sitting underneath when evening comes.*" "*The girl seems to have many dreams.*" After modeling, the teacher can put students into groups of three or four and distribute copies of a poem or reading text that is unfamiliar to each group, then direct students to read and use the think-aloud strategy. Each group should record the responses that were used.

The following are resourceful websites to further use the think-aloud strategy:

- Think Aloud Video: http://int.cysd.k12.pa.us/strategies/Reading/thinkaloud.htm
- Think Aloud Lesson Plan: http://www.readwritethink.org/lessons/lesson_view. asp?id=139
- Thinking Aloud and Reading Comprehension: http://www.readingrockets.org/ strategies/think_alouds
- Teaching students think aloud: https://www.teachervision.com/skill-builder/problem-solving/48546.html

Thumb Up and Thumb Down

This strategy, commonly known as TUTD, is helpful for the ELLs, especially when they cannot express orally. It is also a fun way to test the student's knowledge. The teacher can ask ELLs to use their thumbs to *agree* or *disagree*. For example, the teacher can read a statement and ask students to put their thumbs up if they agree or thumbs down if they disagree with the statement. This technique can be used in a small group or a large group with a follow-up discussion on why they have their thumbs up or down. The teacher can use alternatives for TUTD. For instance, the teacher can ask students to clap their hands: once for *yes* and twice for *no*. Or the teacher can ask students to keep their heads up for *yes* and heads down for *no*. Teachers can also create a *yes* or *no* sign. If they agree with the answer, the students show the *yes* side; if they disagree, they turn to the *no* side. If students need movement, the teacher can ask them to stand up and move to one side if they agree and another side if they disagree after reading the statement. The movement can increase the students' participation and avoids routine boredom.

Teaching Transitional Words and Phrases

Transitional words or phrases can be compared to the *bridges* that carry a reader from section to section in reading. They function as road signs to help a reader understand the direction of thoughts and provide coherence in writing. Transitional words can indicate the relationship, such as cause and effect, compare and contrast, and time sequence. Transitional words and phrases are used between sentences and paragraphs. The teacher can teach ELLs transitions by highlighting, circling, or underlining transitional words in reading. Encouraging students to use different alternative transitional words to restate the sentence is a good strategy. Learning transitional words and phrases also helps ELLs tell the main idea from supporting details and improve their writing. Teachers can help ELLs learn transitional words through a variety of exercises. For example, the teacher can give a list of transitional words and ask students to choose appropriate transitional words they know and give examples of how to use them. The website from McGraw-Hill provides the most common transitional words and phrases: http://www.mhhe.com/mayfieldpub/tsw/tran-cwp.htm

Using comic strips is another helpful way to practice transitions. Teachers can ask students to describe a comic story by using transitional words. This also helps develop ELLs' oral and written English skills. Teachers can find appropriate comic strips online, from newspapers, or books and use them in several ways. One way is to ask students to describe the comic stories orally by using transitional words and connect the ideas between the pictures. Teachers can cut out comics pictures and paste them on index cards and shuffle them, and then show the written scripts of the comics on one side and ask the students put the comics in order. The following website provides many printable comic strips that teachers can use for teaching transitional words: http://www.pinterest.com/pinningteacher/comic-strip-stories/

Teaching Pronouns and Antecedents

ELLs often struggle with identifying pronouns and antecedents in complex sentences. Teachers can provide help on how to identify and use these pronouns and antecedents. This also helps with ELLs' comprehension of text. Teachers should explain to students that when a pronoun is used, an antecedent must be present. Here is an example of reading text and how to teach pronouns with scaffolding:

> The children appeared to have a real fondness for *their* new teacher and *they* were often taking leave of *their* playmates just to spend more time with *her*. *This* was very surprising to the parents who did not expect *she* would become so popular.
>
> "*their*" refers to _____.
> "*they*" refers to _____.
> "*her*" refers to _____.
> "*This*" refers to _____.
> "*she*" refers to _____.

After reading the paragraph, the teacher can ask students to highlight all the pronouns in the reading and their corresponding antecedents, then provide the worksheet and enough time for the exercise. Explicit instruction may be helpful, and teachers can also incorporate meaningful exercises on grammatical structures when practicing the pronouns. This website provides commonly used pronouns: http://www.esldesk.com/vocabulary/pronouns

Teaching Words Ending With -ed and -ing

Words that end with *-ed* or *-ing* are called participles. A participle forms from a verb that can be used as an adjective. The participle ending with *-ing* is called a present participle and a past participle ends with *-e* or sometimes with *-en,-n,* or *-t*. The challenge for ELLs is when to use present participles and when to use past participles to describe in a sentence. Providing examples and modeling can help students understand. When a new participle is learned, try to make a connection to what has been taught. The teacher can provide a list of example sentences and ask students to compare the differences by discussing the subjects, as in the example below, with some commonly used participles.

> Amazing and amazed; annoying and annoyed; bored and boring; confusing and confused; disturbing and disturbed; exciting and excited; exhausting and exhausted; fascinating and fascinated; frightening and frightened; interesting and interested; satisfying and satisfied; surprising and surprised;

We were *amazed* by the show.	The **show** is *amazing* to us.
The **driver** was *confused* by the road.	The **road** is *confusing* to the driver.
People are *disturbed* by the news.	The **news** is *disturbing* to people.
They were *exhausted* by the trip.	The **trip** is *exhausting* for them.
He was *frightened* by the dog.	The **dog** is *frightening* to him.
Fans are *interested* in the song.	The **song** is *interesting to fans*.
Children are *amazed* by the story.	The **story** is *amazing* to children.

The teacher can also ask students to fill in the blanks of the paired sentences with given present and past participles by taking the particles out of the sentences as an alternative exercise, such as, I am _____ by the show; the show is _____ to me (e.g., *bored* or *boring*).

Learning Prefixes and Suffixes

In English, new words can be formed by adding prefixes and suffixes to root words. A prefix or suffix is a grammatical/lingual component attached to a word stem to form a new word, such as *agree* by adding *dis-* to form *dis*agree. Prefixes are placed before and suffixes are placed after a base word to add to new meaning. Teaching prefixes and suffixes helps ELLs increase their vocabulary, and it also adds to their word knowledge. Generally, adding prefixes changes the meaning of the word and adding suffix changes the parts of speech. Teachers can introduce suffixes and prefixes in meaningful contexts and help students understand word structure and also learn words effectively. Many useful websites list common prefixes and suffixes. This following website provides the most common prefixes and suffixes: http:// teacher.scholastic.com/reading/bestpractices/vocabulary/pdf/prefixes_suffixes.pdf. Based on ELLs' English proficiency, teachers can teach appropriate prefixes and suffixes and help students expand their vocabulary and increase word knowledge. For example,

1. At the beginning level, the teacher can introduce basic words with suffixes such as *-er, -or,* or *-ress,* which indicates the person who performs the job.

    act (v); *bank* (v/n); *drive* (v); *run* (v); *teach* (v); *work* (v); *wait* (v); *actor* (n); *banker* (n); *diver* (n); *runner* (n); *teacher* (n); *worker* (n); *waiter* (n); *actress* (n); *waitress* (n)

    Prefixes with *un-* or *re-*: *un + do = undo*; *re + cover = recover*; *un + lock = unlock*

2. At the intermediate level, the teacher can introduce more complicated words with suffixes such as *-tion* or *-ment* and add *-er,* and *-or* if they are from the same word stem.

    assess (v); *entertain* (v); *facilitate* (v); *move* (v); *translate* (v); *assessor* (n); *entertainer* (n); *facilitator* (n); *mover* (n); *translator* (n); *assessment* (n); *entertainment* (n); *facilitation* (n); *movement* (n); *translation* (n)

    Prefixes like *dis-* or *mis-*: *dis + agree = disagree*; *mis + place = misplace*

3. At the advanced level, the teacher can teach those advanced words with suffixes such as *-ion, -ship, -ist* and add the related ending, for example, *-ant* or *-sive* in words such as

    act (v); *consult* (v); *lead* (v); *produce* (v); *submit* (v); *activist* (n); *consultant* (n); *leader* (n); *producer* (n); *submitter* (n); *activity* (n); *consultation* (n); *leadership* (n); *production* (n); *submission* (n); *active* (adj); *consultative* (n); *leading* (adj); *productive* (adj); *submissive* (adj)

    Prefixes with *il-, in-, ir-*: *il + legal = illegal*; *in + complete = incomplete*; *ir + regular = irregular*

This following link provides the most commonly used root words, suffixes, and prefixes for more practice: http://www.readingrockets.org/article/root-words-roots-and-affixes

Teaching Bloom's Action Words

Benjamin Samuel Bloom was an American educational psychologist. In 1956, Bloom edited the first volume of *Taxonomy of Educational Objectives: The Classification of Educational Goals*, which outlined a classification of learning objectives known as Bloom's Taxonomy. Bloom's Taxonomy remains to be foundational to guide teaching and learning in classrooms. However, in the 1990s, a group of educational psychologists revised his old version. See Figure 8.3 for the old and revised versions of Bloom Taxonomy. The new version is more current, and teachers can incorporate the action words by asking questions and checking understanding. It is especially helpful when teachers use Bloom's action words to set learning goals and help students develop critical thinking skills. Of three domains, six levels of the revised critical thinking skills in the cognitive domain are *remembering, understanding, applying, analyzing, evaluating,* and *creating*.

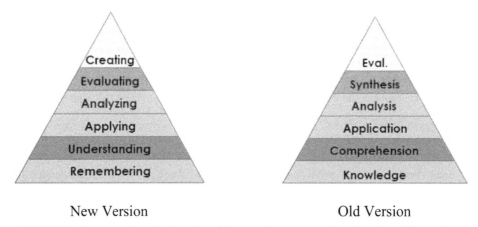

New Version   Old Version

FIGURE 8.3   Compare the revised version of Bloom's Taxonomy to the old version. Information can be found at http://ww2.odu.edu/educ/roverbau/Bloom/blooms_taxonomy.htm

Remembering is basic thinking skills. At this level, a learner is required to recall or retrieve previous learned information. An example is to recite a text. The action words at this level include define, describe, identify, know, label, list, match, name, outline, recall, recognize, reproduce, select, and state. The teacher can use these action words and ask questions (i.e., *who, where, when, what,* and *how*). Answers can be directly located from the text at this level.

Understanding is to comprehend the meaning and interpret instructions and problems. An example is to ask students to explain in their own words the steps for performing a complex task. The action words at this level include comprehend, convert, defend, distinguish, estimate, explain, extend, generalize, give an example, infer, interpret, paraphrase, predict, rewrite, summarize, and translate. Teachers can ask questions such as, "*When the author says ..., what does this mean?*" or "*Why*" questions at this level.

Applying is to use a concept in a new situation. An example is to apply what was learned in the classroom to situations in the workplace. The action words include apply, change, compute, construct, demonstrate, discover, manipulate, modify, operate, predict, prepare, produce, relate, show, solve, and use. The teacher can ask students to provide examples of a natural disaster and explain how it affects people's life.

Analyzing is to separate concepts into component parts so that their organizational structure may be understood. Students are required to distinguish between facts and inferences. Action words include analyze, break down, compare, contrast, diagram, deconstruct, differentiate, discriminate, distinguish, identify, illustrate, infer, outline, relate, select, separate. An example is to ask students to compare the differences between two sets of information.

Evaluating is to make judgments about the value of ideas or materials. An example is to select the most effective solution for a problem. Action words include appraise, compare, conclude, contrast, criticize, critique, defend, describe, discriminate, evaluate, explain, interpret, justify, relate, summarize, support. For example, teachers can ask students to predict what happens in a given situation and evaluate the consequences.

Creating is to build a structure or pattern from diverse elements. Putting parts together to form a new whole, new meaning, or structure is an example. Action words include categorize, combine, compile, compose, create, devise, design, explain, generate, modify, organize, plan, rearrange, reconstruct, relate, reorganize, revise, rewrite, summarize, tell, and write. Asking student to design a class newsletter belongs to this category.

ELLs need to develop skills at all six levels, especially the last three levels, which are considered the higher-order thinking skills. Teachers can use Bloom's action words meaningfully and ask those critical-thinking questions to promote students' academic growth. The following website provides a comprehensive list of these action words that teachers can use as a resource: http://www.highperformancetrainingworks.com/EPSS/TechNotes/Bloom.htm

Visualizing the Characters in Reading

Visualizing is a technique that is essential for building reading comprehension. When students have a mental picture, they comprehend easily. Teachers can help ELLs visualize the character in a story reading. Teachers can encourage students to think and visualize how the characters would think and write down their thoughts. When teaching ELLs to visualize, it is also important to choose the right text. There are many incredible books on the art of creating pictures in a reader's mind. Cynthia Rylant's (1998) *Scarecrow* is a good book for teaching students how to visualize the character. For example, the teacher can instruct students to practice visualizing in these steps:

- Please listen carefully as I read the story.

- Write about what you see as you hear the story.

- Use illustrations, words, phrases, sentences, or combinations.

- Draw and write what you see in your mind; no right or wrong answers but just fill up the paper as you visualize the story characters.

Mei Mei is another character in a Blue Ribbon award-winning book entitled *I Hate English* by Ellen Levine (1995). This story tells about a young girl named Mei Mei, who moves from Hong Kong to New York City. The strangest thing about her new school is that people speak English instead of her Chinese language. The teacher can engage students in using the *visualizing* strategy and do an activity called "Picture the Characters in My Mind" with these steps:

- Using a piece of paper, preferably 8 1/2 × 11 inches, make a hamburger fold and cut it in the shape of the human head.

- Draw a facial picture of Mei Mei on the front side and color it with crayon.

- Write any words or sentences inside on how Mei Mei feels, using the first person "I."

- Punch a hole along the folded edge and tie each student's work with a piece of string to display the work in the classroom with the student's name on the back side.

Making a Flip Book

A flip book is one of the earliest forms of interactive media. It usually involves a series of pictures that vary gradually from one page to the next, and the pictures appear to be animated by simulating motion. Children like to write when writing is interesting. Students also like to see the final products that demonstrates their learning. Making a flip book can arouse children's interest, and it also connects writing with reading to motivate students to write. In the process of organizing ideas and writing down their ideas, the students are creating a book. Depending on the levels of the student proficiency, the teacher can guide

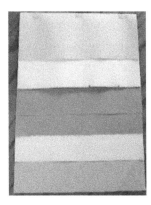

FIGURE 8.4   Example of making a flip book.

students to create a flip book, write sentences or paragraphs, or draw pictures to illustrate their ideas on each page. These steps to make a flip book are as follows:

1. Provide each student with three pieces (or more) of colored paper (8 1/2 × 11 inches) or construction paper, which works even better, although regular copy paper works as well and can be written on clearly. Different colors make a flip book look interesting.

2. Ask the students to line up the colored papers so that they overlap about 1 or 2 inches with a small "tab" left for each color (see Figure 8.4) so that on each page students can write a paragraph or illustrate ideas with pictures about reading.

3. Guide the students to fold the paper over so that you get six tabs in all, and staple the top to make it into a flip book (see Figure 8.4). In addition to writing paragraphs or illustrating ideas, teachers can encourage students to use the flip book for taking notes while reading, making picture books, collecting facts, or creating question and answer booklets.

Writer's Workshop

A writer's workshop, also known as a writing workshop, is a method of teaching writing (Calkins, 2006). It focuses on fostering lifelong writers with four basic principles: (a) students will write about their own lives, (b) they will be engaged in a consistent writing process, (c) they will write in authentic ways, and (d) it will foster their independence. The teacher can use the writer's workshop strategy to develop students' interest in writing. The teacher can guide students with four basic steps in the writing process:

(a) Prewriting: brainstorm, with a minilesson to help students with ideas
(b) Writing: writing and editing the first and second drafts
(c) Conferring: meeting with individuals to discuss their writing progress
(d) Publishing: sharing a clean final copy

In all, the writer's workshop is intended to help students understand the writing process and be good writers. Connecting writing to reading is helpful when using a writer's workshop because reading and writing are reciprocal processes. For more information on the writer's workshop, teachers can find different resources online and this following link is a helpful one: http://www.busyteacherscafe.com/literacy/writing_workshop.html

Interactive Writing

Interactive writing is a method of teaching writing, in which students and the teacher are actively involved in a cooperative way (Swartz, Klein, & Shook, 2001). Dr. Stanley Swartz, a professor of education at California State University, San Bernadino, wrote a book with his colleagues called *Interactive Writing and Interactive Editing*. They believe that the teacher and students should take active roles and negotiate what they want to write. They can literally share the pen to construct joint sentences or writing passages. This method is helpful for ELLs at the beginning level who find writing terrifying. The interactive writing method also helps children learn to view literacy in a more meaningful way through teacher-student interaction. Basic goals to be accomplished through interactive writing usually include

- Learning upper- and lowercase letters
- Becoming more aware of the nature of words
- Increasing vocabulary
- How to organize narrative text
- The nature of correspondence
- How to target writing to an audience

In the interactive writing process, the teacher can use these methods to guide students: writing letters to each other, keeping dialogue journals, and using a message board. Students should be able to choose their own topics. Here is an example of how the interactive writing method works. After reading a passage about hobbies, the teacher can ask students, *"Who wants to talk about your hobbies? Does anyone like to play football?"* Some students may raise their hands and the teacher can ask one student, *"Carlos, do you like football?"* He may nod his head. Then the teacher can say, *"Let's write down a sentence about Carlos's hobby. Where should we start? Can we start in this way—Carlos likes …"* Then, the teacher can invite students to join in the process of constructing the sentence. Together: *"Carlos likes to play football."* The teacher can begin to model writing by writing *"Carlos"* on the board, then invite students to finish the sentence. For more references about interactive writing, please visit Swartz's website about interactive writing at http://www.stanswartz.com/IAW%20excerpt.pdf

Creating Word Walls

Teaching vocabulary is one of the most important activities teachers must do with ELLs and all students. Creating *word walls* provides not only a literacy-rich classroom but also a rich resource for learning vocabulary. A word wall is an organized collection of words prominently displayed in a classroom. This display can be used as an interactive tool for teaching reading and spelling to children. There are different types of word walls, including high frequency words, word families, and names. Some walls can be creative, such as *portable walls*, *words on poster frames*, or *ceiling tiles* (i.e., words on the ceiling to save space). Integrated into instruction, the word-wall strategy can help expend students' word knowledge and learning vocabulary. The basic steps of creating word walls are as follows:

- *Select words for the word walls.* Words should be selected from content units for high frequency words or "must-know" words for the walls. Print the words in a large, simple font so that students can *use* and *refer to* the words from across the classroom. For ELLs, teachers may include daily words.

- *Create word walls with students.* Pasting words on color-coded construction paper to make word walls that provide literacy visual support for children. Words can be categorized by parts of speech or grouped in alphabetical order. For ELLs at the beginning level, grouping words by parts of speech is helpful.

- *Display the walls.* Every time a new word is learned, invite students to add the new word to the wall. Word walls can be displayed in different shapes and sizes. For example, *portable word walls* can be used for categorizing or grouping words, cupboard doors can be used to display words to save space, poster frames can be used to display words within the frame, and tall file cabinet can be used to display words of all types by sticking a small magnet on the back of each word.

- *Practice words on the walls.* Teachers should model how to use the words from the word walls and help students construct meaningful sentences. For example, teachers help students select words and use them in a sentence, find rhyming words, use flashcards, and play word bingo or tic-tac-toe in small groups. For more activity ideas on using word words, this link is helpful: http://www.teachingfirst.net/wordwallact.htm

Integrating Technology With ELLs

ELL students are a fast growing segment of the school population. At the same time, technology has become more and more widely used in classrooms today. To combine these two trends, integrating technology in working with ELLs becomes important. Technology-based projects allow ELL students to draw on their cultural strengths and background experiences through integrating technology in classrooms to make learning accessible fun, engaging, and interactive. Projects that incorporate visual and aural media address a variety of learning styles and modalities. Teachers can incorporate the advantages of technology into their teaching practices, such as using online resources, new technological techniques, and software programs. Several strategies are introduced here to help teachers work more effectively with ELLs through integrating technology.

- *Digital Storytelling*: Digital storytelling is the method of using computer-based tools to tell stories. Teachers can use this technology-related strategy to make learning interesting and engaging. Much like traditional storytelling, digital stories focus on a specific topic. Yet digital stories usually have a mixture of computer-based images, video clips, text, recorded audio narration, and music. Topics can range from personal tales to historical events or from student life experiences to life of other universes. Literally, digital storytelling can cover unlimited topics. Teachers can guide students to appropriately use digital stories, and digital storytelling in classrooms can be used in countless ways. For example, creating personal stories helps students learn important literacy skills of voice in a narrative form and first-person perspective. Since modern communication involves writing with pictures and music, having students create digital stories helps them build media-creation skills. Digital storytelling can also be used to address curriculum areas beyond language arts and media literacy. For example, students can retell an event from the life of a famous person to help themselves and their audience better understand why this person acted the way he/she did. Students can discuss habitat, food, predation, and other life-cycle issues. Public service announcements can be used as both a persuasive writing exercise and a way to address science topics like health and conservation. Telling a digital story successfully depends largely on how teachers can guide students to create their digital stories. Step-by-step procedures on how to create a digital story are provided in Table 8.6.

- *Exploring the basics of using an iPad*: Teachers need to take time and explore the basic use of an iPad so that they can become comfortable and effectively help their students. The more time spent with the iPad, the more comfortable the teacher will be using it. To practice accessing all of the apps to be used, teachers can write down a list of any questions for the things that are important. Spend time to learn and to answer those questions. It is critical to note that introducing an iPad into a classroom requires a lot of time and a great deal of patience. Yet the more teachers use them, the easier it will be for them and their students. Grouping the apps into areas of interest or types of application is important. Stage the use of apps and pair students for use. This will help students explore the app with others. If an iPad Cart is available,

TABLE 8.6 Basic Steps of Creating a Digital Story

	Procedures
Step I: Collect Data	1. Select a topic for a digital story and create a folder on the desktop to store the materials found for the story.
	2. Search for image resources for the story, for example, pictures, drawings, photographs, maps, and charts; save these resources in the folder.
	3. Locate audio resources such as music, speeches, interviews, and sound effects; save these resources in the folder.
	4. Locate informational content, which might come from websites, word processed documents, or PowerPoint slides; save these resources in the folder.
	5. Decide the purpose of the story, that is, to inform, convince, provoke, question.
Step II: Create the story	1. Select the images to be used for your digital story.
	2. Select the audio to be used for your digital story.
	3. Select the content and text to be used for your digital story.
	4. Import images into Photo Story (Note: Photo Story is free software available for download from Microsoft).
	5. Import audio into Photo Story.
	6. Modify images and image order as needed.
	7. Use a computer microphone and record the narration of the script and import the narration into Photo Story.
	8. Finalize the digital story and save it as a Windows Media Video file.

try to use a sign-out sheet with the students for the class session. Or create specific iPad "rules" and a sign-out sheet. Provide basic iPad training for the students.

There are many different ways to use an iPad. First, teachers can use the iPad as a document camera and annotate anything to be observed under the camera. Second, teachers can create multimedia eBooks with iPad. In fact, the iPad can be used for digital storytelling apps, and they can produce much better results with Book Creator for iPad. Over 3 million multimedia eBooks have been created with just this app. You can add text, images, video, audio and more. Choose from over 50 fonts, draw illustrations, and send the finished product to iBooks, Dropbox, or share by email. Third, teachers can collaborate with other classrooms using video conferencing and Subtext. We should never let our students think that their classroom is just the four walls around them. It is essential that students know that the world is their classroom, and the iPad is a great way for students to connect and collaborate with students anywhere in the world. Whether students video conference with Face-Time or Skype (both free) to discuss a book that they read together in Subtext (a social reading app), or to do a Mystery Skype, the iPad opens doors to collaborative learning experiences for students of all ages. Fourth, teachers can review almost any academic topics using the Quizlet app. Quizlet is a completely free resource that allows teachers to create flashcards for their students. Interactive games can also be done on the Web. Students can also practice individually at home for review for upcoming tests. Teachers do not necessarily need the app, as it is a Web-based service and it runs straight from the browser.

- *Learning about using apps*: *App* is an abbreviated form of the word *application*. An *application* is a software program designed to perform a specific function for the user. When an application is opened, it runs inside the operating system until it is closed. Most of the time, more than one application is open at the same time and this is known as multitasking. Applications for desktop and laptop computers are called *desktop applications* and for mobile devices are called *mobile apps*. Types of desktop applications can include word processors. A word processor allows users to write a letter, design a flyer, and create many other kinds of documents. The most well-known word processor is Microsoft Word. Personal finance software, such as Quicken, allows users to keep track of expenses, create a budget, and more. A Web browser is the tool that allows users to access the Web. Most computers come with a Web browser preinstalled. Examples of browsers can include Internet Explorer, Firefox, Google Chrome, and Safari. Many different games allow users to play games on computer. Media players allow users to listen to MP3s or watch downloaded movies. Windows Media Player and iTunes are popular media players. Gadgets are simple applications that are placed on a desktop, such as calendars, calculators, maps, and news headlines.

  Mobile apps are devices like smartphones and tablet computers. Other examples of mobile apps include RedLaser, which can be used to compare prices while shopping. Users can simply scan an item's barcode using the phone's built-in camera, and the app searches the Web for the best price. Word Lens is a language translator app. Like RedLaser, it uses your phone's camera to take a picture of a sign, menu, or other text you want to translate, and it displays the translation for you. Compared with traditional applications, mobile apps are relatively cheap. Many of them cost as little as $0.99 and many others are free. If the mobile device has an Internet connection, teachers can download apps directly onto the mobile device. Otherwise, you can download them to your computer and then transfer them over. The following apps are great to have and work with ELL students: Dropbox, Show Me, Google Earth, Idea Sketch (mind mapping tool), InkFlow, Visual Notebook, or TeacherKit. More information on apps and ideas can be found at AppsGoneFree. For example, Google Earth is a free Internet tool that introduces the Earth's geographic features. It allows students to view anywhere on Earth with satellite maps, terrain, 3-D images from galaxies in outer space to the canyons of the ocean, and it provides geographical information. It maps the Earth by the superimposition of images obtained from satellite imagery, aerial photography, and geographic information system (GIS) 3-D globe. Teachers can use it to teach content lessons. For example, it can take ELL students to a new place to learn about the geographic features of this place for teaching social studies and geography classes.

Educational apps and technology tools can help teachers to connect with other teachers or organize files. The following resources provide more information for teaching ELLs:

- *Uen.org* is a website that provides resources related to teaching ELLs as well as many useful links on the topics of teaching ELLs. Some of these websites include WIDA ELP Standards, Everything ESL, Lanternfish, Colorín Colorado, Dave's ESL Café, USOE's English Language Learners Web Page, One Stop English, Learning the Language. The website can be assessed at http://www.uen.org/k12educator/ell/.

- *Dave's ESL café* is an Internet meeting place for ESL teachers and students around the world. It provides a resource for students of all ages learning English and teachers to teach English as a foreign language. Features include grammar lessons, idioms, phrasal verbs, pronunciation, quizzes, slang, student forum, a Job Center, and discussion groups for students and teachers. The website link is www.eslcafe.com

- *Everythingesl.net* is a useful website that provides teaching tips, lesson plans, and resources to teach ELLs. Judie Haynes left her teaching job in June 2008 and became an educational consultant. She created this website with resources and strategies for ESL teaching and learning community, such as lesson plans and teaching tips. Teachers can also ask questions. The website link is http://www.everythingesl.net/

- *Lantern fish* provides worksheets, flashcards, lesson plans, jobs, and a forum for ESL and TEFL teachers. It also includes many activities such as crosswords, phonics skills, alphabet, e-books, proverb communication, word skill games, and lesson plans. The website can be accessed at http://bogglesworldesl.com/worksheets.htm

- Onestopenglish is packed with resources for English language teachers, with information on ESOL, grammar, exams, skills, games, and teaching support. There are free resources or teachers can pay for a subscription to get access to even more. The website link is http://www.onestopenglish.com/

- *Edmodo* is an educational website that takes the ideas of a social network and makes it appropriate for a classroom. The users of Edmodo can post assignments, create polls for student responses, embed video clips, create learning groups, post quizzes for students to take, and create a calendar for events and assignments. Students can also turn in assignments or upload assignments for their teachers to view and grade. The website link for *Edmodo* is https://www.edmodo.com/

- *Colorín Colorado* is a bilingual website with many resources for educators, administers, and families of English language learners. For example, it provides topics on common cores and ELLs, ELL topics from A to Z, and ELL research, reports, and toolkits. The website link can be accessed at http://www.colorincolorado.org

- *Activities for ESL Students* is a website that offers activities in classrooms, for example, quizzes, tests, exercises, and puzzles to help ELL students learn English as a second language. This project of *The Internet TESL Journal (iteslj.org)* has thousands of contributions by many teachers. The website link is http://a4esl.org/

- *ESL Kids Lab* is a website that provides English (ESL, EFL, ELT, ESOL) learning and teaching materials for young learners, preschoolers, beginners, elementary, and pre-intermediate. The materials are designed to appeal to all learning styles, with resources on handouts, lessons, flashcards, phonics activities, and even shop related to help ELLs. The website link is http://www.eslkidslab.com/

- *ESL Partyland* is a webpage designed to provide teachers with the resources and connections they need to become better ESL teachers with great activities. The Teacher Page is where information and resources related to teaching ELLs from K–12 grads are provided. Teachers and students can have fun while learning English as a second language. The website link is http://www.eslpartyland.com/

- *About.com ESL Guide* provides resources and information related to English as the second language (ESL). Resources provided range from food, health, home to quizzes and tests for different levels. The website link is http://esl.about.com/

- *ESLAmerica.US* is a resourceful website where everything has sound, and it provides resources to practice conversation, vocabulary, grammar, reading, writing, holidays. Because everything has sound, it allows ELLs to listen to pronunciation and even to their own voice. The website link is http://www.eslamerica.us/

- *English Page* offers free English lessons and ESL resources with English grammar and vocabulary exercises online. Hundreds of English lessons help ELLs learn English and practice four domains of language skills (i.e., speaking, listening, reading and writing). Some resourceful topics include weekly lessons, vocabulary, grammar, verb, articles, reading, and listening. The site is at http://www.englishpage.com

- *TESOL International Association* is Teachers of English to Speakers of Other Languages. The TESOL association has a mission to ensure excellence in the English language. The TESOL website provides many professional resources related to teaching ELLs. The official website for TESOL is http://www.tesol.org/

Technology opens a new door for teaching and learning. Integrating technology to work with ELLs adds a new dimension to traditional teaching and learning in classrooms. Teachers should avail themselves of the advantages that technology offers and also take time to avidly explore and become comfortable with technology to make teaching and learning more connected and productive.

Summary

This chapter discusses planning to teach with the SIOP model, TPR, teaching strategies, and tips to work with ELLs and all students. The SIOP model, *Sheltered Instruction Observation Protocol*, is an empirically tested approach that helps teachers prepare ELLs and all students to become college and career ready. TPR stands for the *Total Physical Response*, a method that incorporates physical movement to facilitate student learning. Strategies cover four areas: using visual aids, relating to existing knowledge, presenting contextual information, and integrating technology for working with ELLs. These strategies are intended to help teachers better work with ELLs and all students and produce positive learning outcomes.

References

Allen, R., & Franklin, J. (2002). *Acquiring English: Schools seek ways to strengthen language learning.* Alexandria, VA: Association for Supervision and Curriculum Development. (ERIC Document Reproduction Service No. ED 471 636)

Bloom, B. (1956). *Taxonomy of educational objectives, handbook I: Cognitive domain.* White Plains, NY: Addison Wesley.

Byram, M. (2000). *Total physical response. Routledge encyclopedia of language teaching and learning.* London, UK: Routledge.

Calkins, L. (2006). *A guide to the writing workshop, grades 3–5.* Portsmouth, NH: First Hand.

Drucker, M. J. (2003). What reading teachers should know about ESL learners. *International Reading Association.* Retrieved from http://read4343.pbworks.com/f/Drucker.pdf

Echevarria, J., Vogt, M. E., & Short, D. (2010). *Making content comprehensible for English language learners: The SIOP model.* Boston, MA: Allyn & Bacon.

Egbert, J. L. & Ernst-Slavit, G. (2010). *Access to academic: Planning instruction for K–12 classrooms with ELLs.* Boston: MA: Allyn & Bacon.

Francis, D., Rivera, M., Lesaux, N., Kieffer, M., & Rivera, H. (2006). *Practical guidelines for the education of English language learners: Research-based recommendations for instruction and academic interventions.* Portsmouth, NH: RMC Research Corporation, Center on Instruction.

Goldenberg, C. (2008). Teaching English language learner: What the research does—and does not—say. *American Educator*, 8–44.

Harvey, S., & Goudvis, A. (2000). *Strategies that work: Teaching comprehension to enhance understanding.* Portland, ME: Stenhouse.

Hughes, L. (1926). *Dream variations. Langston Hughes collection: The Billops-Hatch Archives.* Atlanta, GA: Emory University Manuscript, Archives, and Rare Book Library.

Hunter, M. (1982). *Mastery teaching.* El Segundo, CA: TIP.

Jensen, E. (2005). *Teaching with the brain in mind* (2nd ed.). Alexandria, VA: Association for Supervision and Curriculum Development.

Jong, E., & Harper, C. (2005). Preparing mainstream teachers for English language learners: Is being a good teacher good enough? *Teacher Education Quarterly, 32*(2), 101–124.

Levine, E. (1995). *I hate English!* New York, NY: Scholastic.

National Clearinghouse for English Language Acquisition. (2012). *The growing number of English Language Learners: 1995–2005.* Washington, DC. U.S. Department of Education Office of English Language Acquisition.

OELA Report. (2010). *The Biennial Evaluation Report to Congress on the Implementation of the Title III State Formula Grant Program for School Years 2008–2010.* Washington, DC: Office of English Language Acquisition.

Pearson. (2013). The SIOP Model: Sheltered Instruction Observation Protocol. Retrieved from http://siop.pearson.com

Peregoy, S. F., & Boyle, O. F. (2005). *Reading, writing, & learning in ESL: A resource book for K–12 teachers.* White Plains, NY: Longman.

Reed, B., & Railsback, J. (2003). *Strategies and resources for mainstream teachers of English language learners.* Portland, OR: Northwest Regional Education Laboratory. (ERIC Document Reproduction Service No. ED 478 291)

Rylant, C. (1998). *Scarecrow.* San Diego, CA: Harcourt Brace.

Swartz, S., Klein, A. F., & Shook, R. E. (2001). *Interactive editing and interactive writing.* Parsippany, NJ: Pearson Learning/Dominie.

Thrower, I. M. (2009, August). *What is SIOP: SIOP is good teaching PLUS+ purposeful teaching of the language necessary for ELLs to understand content.* Retrieved from http://www.houstoncte.org/SIOP/SIOPOverviewHandouts.pdf

U.S. Department of Eduction. (n.d.). *Developing programs for English language learners: Lau v. Nichols.* Retrieved from http://www2.ed.gov/about/offices/list/ocr/ell/lau.html

Zacarian, D., & Haynes, J. (2012). Educating newcomer ELLs with limited schooling: An overview. *¡Colorín colorado!* Retrieved from http://www.colorincolorado.org/article/55784/

Chapter 9

Ideal Classroom Conditions for Adolescent Newcomer English Learners

Lynn David Tarvin

Glossary

Term	Meaning	Usage
Additive bilingualism	Acquiring fluency in an L2 while maintaining fluency in the L1	A view of the student's L1 in positive terms and often uses the L1 to support L2 development (contrasts with subtractive bilingualism).
BICS	Basic interpersonal communication skills	Social language that is acquired more quickly; in school settings refers to language typically used on the playground, at lunch, etc.
Brick words	Content-specific words, often found in boldface within a textbook, chapter, or glossary	Words that teachers want to call attention to for their language learners
CALP	Cognitive academic language proficiency	Academic language that is acquired more slowly; in school settings refers to the language needed to take in content instruction and to display content understanding
Deficit model	An approach that focuses on the skills that are lacking rather than students' existing skills/funds of knowledge	Used in contrast to asset model. When teachers and others working with CLD students only view students in terms of language and knowledge deficiencies.
ELP	English proficiency level	A description of a person's ability to understand, speak, read/view, and write English; may be reported using word descriptors (beginner, intermediate, advanced) or numbers on a scale (often 1 to 5 or 6)

(Continued)

Term	Meaning	Usage
Genres	Text types that are socially constructed, repeated, and specific to a given culture	In language instruction, various genres are used to help students recognize patterns of language features.
L1	First language	The language a student acquires growing up in a family household; typically the same as the parents' primary language, but not always
L2	Second language	The new language the student is acquiring; also called target language
Language functions	Types of communication interactions that follow typical expected patterns	In school settings includes inform, narrate, inquire, explain, argue, discuss, among others
MALP	Mutually adaptive learning paradigm	An instructional approach that uses students' home country educational practices at first, then transitions to U.S. educational practices over time
Mortar words	The language pieces necessary to hold the content words together to communicate complete ideas	Used in contrast to brick words, mortar words are often prepositions, articles, and adverbs that support the main words of a text.
Realia	Authentic objects materials used in daily life	In language instruction, refers to tangible items used to create more authentic instruction. For example, a teacher teaching a unit on food may bring in various foods to let students see, touch, and taste.
Register	Group of language choices that define the relationship between the speaker/writer and listener/reader	Used in reference to formal or standard (school, professional) versus informal or nonstandard (slang, casual) language; can also refer to publicly acceptable versus publicly forbidden (expletives)
Sentence frame	A partially completed sentence that can be used repeatedly by filling in different content information	Often supplied by teachers to help language learners keep up with instruction and focus on important content ideas
Silent period	First 6 to 18 months after arrival when ELs may not initiate spoken or written communication	Important stage of second language development for teachers to be aware so as not to force students to speak before they are ready
SLIFE	Students with limited or interrupted formal education	Students who never attended school, had gaps in their education, or had limited education due to lack of resources

Term	Meaning	Usage
SFL	Systemic functional linguistics	Concerned with identifying typical language choices used in specific settings; these choices are language functions that need explicit instruction—includes a focus on "field" (the general topic of a text), "tenor" (the relationship between the author and the reader), and "mode" (the method of communication, i.e., written, oral, or digital)
Teaching-learning cycle	A lesson/unit structure that involves a gradual movement from the teacher demonstrating language use to joint construction of a text and then to individual student use of that language	A form of gradual release model, with a focus on the teacher modeling appropriate contextual language use
WIDA	Formerly, World-Class Instructional Design and Assessment; according to WIDA, initials no longer refer to specific words.	A consortium of 35 states that provides an annual English proficiency assessment, as well as many instructional resources to help teachers support students based on their English proficiency level
WIDA proficiency scale	A scale from 1.0–6.0	Indicates the level of English students are able to understand and use

Case Scenario

....

*Anai (ah-NAH-ee) and Roberto (pseudonyms) are 2 of 26 real students in a newcomer **English language development (ELD)** class at ABC High School in a suburb in the Midwest. They spend much of their school day together with the other newcomer students, but Anai and Roberto have had very different educational experiences than the rest of their class. (In this school district, a newcomer student is defined as having experienced less than 1 year of U.S. schooling and having an **English proficiency level** of 1.0–1.9 on the **WIDA** Proficiency Scale; that is, the student can only speak or understand a few words of English at a time and is unable to speak or understand sentences or longer discourses.)*

*From Guatemala, Anai's first language **(L1)** is an indigenous language, Q'eqchi'. However, Anai learned Spanish in school and heard it at Mass and in the market. Her mother and father only attended school until sixth grade, and then they started working in the family business. Anai was able to attend school in Guatemala until seventh grade, but she did not attend school for the last 2 years, so at age 16 she is starting U.S. high school in ninth grade. Typically, students are placed*

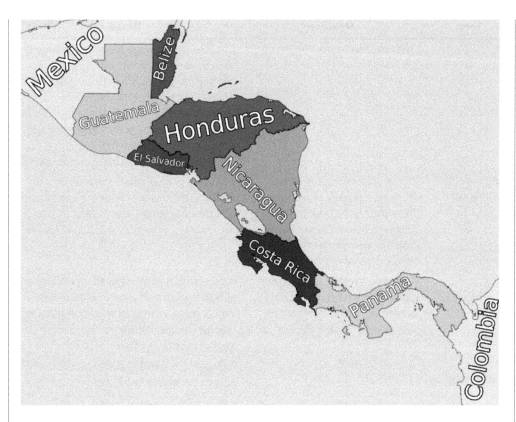

FIGURE 9.1   Many recent immigrants to the United States come from Guatemala, El Salvador, and Honduras.

Source: Copyright © by Luveha (CC BY-SA 4.0) at https://commons.wikimedia.org/wiki/File:Map_of_Central_Amer-ica-New.png.

in the same grade as peers who are the same age, regardless of their English proficiency level. Anai missed eighth grade completely, and she should be in tenth grade by her age. However, she is placed in ninth grade because she is not bringing in any high school credits. Anai's family sent her to live with cousins who lived in this high school's school district, but she had never met these cousins before coming here. Her trip from Guatemala to the Midwest took about 4 months, and some of it was quite dangerous. She doesn't like to talk about the trip very much, and she often cries softly at her desk.

From Honduras, Roberto's L1 is Spanish. His family supports education and encourages him to speak English as much as he can, but when he arrived in the United States Roberto still met the definition of a newcomer, scoring at a 1.0 on the WIDA ACCESS placement test. At 14, Roberto is also in ninth grade. He did not miss any years of school, but sometimes he did not get to attend school, so he had to stay home at times when it was not safe. He also had to stay home when his family could not pay his school tuition; he would have to wait for the family to save up enough money to return to classes. In Honduras, Roberto lived with his father and grandmother. His mother moved here to this school district 5 years ago, to prepare for a better life for her children. This year, she saved enough money to send for Roberto. She hopes to be able to send for her other children in the next 5 to 10 years. Roberto has not seen his mother since she left, and his father and grandmother allowed him a lot of independence. Roberto has a hard time learning to follow adults' directions again, and this is a source of conflict between Roberto and his mother.

Both Anai and Roberto are happy to experience the better futures their families have planned for them, but they miss their families back in their home countries terribly.

ABC High School is the first U.S. educational experience for almost all of the students in the class, and all have beginning English proficiency (1.0–1.9 on the WIDA ACCESS placement test). The 26 English Learners (ELs) in this class, 12 girls and 14 boys, come from a variety of countries (Central America—14; Chile—1; Cuba—2; Dominican Republic—3; Mexico—2; Puerto Rico—2; and Vietnam—2), with seven students transferring to other districts during the school year. Although 10 students immigrated simultaneously with their parents, 8 students joined a parent who had immigrated several years previously, and 8 students moved in with an aunt, uncle, or family friend already established in the school district. The students' average age when they started in the school district was 16.0, with a minimum of 14.3 and maximum of 19.0, and 84.6% receive free or reduced lunches.

*These students' experience five hours of ELD support daily, mostly in a separate classroom: 1 hour of social English, or **basic interpersonal communication skills (BICS)** (Hill & Flynn, 2006); 1 hour of academic English, or **cognitive academic language proficiency (CALP)** (Hill & Flynn, 2006); a co-taught physical science class (in a mainstream classroom setting); a sheltered pre-algebra course; and a study skills homework resource hour. The students experience a continuum of interactions from English classes with highly communicative settings to math class with somewhat communicative content-based instruction, to science class in which they communicate, and perhaps understand, very little.*

Most students express interest in pursuing studies after high school, but many will need further English studies after high school to be ready for postsecondary coursework. Most of the students from Central America and the Dominican Republic, and one from Vietnam, seem to lack strong educational knowledge, study skills, and formal L1 literacy, so they encounter more obstacles than students with stronger educational backgrounds (those from Mexico and Chile, and one from Vietnam). The students who did not immigrate with their parents also experience more instability that they display through significant misbehavior and difficulty with studies.

Introduction

The students in the case scenario all need to learn English in order to be successful in school, but how and what they need to learn can vary widely based on their backgrounds. Adolescent newcomer ELs (as well as every other English learner) need a classroom setting where they interact with the teacher and each other to learn content and language simultaneously. This approach will be reviewed throughout the discussion that follows. Students also need to have their L1 language and culture integrated into lessons, with instruction focusing on the language discourses and forms that they will need for social, educational, and work pursuits. In the ideal classroom environment for adolescent newcomer ELs, teachers will (a) utilize SIOP as a framework to build lessons and SFL to identify and instruct the content area language, (b) encourage L1 use as a tool to reach **L2** understanding, and (c) develop a classroom dynamic where students and their families feel safe and acceptable as positive contributors to the learning process.

Ideal Classroom Conditions

The goal for these students is that they may develop their academic English and obtain a high school diploma. Due to their entry ages, many students understand that they will not achieve peer-like fluency in academic English before graduation, but they can develop foundational skills necessary to continue in post–high school ELD coursework if they so desire. To realize these goals, the ideal classroom will utilize and implement several methods and approaches that the research literature shows to be most effective for improving language growth and academic success among newcomer ELs. These notions will be developed in light of methods and materials, lesson structure, activities, interactions, and room organization.

Methods and Materials

The methods that teachers use with ELs set a foundation for many of the other choices teachers make in creating ideal classroom conditions. Two complementary methods or pedagogical approaches appropriate for use with adolescent newcomer ELs include the **sheltered instruction observation protocol (SIOP)** model and **systemic functional linguistics (SFL)**. SIOP deals with instructional choices that make certain all students have comprehensible access to the content, the how of good EL instruction. SFL deals with identifying the language in context that students need in order to understand the content, the what of good EL instruction. Integrating the two together provides a strong foundation in which adolescent newcomer ELs can excel. The following sections will describe each in more detail, along with research demonstrating their effectiveness.

Sheltered Instruction Observation Protocol Model

SIOP creates ideal conditions for adolescent newcomer ELs because it helps teachers think reflectively and plan with detail, integrating content and language together intentionally so that both are accessible to all students, including ELs. Using **content** and **language objectives** to guide lesson preparation, SIOP leads teachers to reflect on how they will connect to prior learning (background knowledge), scaffold (provide supports for) new concepts, use and assess all four language domains (reading, writing, listening, and speaking) while also assessing content, group students intentionally, and provide application for the content being learned (Echevarria et al., 2010). SIOP's 30 features provide a checklist to fully develop these areas of lesson preparation.

The 30 SIOP features are summarized briefly here (Echevarria et al., 2010) with specific examples highlighted throughout this chapter. Teachers write objectives for both content and language, adapt their rate of speech, and use supplementary, modified materials based on students' proficiency levels. Highlighting key vocabulary and linking to prior knowledge, teachers approach the content and the language using a variety of techniques and higher-order thinking questions to scaffold the lesson for ELs. Teachers intentionally plan for a great deal of interaction with and among students, using appropriate groupings and allowing wait time in which ELs can process the new materials. Teachers use hands-on materials to help ELs apply new knowledge, and they lead students to use all four language skills in the lesson. Students should be engaged at least 90% of the class time by pacing the materials to meet students' needs. Teachers should provide feedback on both content and language growth throughout the lesson, not just at the end.

Using **sheltered instruction** (**SI**), and specifically the SIOP model, can effectively lead ELs to access mainstream course content. "In highly effective SI classrooms, explicit language instruction targeted to and slightly beyond students' level of English proficiency ... is presented in every lesson" (Echevarria et al., 2006, p. 207). ELs in SIOP classrooms made more gains in writing than ELs in other SI classrooms. Though teachers' content area knowledge is important, the other skills are necessary to make content language accessible to ELs.

FIGURE 9.2 Visuals such as this globe help newcomers understand classroom instruction better.

Source: Copyright © by Intisar Ali (CC BY-SA 4.0) at https://commons.wikimedia.org/wiki/File:World_Globe_Map.jpg.

One example of best practices for working with newcomers comes from a high school world geography teacher working with ELs who had spent less than 1 year in the United States

(Salinas et al., 2008). The teacher employs a great deal of the SIOP features in her lessons. She uses a variety of visuals, including wall maps, transparencies, and a globe to help students understand the new ideas. She also has students physically move to represent ideas such as the earth's rotation and revolution. The teacher differentiates lessons by having stronger readers find definitions in the textbook and read aloud to the class, while all the class is expected to participate in discussions that build content and language knowledge. She asks questions in multiple manners, with the visuals as a reference point, to help students develop their ideas. When students voice their ideas, she writes them down on the board for all to see in print. She has students use a graphic organizer to organize those ideas, but she makes sure to model how to use the graphic organizer first before asking students to work in pairs.

Another example comes from a high school science teacher who uses several SIOP features in his lessons for newcomer students. Students in the class scored a 2 or less on the WIDA proficiency scale; thus, the strategies described should be a good match for the described learner population (Tretter et al., 2014). The notion of brick and mortar language can help teachers and students classify the content language. **Brick words** are content-specific words, often found in boldface in a textbook chapter and in the glossary. **Mortar words** are the language pieces necessary to hold the content words together to communicate complete ideas. The classroom teacher considers the overarching ideas of a unit and identifies language structures necessary to understand those ideas. Concentrating on a language structure for about a week, the teacher uses explicit and repetitive instruction to help students acquire both the language structure and the science content. Wall charts provide explicit language examples for specific scientific functions, such as comparing, and language journals help students to demonstrate their understanding of new vocabulary, including a self-rating scale. The teacher instructs students how to use sentence frames (e.g. "_____ (something is) as _____ (adjective) as _____ (adjective)" [p. 42] to show similarity), and then he has the students use the sentence frame to talk and write about the unit content. Finally, the teacher assesses students' mortar vocabulary to monitor growth and gaps.

Systemic Functional Linguistics

SFL creates ideal conditions for adolescent newcomer ELs because it breaks down the language of a lesson, identifying the **language functions** or purposes that the language serves in the lesson context. Teachers may feel ill-equipped to recognize the language ELs need to process the lesson content; SFL provides a framework to address this concern. SFL pedagogies can "involve apprenticing ELLs to using school-based genres and registers" (Gebhard & Harman, 2011, p. 49). SFL identifies **genres** as text types that are socially constructed, repeated, and specific to a given culture. When newcomers learn the genres they should expect to see in their classwork, they can focus more on the content to be learned and less on the language. Students experience many genres across the content areas, many of which are included in the following list.

1. Language arts/foreign language: Narratives (stories), arguments, poetry, plays (including opinion and persuasive communication)
2. Math: Word problems, explanations, critiques of others' explanations, proofs, charts/tables/graphs
3. Science: Explanations (how and why things occur), observations, procedures, lab reports
4. Social studies/history: Nonfiction narratives, letters, legal documents, time lines, charts/tables/graphs
5. Practical arts: Recipes, procedures, explanations, business proposals, diagrams
6. Fine arts: Sheet music, procedure, description, historical narrative (of musicians and artists), critique, scripts
7. Physical education: Diagrams, instructions, explanations

Teachers can lead students to understand the typical patterns they should expect in each of these genres by applying SFL analysis principles. Students should be aware of the general topic of the text (the **field**), the relationship that exists between the author and the reader (the **tenor**), and the medium of communication—written, oral, or digital (the **mode**). SFL analysis can be used by teachers to lead students to an understanding of how to mimic the structure and language choices of dominant forms (Gebhard & Harmon, 2011).

In the classroom setting, SFL can be put into practice using the **teaching-learning cycle** (Figure 9.3) that consists of five phases (Gebhard & Harmon, 2011; Pavlak, 2013). This teaching-learning cycle mirrors the gradual release of responsibility model (Archer & Hughes, 2010; Hollingsworth & Ybarra, 2009) but extends the model further by focusing on students' use of metacognition to understand the language choices needed for successful communication and then to evaluate their communication in light of expected cultural norms.

The students in the case scenario experienced several lessons applying SFL to the teaching-learning cycle in several content

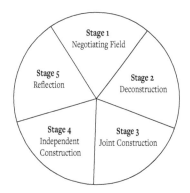

FIGURE 9.3   Teaching-learning cycle.

TABLE 9.1 Stages of the Teaching-Learning Cycle

	Description of Stage	Example in Action
Stage 1: Negotiating field	Students build background knowledge of a genre by understanding its typical use and associated language. Students need to see multiple examples of the genre addressed in the unit, so they can observe the similarities that create a specific genre but also recognize variations that might be encountered.	After reading and analyzing several children's stories as mentor texts, students noticed the typical narrative story genre pattern of exposition, conflict, and resolution (the overarching text structure) and the strong use of visuals to support the reader's comprehension. The field of most of the stories involved children interacting with friends and family at school and home. The tenor of most of the stories was impersonal but not formal; the author did not speak directly to the reader, but the vocabulary was simple and accessible to children ages 4 to 8. The mode of all the stories was written.
Stage 2: Deconstruction	Teachers lead students to analyze model texts. (a) What is the overall topic (field)? Is the text about animals or an important battle or a musical instrument's tone quality? (b) What is the relationship between the author and the reader (tenor)? Is the language formal and distant or informal and casual? Why? (c) What is the medium of communication (mode)? Is this a written text? Is it a spoken conversation or monologue? Is it an audio-visual digital communication? (d) How is the text organized? What happens typically in the beginning, middle, and end of the model texts? Is there a repeated phrase across the model texts, such as "Once upon a time ..."? Are there similar kinds of headings, bullet points or numbering, etc.?	The teacher provided another illustrated story about a boy whose house burned down when he was 15. The students and teacher analyzed the story together for types of language used, the setting and character description in the beginning of the story, the conflict of the house burning, and the resolution of the boy finding a new home. After reading the story, the students discovered that the boy in the story was actually their teacher. They learned about a specific type of nonfiction story called a personal narrative.

(Continued)

TABLE 9.1 (*Continued*)

	Description of Stage	Example in Action
Stage 3: Joint construction	The teacher and students use their understanding of patterns and typical language structures from the first two phases to jointly construct a new text that meets the expectations of the genre. Together, the teacher and students can decide on the field, tenor, and mode of their new text. They also decide together how to organize their writing to follow the pattern of the mentor texts, developing their new ideas by generally following what they discovered in stages 1 and 2.	The students and the teacher wrote another story together, being sure to include an exposition, a conflict, and a resolution, like they found in the mentor texts, and illustrated the story to help others understand what they wrote. And, just like the children's stories, they searched for images online to support the meaning of the story.
Stage 4: Independent construction	Only after working through the first 3 stages are students asked to try to write something independently. Teachers should encourage students to continue referencing the model texts, text analyses, and joint texts as students start to create their own texts. Students' work will likely be less refined than the model texts; it is important for teachers to validate the language students are able to create based on their proficiency levels.	Students wrote their own individual stories about loss, using the mentor texts and joint construction as guides for how to pattern their writing. They made sure to establish a setting and identify a main character, describe a problem or conflict, and develop a solution.
Stage 5: Reflection	Students and teachers evaluate the newly constructed texts in light of what was learned in the first two stages. Students compare their own writing with the model texts and joint construction in terms of field, tenor, mode, and text organization. Students may choose to refine and revise their writing as they discover how to make their own writing conform more closely to the expectations of the genre.	Students presented their writing to each other and the class, and the students and teachers together reflected on how well their stories matched the expectations of the narrative genre. They were given opportunities to revise their thinking and their writing, making improvements as they understood more about the genre's typical patterns.

areas. Following is a description of the five stages of the cycle, along with an example, including a narrative writing unit focused on loss.

Through the process of this unit, students in the case scenario learned about and wrote using the personal narrative genre; they also had an opportunity to communicate about the losses they had experienced as immigrants. When possible, it is ideal to contextualize lessons in students' own experiences.

SFL leads to desired language and content growth in the classroom (Gebhard & Harman, 2011). Student engagement increases due to deconstruction and joint construction, which serve as scaffolds to prepare the students for independent construction. These stages do not necessarily form a linear process, but throughout the cycle "responsibility for constructing text is gradually released from the teacher to students" (Pavlak, 2013, p. 407). Students who participate in coursework implementing an SFL pedagogy are able to discuss history with greater depth than teachers have experienced with other methods. They also demonstrate more improvement on state exams, with EL students being among those whose scores increase the most. Current research trends are expanding application beyond history into other content areas as well.

One application of SFL to the classroom is the genre theory approach (Gebhard & Harman, 2011). For example, a high school biology teacher and an ELD teacher could collaborate together to identify "the types of texts biology students are required to read and produce (e.g.[,] class notes, reading logs, illustrations of biological structures, diagrams of biological processes, lab reports, and textbooks)" (Gebhard & Harman, 2011, p. 48). The ELD teacher can unpack the structures of these text types to help ELs be more successful in the mainstream biology class.

Research supports the value of SFL for adolescent newcomer ELs. Teachers need to "help students notice [language] and unpack it to enter into the content, develop their understanding, achieve their goals, and carry out actions … . [This] is especially important for English Language Learners" (Understanding Language, 2012, p. 10). "Secondary students need to engage with a range of **registers**—oral and written, formal and informal, in a range of subject areas … . Newly arrived immigrants of secondary school age with little or no proficiency in the L2 need intensive support for language development" (Schleppegrell & O'Hallaron, 2011, p. 4). This describes the case scenario students exactly. Secondary teachers should consider themselves as language teachers of their content, and they may need to make changes to packaged curricula in order for ELs to access their content (Schleppegrell & O'Hallaron, 2011).

The ideal classroom conditions for these students involve each content teacher identifying and making students aware of the language structures (active or passive voice, verb tense, typical sentence frames, transitional words), patterns (paragraphs, listing and heading formats, types of vocabulary, text density), and choices (level of formality, use of visuals, use of standard or colloquial language) that are expected within that content area. Content teachers should think of not only individual lessons but also the lesson progression as they consider the language that students will need to build in order to process and respond to the content instruction. In the ELD classroom, the teacher can pre-teach and reinforce the content academic language expectations so that newcomers are better prepared to process the content language when they enter those classes.

One aspect of a newcomer program not often discussed is discerning when a student should move on to more linguistically challenging classes. Often, students may not perform well on English proficiency placement tests, but they may have much more English proficiency than true non-English speakers. WIDA's (World-Class Instructional Design and Assessment, 2014) six-point proficiency scale, which is used for both placement and annual assessment in Missouri, along with more than 30 other states, remains ambiguous as to the nuanced differences between proficiency levels and why the higher levels are more linguistically complex (O'Dowd, 2012). When teachers use an SFL framework to specify the ideational (language as processes, participants, and circumstances), interpersonal (language as tone or voice), and textual (language as structure) development of a lesson's language, they can know where ELs are making progress and where they still need help. This more refined awareness of students' language progress could help students more quickly access the more challenging curriculum recommended across the literature.

SFL provides a framework to respond to the high-stakes testing environment in which ELs must participate. "The amount of time that students are expected to spend interacting and talking with peers about content is unprecedented" (Hakuta et al., 2013, p. 453). Students must write clear explanations and arguments appropriate to each content area. In order to meet these challenges, teachers must (a) support ELs as they engage in reading complex texts rather than simplifying those texts; (b) activate ELs' prior knowledge and L1 skills in writing, using mentor texts for support; and (c) lead ELs to listen and speak in different group sizes using extended discourses about content texts. In math, teachers must (a) focus on ELs' reasoning skills as they build language fluency and accuracy; (b) teach complex math language rather than avoiding it through simplification; and (c) use multiple modes, representations, and types of written and spoken interaction of mathematical concepts to make them accessible to ELs. Echoing SFL pedagogy, "students must participate in classroom activities and discourses that reflect the practices of each content discipline" (Hakuta et al., 2013, p. 453), but ELs must balance their need to participate in the disciplines with the need for sufficient language proficiency to access the disciplines in the first place.

SIOP calls for teachers to include language objectives in parallel with content objectives, but it does not directly help teachers identify the language in their content that needs to be sheltered. SIOP's developers refer teachers to their state English language proficiency (ELP), communication arts, or content standards, the TESOL national ELP standards, or the WIDA Can Do Descriptors (Echevarria et al., 2010). SFL's notions of field (the social context and ideas), tenor (the relationship between speakers or author and readers), and mode (the method of communication) can help teachers break down the language they are teaching so as to identify the recurring language forms necessary for understanding and responding to the content. Teachers can use the SFL paradigm as a method to notice language that they take for granted in their curricula and use the sheltering strategies of SIOP to make the language and content accessible to students.

Associated Materials

Adolescent newcomers face the challenge of acquiring new language while their native English-speaking peers are also moving forward in content. **Students with limited or interrupted formal education (SLIFE)** must work even harder, learning missed content to be ready for peer-level work. Teachers must teach ELs how to obtain materials whose access native English speakers take for granted, and they must modify some complex, grade-level materials using SIOP techniques as well. ELs find success when materials use lots of visuals that are easily understood and when content is redundant through text and other representations. Students also appreciate technology that allows them independent access to images and translations to understand difficult texts.

To implement SIOP and SFL, various resources are necessary as part of effective instruction. For SIOP, research shows that realia, models, visual aids, graphic organizers, manipulatives, and foldables help ELs "make more rapid progress in mastering content objectives" (Echevarria et al., 2010, p. 143). Picture dictionaries can make the content more accessible. Gap activity forms and cloze dictations can help scaffold lessons. For SFL, model texts and other authentic documents provide the launch point for the teaching-learning cycle, and student-teacher joint constructions extend students' support further (Gebhard & Harman, 2011).

A world geography teacher uses globes, graphic organizers, and other visuals to make the content accessible to her students (Salinas et al., 2008). Another social studies teacher makes use of digitized primary sources to allow her students "opportunities to link complex ideas to their own lives and the lives of others" (Fránquiz & Salinas, 2013, p. 344). In her newcomer sheltered American History class, the teacher has students with strong L1 literacy and content knowledge, but she also has students with interrupted formal education (SIFE) who struggle academically in both their L1 and L2. In sheltering her students' lessons, the teacher "note[s] three elements of historical inquiry that were instrumental" for ELs in her classes: (a) primary documents that are not dense with text such as letters and maps; (b) other, non-dominant perspectives that challenge the accepted, written history found in a textbook; and (c) historical documents that are visual in nature such as photographs (Fránquiz & Salinas, 2013, p. 344). Using these documents and perspectives, the teacher leads students to respond to document-based questions (DBQs). In a scaffolded manner, the DBQs allow the students to write using text evidence and draw their own conclusions.

Lesson Structure

Both SIOP and SFL influence the structure of the lessons that teachers use with adolescent newcomer ELs. Strong lesson design for supporting ELs begins with the teacher constructing most of the language and moves toward individual accountability, as enacted by the teaching-learning cycle (see Figure 9.3) (Gebhard & Harman, 2011; Pavlak, 2013). Although many of the students in the described case scenario are in the **silent period** at the beginning of the year, they can still respond to yes/no questions and use nonverbal or L1 responses to participate actively in a lesson. It may not be possible to focus on all four language domains in each specific lesson, but across a unit arc students should experience specific activities in listening, speaking, reading, and writing to learn about and display understanding of the content, with assessment of both content objectives and language objectives (Echevarria et al., 2010).

SIOP provides templates that outline lesson structure (Echevarria et al., 2010). Teachers should pace the lesson activities and their speech rates to match the ability of these newcomers. Lessons should begin with overt statements of language and content objectives, so students are directed toward the learning targets. Teachers should use **realia**, visuals, movement, and other sheltering techniques to activate prior knowledge and present new material. Teachers should make explicit the targeted key vocabulary and language forms and then should use redundant manners of explaining the academic tasks to which students should attend. In order for ELs to have the opportunity to hear good L2 models as well as practice listening and speaking skills, a great deal of teacher-student and student-student interaction should occur. Student-to-student interaction should occur in smaller, probably heterogeneous groups so as to lower ELs' affective filter and to reduce their likelihood to hide from academic work. Students should experience a closure to lessons, including a review of language and content before assessment, with teachers giving feedback on the quality of students' language, content, and effort throughout the lesson.

In the sheltered American History class mentioned, students might be working on a lesson over the Declaration of Independence. The content objective might be "I can identify major grievances that caused the colonies to declare independence from the United Kingdom." The language objective might be "I can state a formal complaint with logical reasoning." Students might watch a clip from the musical *1776* to get some background knowledge context. The teacher might show students examples of formal complaints from several different situations. Students might have leveled readers, with students at low proficiency levels having L1 supports, that address the reasons leading up to the formal declaration, and students, through discussion and graphic organizers, could display their content understanding. The class could write a joint complaint to someone in the community or school about something that upsets them. Then, students could work in partners to write a formal complaint to a business. Finally, students could work individually to write a formal complaint. This final complaint could be differentiated by students' proficiency levels.

Activities

Ideal classroom activities for adolescent newcomer ELs will engage students and lead to content mastery and language proficiency growth. Learning activities for newcomer ELs focus on content area instruction, BICS and CALP language instruction, and exposure to L2 culture. As mentioned in the SIOP section, students should be using higher-order thinking skills, even when they are just beginning to learn the language (Echevarria et al., 2010). Teachers should use sentence frames to help students express their understanding of the content. Students can draw, sort pictures or words, and use graphic organizers, all with L1 and partner support, to demonstrate higher understanding (WIDA, 2014). Also mentioned in the SFL section, teachers should expose students to a variety of mentor texts, deconstruct those texts, jointly construct a new text of the same genre, and then have students independently construct an original text of the same genre, as discussed in the example (Gebhard & Harman, 2011).

Even though ELs should never be forced to accept U.S. cultural norms in lieu of their heritage norms, teachers do need to make explicit what expectations teachers and society in general will have of adolescents. Some examples of typical U.S. cultural school norms include teachers expecting students to give direct eye contact, especially when being disciplined, and teachers holding each student individually accountable for content learning. In other cultures, looking down as an adult speaks to a student may be seen as a mark of respect, while looking directly at the adult may be seen as a disrespectful challenge to authority. Other cultures may value the learning of the group as a whole; students might not be used to being held individually responsible. When teachers make these U.S. expectations explicit, newcomers can begin to understand the intercultural breakdowns that might occur. Teachers can also explain that people can follow different norms at home than they do at work or school, so students can see that they do not have to give up all of their heritage identity. As an extension of **additive bilingualism** (Lightbown & Spada, 2013), culture can also be additive rather than subtractive. Students may or may not choose to take up L2 cultural aspects, but at least they should have L2 culture made explicit to them so they have the choice.

Interactions

Ideal interactions with adolescent newcomer ELs will be responsive to students' L1 cultural backgrounds. First, teachers will encourage students to use their L1 in order to achieve L2 proficiency. Second, teachers will recognize challenges that students will have to overcome and leverage all of the ELs' resources, including family, to help them find academic success. Third, teachers will provide a safe classroom setting where students are honored and challenged. These conditions create an atmosphere where ELs are more likely to learn content, develop English language proficiency, and persist to graduation.

First Language Use

The ideal classroom for adolescent immigrants who have been in the country less than a year will include multilingual interaction between teacher and students as well as among students. Students' L1s will be valued and included in the instructional process in order to allow students to process and respond to content before English L2 language is available. In the case scenario, Spanish was the most frequently spoken L1. However, minority L1s (students whose language does not occur as frequently as the majority L1, such as Chinese, Vietnamese, Hmong, Pohnpeian, etc.) will have equal standing in processing alongside the majority L1, making use of technology, parents, and other community resources to connect with L1s that the teacher does know. Other nonverbal communication skills, such as drawing and student technology use, will be encouraged to allow students to express their questions, thoughts, and understandings as much as possible. The teacher will encourage students to participate in the classroom, school, and community. The teacher will also provide corrective feedback that is situated within the learning context and that will lead students to notice forms that need improvement.

When considering student-teacher interaction, there must first be recognition of how much time students have been in the United States. As mentioned before, most of the students in the case scenario have been in the United States fewer than 12 months. For most of these students, their first day of school in the United States happens in this environment. Although they may have studied some English in school in their home countries, by definition these students are non-English speakers (NES) if they are in this program, based on their English proficiency screener scores. A student in the first 6 (to 18) months is often considered to be in the silent period because most likely the student will not speak much English during this time. He or she "has minimal comprehension, does not verbalize, nods 'Yes' and 'No,' and draws and points" while a student in the 6 months to 1 year time period "has limited comprehension, produces one- or two-word responses, participate[s] using keywords and familiar phrases, and uses present-tense verbs" (Hill & Flynn, 2006, p. 15). These time

TABLE 9.2 Typical Time Needed for Proficiency

0 to 6 Months	6 to 12 Months	1 to 3 Years	5 to 10 Years
• Silent period (up to 18 months) • Minimal comprehension • One word responses • Draws and points	• Limited comprehension • One- to two-word phrases • Uses keywords and familiar phrases • Uses present tense verbs	• Acquires fluent BICS language • Can appear to be fluent on social topics • Still needs help with academic language	• Acquires fluent CALP • Can use L2 academic language as well as English-only speaking peers

periods are not fixed, but they do represent stages most newcomer ELs will experience. By the time an EL "can produce simple sentences," he or she has typically moved on from the beginning proficiency level of the students in the case scenario to a more advanced level (Hill & Flynn, 2006, p. 15).

L1 use in the classroom can benefit students in many ways. Multilingual classrooms are important, especially for newcomers, for several reasons: (a) New L2 language cannot build on background knowledge if L1 literacy is discouraged or ignored; (b) translation is a valuable skill for EL students; (c) teaching for transfer, such as by a focus on cognates, allows students to build L2 vocabulary more quickly; (d) newcomers who first write in their L1 and then translate to L2 build higher-order thinking skills not possible in English-only classrooms; (e) bilingual dictionary use is more effective for vocabulary development than monolingual dictionary use; and (f) L1 use validates a student's identity as having equal standing with students of the majority culture (Cummins, 2009). When newcomer ELs can use their L1s in the classroom, they are able to reduce their affective filters, participate more quickly, and refute assumptions that "students' home languages are a major cause of underachievement" (Cummins, 2009, p. 320).

Some states, such as Massachusetts, California, and Arizona, have been strongly criticized for forcing English-only classroom settings for ELs (Adams & Jones, 2006). Newcomer ELs learning content knowledge and language simultaneously without L1 support is "not realistic or fair to both teacher and EL student" (Adams & Jones, 2006, p. 17) because, although social language development can happen within 2 years, academic language development might require 5 years or more (Adams & Jones, 2006; Leckie et al., 2013) and even up to 10 years. In Arizona, the single year of available sheltered English instruction is insufficient to lead students to proficiency (Leckie et al., 2013). These students in the case scenario likely will never reach peer-level academic language development in their first year. Nevertheless, they are able to process and produce content knowledge, as long as L1 communication is allowed in the learning process. The ELD and content teachers may not know all of the students' L1s, but this should not prevent ELs from being able to use their strengths (i.e., their L1s), as a bridge to L2 academic proficiency.

Recognition of Cultural Influences on Learning

Adolescent newcomer ELs often have challenges that they must overcome in order to be successful academically. The **mutually adaptive learning paradigm (MALP)** is one method teachers can use to help students with limited or interrupted formal education (SLIFE) overcome educational gaps (DeCapua & Marshall, 2010). While exact numbers of SLIFE are unavailable due to differences in definitions and data collection patterns, it is clear with the overall increase of immigrant students that likewise there is a significant increase in the number of SLIFE in U.S. schools (DeCapua, 2016). "Some may have had no prior schooling and will be unfamiliar with common school routines ... and have difficulty sitting at desks for class duration" (DeCapua, 2016, p. 226). Like the students in the case scenario, these students might have missed years of school due to financial or other reasons, or the school they attended might have been limited due to inadequate school resources. These students' teachers may have had little pedagogical training, and they may not have had many textbooks. Learning is often based on rote memorization and copying rather than the higher-level thinking typical of U.S. schooling. Therefore, SLIFE "will have developed different ways of thinking and learning than those expected and valued in formal [i.e., U.S.] education" (DeCapua, 2016, p. 226). "This population of ELs is particularly challenging for educators, especially at the high school level, where students have a relatively short time to develop English language proficiency while simultaneously developing literacy skills and catching up in academic content knowledge" (DeCapua & Marshall, 2010, p. 50). Many of the students in the case scenario fit the definition of SLIFE, and clarifying the formal education these students have experienced can be very difficult.

Recommending many of the same teaching strategies as SIOP with a focus of also making the content relevant to students' L1 cultures, MALP recognizes that SLIFE often come from **collectivistic** cultures that view learning very differently than the dominant individualistic culture in the United States (DeCapua & Marshall, 2010). The goal of MALP is to move students along a continuum, with teachers initially accepting and using students' cultural views of learning in instruction while moving students to be able also to work in a U.S. learning structure as well. Initially, learning is about more immediate and pragmatic concerns, where students are encouraged to depend on each other through the learning process. Oral interaction carries a significant role in instruction. Over time, the teacher scaffolds students toward doing more independent, academic work and using written text by linking students with the text through oral interaction first. "Oral and written [language] need to be continuously connected so that SLIFE learn to derive meaning from print" (DeCapua & Marshall, 2010, p. 54).

Newcomers typically have two reasons to immigrate: (a) fear of staying in their home country and (b) desire of upward social mobility (Deckers & Zinga, 2012). This correlates with some of the fear-based stories shared by the case scenario students and their families from Central America and Mexico, along with the "better future" desires expressed by most of the other students (Deckers & Zinga, 2012). ELs whose immigration is motivated by fear tend to be less involved in their school and community. They tend to view their immigration as temporary, with the hope of returning when it is safe again. Those seeking social mobility indicate a desire to visit their home country, but they see their new home as being fairly permanent. They are more likely to become involved in the school and community.

School and community involvement is correlated with greater academic success, as it provides opportunities to practice English and to develop relationships. "Having even one native English-speaking friend [helps ELs] acquire English skills more quickly and proficiently" (Suárez-Orozco & Suárez-Orozco, 2007, p. 255).

In order to support immigrants fearful of staying in their home country and those desiring upward social mobility, teachers can provide information about available community and school resources, especially sports, and include L1 cultural awareness in course activities (Deckers & Zinga, 2012). When students have immigrated for fearful reasons, teachers must be careful to promote community involvement as a means to achieve students' personal goals of language and skill development rather than pushing students toward the idea of the L2 culture as permanent. "As the importance of parental influence was continually noted by the youth, it would be beneficial for teachers to receive specific training on how to engage parents within their classrooms" (Deckers & Zinga, 2012, p. 43). Although a challenge when parents must work multiple jobs to meet their families' needs (Suárez-Orozco & Suárez-Orozco, 2007), it seems an ideal classroom would engage the students along with their parents in order to help these students find academic, as well as social, success.

Parental involvement can help engage students who might otherwise not find success in schools. A monolingual, rural school teacher in North Carolina, Siefert (2010) looks for ways to add her Latino newcomers' **funds of knowledge** (Moll et al., 2005) to the classroom by having the students, and their parents, provide Spanish parallel instruction to the mainstream English curriculum. She views this as continuing L1 literacy while "learning English in an additive manner" (Siefert, 2010, p. 95). Siefert feels that engaging parents to help English speakers understand more Spanish is an authentic reason for these parents to participate in a school setting. Siefert promotes bilingual social language within the classroom and develops word walls and classroom labels in both English and Spanish. She suggests leveraging community resources such as parent-teacher organizations, bilingual churches, and so on to find tutors who can help in both languages. Rather than feeling that including Spanish in her classroom culture takes away from completing the curriculum, she feels that doing so increases all students' understanding and literacy growth.

Interpersonal Interactions in the Classroom

Ideal classroom conditions for adolescent newcomer ELs also include an environment where students do not have to fear criticism, racism, or being ignored due to their English proficiency level and where the ELs' interests and points of view actually matter. Ideal interactions between students and teachers are based on genuine questions seeking legitimate answers or information rather than display questions for which the teacher already knows the answer (Lightbown & Spada, 2006). Teachers must create a safe atmosphere where students feel like they can take risks in producing language, and this could include allowing some interactions that might not be permitted in a traditional classroom.

Examples of nontraditional interpersonal interactions:
- Allow students to use whiteboards to draw what they are trying to communicate when they do not have the words to do so.
- Allow students to take the teacher's hand so the students can lead the teacher to what they want to talk about.
- Use visual or oral cues to affirm L1 response, even if the teacher does not understand, because the teacher does not want to prohibit the students from attempting to process content and language understanding (de Oliveira & Athanases, 2007).

Teachers can increase ELs' feeling of security in the classroom by building an "intentional classroom learning community" (Rance-Roney, 2008, p. 19). "For a new learner of English to take the risk of using the fledgling language in spite of the fear of being misunderstood or laughed at, the learner must believe that there is a substantive payoff in the language use" (Rance-Roney, 2008, p. 19). In order to ELs access her language arts curriculum, Rance-Roney asks for student volunteers to form a culture share club. These volunteers then form cooperative learning groups with whom the ELs work all year long. As an alternative to SIOP's jumpstart lessons, Rance-Roney (2008) has Culture Share club members develop jumpstart packets to preview the upcoming literature piece, including "(1) a preview of essential vocabulary; (2) visual scaffolding of the content; and (3) proficiency-appropriate prereading text that parallels the upcoming class readings" (p. 21). This packet might include annotations of the text or recorded audio, with commentary, of the text. By utilizing willing students, Rance-Roney is able to differentiate her instruction much more than if she had tried to do it all herself. She finds that her students appreciate helping their classmates and discover that they are better prepared for the literature pieces themselves. Rance-Roney also has the ELs prepare a "jumpstart" packet for the native English-speaking students when she does a unit on poetry in the ELs' L1. The ELs are considered the experts whose knowledge the rest of the class needs to translate and understand the literature. In this way, Rance-Roney not only finds L2 peers who are sympathetic and supportive of her newcomer ELs, she also finds a way to make them equal contributors to the class as a whole.

Integrating good instructional strategies with an understanding of students' L1 culture can increase ELs' academic success. The high school world geography teacher mentioned before implements a great deal of the SIOP model characteristics in a single lesson, but she also is very intentional about what she chooses to teach (Salinas et al., 2008). She includes references to students' L1 cultures when possible, and she allows honest evaluations of the effects of European colonialism on Native Americans and Mexicans. By respecting the students' heritage, she leads them to be more engaged in the learning process.

Teachers must find ways to explicitly value students' L1 cultures, especially by establishing a classroom atmosphere that reduces anxiety and shows "respect for native language and culture" (Klein, 2008, p. 43). Students who feel safe are more likely to take academic and linguistic risks. When students take more risks and produce more language, they have more opportunities to receive feedback and improve their English and their content knowledge.

Teachers must recognize the importance of L1 cultural awareness in building lesson plans for students. Students might come from field-dependent cultures, including Hispanic cultures, and thus react to elders and peers in different fashions than field-independent cultures, including Anglo-European cultures. Lessons should build on students' L1 cultural and linguistic competences, rather than treating students as blank slates. Class activities should be authentic, and artifacts from students' casual culture should be used to make connections that lead to deeper thinking.

ELs need to feel safe, but they also need to be challenged. Such a culture exists in the international schools in the New York City public school system (Jaffe-Walter & Lee, 2011). EL newcomers often come from working-class and poor families, and they experience "emotional and psychological strains of migration" (Jaffe-Walter & Lee, 2011, p. 285). However, these students can achieve success in learning English and addressing the mainstream skills and concepts while using higher-order thinking skills. In this setting, teachers create an expectation that college, in some form, is available for all students, and EL students accept this as possible. Clearly refuting a **deficit model** of understanding EL students, teachers call students to use their cultural backgrounds as launching points for essays and discussions. Students are allowed to make use of L1 as needed to process complex topics discussed in class, and teachers understand that they are teaching language and content, together. Teachers work in instructional teams, including school counselors, to develop curricula and differentiate instruction. Thus, all students, regardless of English proficiency level, can access course content. Many of the assignments across various courses are designed as a preparation for college applications and essay writing, and students clearly understand that the rigor they experience is college preparatory.

Room Organization

In order for student-to-student interaction to take place, student desks should be placed such that this can occur easily, in pairs or pods of four. SIOP calls for a gradual release from teacher–whole class to small groups to individuals (Echevarria et al., 2010). When desks are already arranged in this fashion, students may move quickly back and forth between

- Tie in students' L1 culture and language to lessons whenever possible. Consider what music, art, famous people, and names from your student's home culture might be integrated into your lessons.

- Find out what schooling is like in the country your newcomer student comes from.

  1. What did the school building look like?

  2. How long did students stay in one room?

  3. Were students given breaks? Did they each lunch at school?

  4. How many students were in the school?

  5. Did one teacher teach all the subjects, or did students and/or teachers change rooms with different teachers teaching different subjects?

- Be sure to know the language structures typically found in your content area. What are the most common types of writing students must create? How are they organized? What word banks or sentence stems could you create to help students focus on the content of your course?

- Use resources related to students' English language proficiency levels to discover nonverbal ways for ELs to demonstrate understanding. Encourage nonverbal representations of understanding, with students verbally explaining more as their language develops.

- Be sure to have books available in students' L1s in your school. Students need to maintain their L1 in order to add English skills.

- Be aware of any culture shock students might be experiencing. If you are not sure how they are feeling, try to find someone to help you with language breakdown, especially if the student does not engage at all. Don't assume they are upset; they could be demonstrating L1 culturally appropriate expressions of emotion. If you do discover they are struggling emotionally, seek help from the school counselor and other ELD staff.

whole-group and small-group activities. Traditional rows may be unsuitable for communicative activities; instead, teachers should use a variety of desk groupings in order to encourage student academic talk (Scrivener, 2012). SIOP features require other practical configuration concerns, as well. All students need to be able to clearly see and hear when the teacher models or displays realia. Also, students need to be able to clearly see language presented on wall posters or projected on a screen that they will use in speaking or writing about lessons. If possible, there should be room for students to move about the classroom as a kinesthetic response to instruction. Ideally, books will be available in the room at students' independent and instructional reading levels (Echevarria et al., 2010).

Conclusion

In developing a profile of ideal classroom conditions for adolescent newcomer ELs, two methodologies, the sheltered instruction observation protocol and systemic functional linguistics, guide many of the recommendations. Adolescent newcomer ELs, especially students with limited or interrupted formal education, may experience difficulties transitioning to U.S. school settings, so an approach such as the mutually adaptive learning paradigm can help teachers work with these students to overcome cultural differences in schooling. By using SIOP to understand how to make instruction more accessible, SFL to understand what language choices are necessary to access the content, and MALP to help students become accustomed to U.S. school culture, teachers provide these students with opportunities to engage effectively in schools. Furthermore, allowing students' L1 use and valuing students' L1 cultures can help teachers motivate these students to engage in lessons. In doing these things, teachers can create ideal classroom conditions where adolescent newcomer ELs can increase their academic English and graduate from high school.

Questions to Consider

1. How might ELs immigrating from other countries react when faced with U.S. schooling practices, especially if they have missed a year or more of school or have experienced education that was much more practical and less abstract?
2. Think about a unit of study you have reviewed or created recently. What are some brick words and mortar words that students will need to be successful in that unit?
3. For the unit of study from question 2, what is one genre or text type students are expected to produce? What are some language features (e.g., organizational patterns, types of vocabulary, verb tenses, sentence patterns, etc.) that students need to know to produce this genre successfully?
4. Identify at least one content objective and one language objective students would need to master to be successful in the unit from question 3.
5. Describe the teaching-learning cycle. Write a summary of putting the cycle into practice for the genre and unit you described in question 3.

6. What are three sentence frames for this same unit that you might supply students to help them communicate their content understanding?
7. How might you discover some of the learning patterns students experienced in other cultures so you might implement MALP in your classroom?
8. How might your classroom look and sound different if you have a newcomer EL?
9. Review the section on interpersonal interactions in the classroom and think about the language students would use to process the learning of the unit, to discuss it with classmates, and to present their learning formally.

References

Adams, M., & Jones, K. M. (2006). Unmasking the myths of structured English immersion. *Radical Teacher, 75*, 16–21.

Archer, A., & Hughes, C. (2010). *Explicit instruction: Effective and efficient teaching*. Guilford.

Cummins, J. (2009). Multilingualism in the English-language classroom: Pedagogical considerations. *TESOL Quarterly, 43*(2), 317–321.

de Oliveira, L. C., & Athanases, S. Z. (2007). Graduates' reports of advocating for English language learners. *Journal of Teacher Education, 58*(3), 202–215.

DeCapua, A. (2016). Reaching students with limited or interrupted formal education through culturally responsive teaching. *Language and Linguistics Compass, 10*(5), 225–237.

DeCapua, A., & Marshall, H. W. (2010). Serving ELLs with limited or interrupted education: Intervention that works. *TESOL Journal, 1*(1), 49–70.

Deckers, C. M., & Zinga, D. (2012). Locating home: Newcomer youths' school and community engagement. *Canadian Journal of Education, 35*(3), 30–47.

Echevarria, J., Short, D., & Powers, K. (2006). School reform and standards-based education: A model for English-language learners. *Journal of Educational Research, 99*(4), 195–210.

Echevarria, J., Vogt, M. E., & Short, D. (2010). *Making content comprehensible for secondary English learners: The SIOP model*. Pearson.

Fránquiz, M. E., & Salinas, C. (2013). Knowing English is not enough! Cultivating academic literacies among high school newcomers. *The High School Journal, 96*(4), 339–357.

Gebhard, M., & Harman, R. (2011). Reconsidering genre theory in K–12 schools: A response to school reforms in the United States. *Journal of Second Language Writing, 20*(1), 45–55.

Hakuta, K., Santos, M., & Fang, Z. (2013). Challenges and opportunities for language learning in the context of the CCSS and the NGSS. *Journal of Adolescent & Adult Literacy, 56*(6), 451–454.

Hill, J. D., & Flynn, K. M. (2006). *Classroom instruction that works with English language learners*. Association for Supervision and Curricular Development.

Hollingsworth, J., & Ybarra, S. (2009). *Explicit direction instruction (EDI): The power of the well-crafted, well-taught lesson*. Corwin.

Jaffe-Walter, R., & Lee, S. J. (2011). "To trust in my root and to take that to go forward": Supporting college access for immigrant youth in the global city. *Anthropology & Education Quarterly, 42*(3), 281–296.

Klein, A. M. (2008). Sensitivity to the learning needs of newcomers in foreign language settings. *Multicultural Education, 16*(2), 41–44.

Leckie, A. G., Kaplan, S. E., & Rubinstein-Ávila, E. (2013). The need for speed: A critical discourse analysis of the reclassification of English language learners in Arizona. *Lang Policy, 12*(2), 159–176.

Lightbown, P. M., & Spada, N. (2013). *How languages are learned* (4th ed.). Oxford University Press.

Macías, A. H., Fontes, A. D., Kephart, K., & Blume, M. (2013). Sheltered instruction for English language learners: Insights and challenges. *TESOL Journal, 4*(1), 83–105.

Moll, L. C., Amanti, C., Neff, D., & Gonzalez, N. E. (2005). Funds of knowledge for teaching: Using a qualitative approach to connect homes and classrooms. In N. Gonzalez, L. C. Moll, & Amanti, C. (Eds.), *Funds of knowledge: Theorizing practices in households, communities, and classrooms* (pp. 71–88). Lawrence Erlbaum Associates.

O'Dowd, E. (2012). The development of linguistic complexity: A functional continuum. *Language Teaching, 45*(3), 329–346.

Pavlak, C. M. (2013). "It is hard fun": Scaffolded biography writing with English learners. *The Reading Teacher, 66*(5), 405–414.

Salinas, C., Fránquiz, M. E., & Reidel, M. (2008). Teaching world geography to late-arrival immigrant students: Highlighting practice and content. *The Social Studies, 99*(2), 71–76.

Schleppegrell, M. J., & O'Hallaron, C. L. (2011). Teaching academic language in L2 secondary settings. *Annual Review of Applied Linguistics, 31*, 3–18.

Scrivener, J. (2012). *Classroom management techniques.* Cambridge University Press.

Siefert, B. (2010). Success with ELLs: Spanish in the mainstream—finding middle ground for Latino/ Latina immigrant newcomers. *English Journal, 99*(3), 95–97.

Suárez-Orozco, M., & Suárez-Orozco, C. (2007). Moving stories: Immigrant youth adapt to change. *Du Bois Review, 4*(1), 251–259.

Tretter, T., Ardasheva, Y., & Bookstrom, E. (2014). A brick and mortar approach: Scaffolding use of specific science language structures for first-year English language learners. *The Science Teacher, 81*(4), 39–44.

Understanding Language. (2012, April). Challenges and opportunities for language learning the context of Common Core State Standards and Next Generation Science Standards. Conference overview paper from the Understanding Language Conference, Stanford, CA.

World-Class Instructional Design and Assessment. (2014). *WIDA's Can Do descriptors by grade level cluster.* https://wida.wisc.edu/resources?keys=&field_category%5B12%5D=12

Chapter 10

Lessons Learned
Insights Into One Teacher's Experience Working With
Karen Refugee Students in the United States

Daniel Gilhooly
University of Central Missouri

Glossary

Term	Meaning	Usage
Acculturate	The process of adapting to a new culture while also maintaining a connection to one's heritage culture	Often used in contrast with assimilation, which indicates a rejection of the heritage culture in favor of the new culture
Bifurcate	Divided into two parts	A term often used to describe some culturally diverse students who often live in two distinct worlds of home and school
CRP	Culturally responsive pedagogy	The inclusion of students' cultural beliefs, language, values, and learning into instruction
Cultural dissonance	A term used to explain the difficulties some immigrants face as they adapt to new culture, language, and society	Often there is great variation between children and their parents when it comes to adapting to their new culture. This can lead to cultural dissonance within families.
Deficit perspective	A perspective that only views diverse students in terms of what they cannot do	Too often teachers and schools view their culturally diverse students in terms of their deficits in language and culture.
Diaspora	The dispersion of a people from their native country due to persecution or other conditions	Diasporic students are often refugee or other immigrants who come from regions where they were forced to flee their homeland due to persecution or other traumatic experiences.

(Continued)

Term	Meaning	Usage
Funds of knowledge	Refers to those historically developed and accumulated strategies (skills, abilities, ideas, practices) or bodies of knowledge that are essential to a household's functioning and well-being (González & Moll, 1995 p. 446)	The recognition by teachers that culturally diverse students are an asset as they bring unique knowledge and skills into classrooms and schools.
IRB	Institutional review board	An administrative body established to protect the rights and welfare of human research subjects.
Karen people	An ethnic minority group from Burma who have been resettled throughout the United States since 2006	Ethnic Karen in the United States are typically either Pwo or Sgaw Karen. Each group has their own culture and language.
Mae La Refugee camps	The largest refugee camp on the Thai-Burma border	Many of the refugees from Burma will be from this camp.
Refugee resettlement	The process of settling refugees from refugee camps to host country communities like the United States.	Refugees do not have a choice on where and when they will be resettled, and thus extended families are often settled in different states.
Secondary migrant	An immigrant who moves from their original place of settlement	A term often used to describe immigrants and/or refugee groups who move from their original place of resettlement
Transnational	Operating between national boundaries	A term usually applied to individuals who have deep familial connections in their country of origin and their host country
First generation	A term referring to those adults who first immigrate to a new country	Often times parents immigrate to new countries and represent the family's first generation in the host country. First generation is often synonymous with language and cultural difficulties.
1.25 generation	Those who immigrate as a youngster between the ages of 6 and 12	Often these children share many commonalities with their parents as they may struggle with the new language and adjustments to U.S. schools.
1.5 generation	A term referring to immigrant children who immigrate between 13 and 17 years old.	These children often speak both the home language as well as the new language but with varying degrees of proficiency.

Term	Meaning	Usage
1.75 generation	A term referring to immigrant children who immigrate between 0 and 5 years old.	These children often adapt well to a new language and schooling. These children may lose their home language.
Second generation	The children of immigrants born in the United States.	Second-generation youth are often more acculturated to the host country than their parents and older siblings.

> I want people to know that I am not Mexican and I am not Chinese or Burma people! I was born Thailand but I am Karen! Why it is so difficult? (Julie Htoo (pseudonym), age 13, 2013, Georgia)

THIS EXCERPT FROM AN EXACERBATED KAREN girl was one of the motivations behind this chapter. Her frustrations and pride in her Karen identity speak to the experiences of many immigrant children who face similar challenges of living in the bifurcated worlds of home and school. Moreover, it speaks to the ambivalence of many Americans toward Asians in their neighborhoods and classrooms. The following pages represent my story and the lessons learned from teaching and assisting a Sgaw Karen community in rural Georgia, USA.

Background

From May 2010 to June 2014, I worked as a language tutor in a nearby rural Karen community while pursuing my doctoral degree in Teaching English as a Second Language (TESOL) at a large public university. This particular chapter is also informed by a larger qualitative study on Karen resettlement. In 2011, I conducted a participatory action research (PAR) project alongside three Karen brothers who were my students in the small rural community of Sandville (pseudonym), Georgia.

That PAR study looked at a wide variety of issues related to Karen resettlement in four different Karen communities, two in the Midwest and two in the southeastern part of the United States where we conducted interviews, distributed questionnaires, and video recorded our research experiences. That study and an earlier research project based on my participant observations on the schooling experiences of those three Karen brothers, both received Institutional Review Board (IRB) approval and are the primary sources of data for this chapter. The primary research questions that guided this chapter are:

1. What important cultural and historical considerations can help inform those working with the Karen?

2. What are the primary issues and concerns of Karen students, parents and their teachers as Karen families navigate the U.S education system?

3. How might teachers integrate Karen students' *funds of knowledge* into their classrooms?

Theoretical Framework

This chapter intends to follow in the tradition of the ethnographic work of teachers/researchers like Donald Hones. Like Hones (2002), I believe that teachers can be more effective in addressing immigrant students if they become knowledgeable about their cultural, historical, and linguistic backgrounds.

Like Hones, I contend that teachers need to apprise themselves of the unique cultural and historical backgrounds of their students. Therefore, I first draw on *culturally responsive teaching* as presented by Geneva Gay (2010, 2002). According to Gay (2010), teachers need to become aware of their students' cultures and lived experiences in order to address their needs as well as to legitimize their cultural heritage. More importantly, as Gay contends, such awareness can improve instruction for those children who are currently falling through the educational cracks. For transnational students like the Karen, I believe it is important that teachers become aware of students' immigration (*transnational, diasporic, immigration and secondary migration*) experiences so as to better address their emotional, psychological, social, and academic needs.

This chapter is also informed by *funds of knowledge* as presented by Norma Gonzalez and Luis Moll (1993, 1995, 2005). According to Moll et al. (1992), *funds of knowledge* refers to the "knowledge and skills found in local households" (p. 132). The goal is for teachers to recognize their students' diverse home cultures in order to integrate the students' home knowledge and skills into their classroom teaching. I specifically address ways teachers can utilize students various funds of knowledge in the final implications section of this chapter.

Both culturally responsive teaching and funds of knowledge offer an alternative to the *deficit model* (Gonzalez & Moll, 1993) or *cultural deprivation paradigm* (Gay, 2010) that often view immigrant children as inherently lacking in cultural/social capital and the skills needed to succeed academically and socially in the classroom. Rather, both funds of knowledge and culturally responsive teaching consider the many ways students bring valuable cultural, linguistic, and social practices with them into their American classes. Towards this aim, I present a brief background of the *Burmese* students entering American classrooms.

Burmese Refugees

The Karen (pronounced kuh-REN, sometimes referred to as Kayin) people and their resettlement to the U.S. has garnered little public attention over the seven years since they began resettling to the U.S. Therefore, I have elected to provide a short history of the people and offer a description of their journey from Burma to Thailand and, ultimately, to the United States. Firstly, some clarification is warranted regarding who is resettling from the refugee camps along the Thai-Burma border.

Although refugees originating from Burma[1] are designated as *Burmese* by the U.S. government, the designation Burmese[2] is somewhat misleading. In fact, the United States has been resettling multiple ethnic groups under the designation *Burmese*: Burman (3.81%), Chin (33%), Karenni (8%), and the largest group, Karen (47%) (Refugee Processing Center, 2014). Moreover, the Karen are not a homogenous ethnic group; they consist of multiple language groups; namely Sgaw, Pwo, and Bwe. This study looks at the largest Karen sub-group coming to the United States, Sgaw (also spelled Sgau or Skaw) Karen. Importantly, much of the confusion surrounding the ethnicity of students arriving from Burma originates in the children. For instance, in all my interactions with Karen in the U.S., respondents invariably answered "Thailand" when asked, "Where are you from?" This response often leads teachers and those working with the community to misidentify these students as Thai.

The Karen: From Missionaries to Main Street

The people known as Karen come from various regions throughout Burma and the eastern hills of Thailand. Most originate in the Karen state, which lies on Burma's eastern border with central Thailand. Historical animosity between Karen and Burman[3] intensified with the near simultaneous arrival of American missionaries and the British colonial enterprises in the early nineteenth century (Harriden, 2002; Smith, 1999; Thawnghmung, 2008).

The Karen people remain relatively anonymous in the United States despite a vast amount of anthropological and ethnographic literature dedicated to them and their current presence in all 50 U.S states. Surprisingly, despite this anonymity the Karen have a long history with Americans as Adoniram and Anne Judson established the first American mission abroad in Burma in 1813[4]. The Karen represent the Judson's and later missionaries' greatest success. Many Karen supported the American missionaries and the British colonial enterprise. Karen served in the colonial police, civil service, and military forces under the British (Thawnghmung, 2012). These alliances played a critical role in the development of Karen culture, education, identity, nationalism, and religion over the ensuing 200 years (Cusano, 2001; DeLang, 2000; Harriden, 2002).

The role of Christianity on Sgaw Karen culture, history, and language cannot be underestimated. Karen conversion to Christianity introduced not only religion but provided the Karen access to Western education, medicine, and protection from their historical adversaries, the Burmans. Today, between 20% and 30% of Karen are Christian and most resettling to the U.S. are either Baptist or Seventh Day Adventist.[5]

After independence from the British in 1948, many Karen political organizations competed for representation of all Karen people (Falla, 1991; Thawnghmung, 2008). This division led to disparate goals regarding a path forward post-independence. One route was an armed insurgency instituted by various paramilitary organizations. The Karen National Union (KNU), the largest Karen political group, has continually called for an independent Karen state and their military wing, the Karen National Liberation Army (KNLA), has fought subsequent Burmese governments using guerilla style tactics for over six decades. This insurgency and its suppression by the Burmese military has led to the displacement of hundreds of thousands of Karen and other ethnic minorities.

Ethnic minorities, including the Karen, have faced persecution in the form of forced labor, rape as a weapon of war, forced conscriptions into the military[6], burning and looting of villages, mass killings, and forced relocation of villages (Malseed, 2008; Milbrandt, 2012; TBBC, 2008). The civil war has led to both internal and external displacement. The Karen students arriving in U.S. classrooms are part of this diaspora.

Resettlement to the USA

The United States government began resettling Burmese, namely Karen, refugees in earnest in 2006. To date, an estimated 50,000 Karen have been resettled in states across the U.S. with the majority settling in Minnesota, New York, Texas and California (Refugee Processing Center, 2014). Although registration for group resettlement ended in January 2014, Karen and other Burmese refugees are expected to continue resettling into 2015.

The Karen of Sandville, Georgia

The Karen began arriving in Sandville, GA, in 2006. A non-profit Christian service community that offers assistance to sponsoring agencies to resettle refugee families, resettled the initial family in the area in late 2006. The community grew from that first family (five members) to 12 families (54 members) by October, 2013. The members of two extended families account for 45 of the 54 Karen residents in the area. Each of the families is employed at a nearby chicken processing plant. The burgeoning Karen community now has an active Karen church (they rent a vacant church) and a Karen grocery store that sells Thai and Karen products.

Each of the Sandville-Karen families resettled to the United States from Mae La Refugee camp, the largest camp serving Karen and other ethnic minorities along the Thai-Burma border. Each of the families spent between ten and twenty years in Mae La and/or other camps. The education levels of all the Karen adults with school-aged children in Sandville vary; eight adults reported no formal education while six attended primary school and a one attended high school. All of the adults can read, speak, and write Sgaw Karen and four adults can speak, read, and write in English with varying degrees of proficiency.

According to the U.S. Census, the county, at 3.7%, is well below the state average of 12.9% non-English speaking population. The county of approximately 14,000 is predominantly white (80%) and 17% Black. The Karen community in Sandville represent the entire Asian population in the county. Although the elementary and high schools each had an ESL teacher prior to the arrival of Karen students, the district was unprepared for the arrival of such a unique population as the Karen. One ESL teacher explained the arrival of Karen students in her school this way when asked about her preparedness for their arrival:

> I didn't hear about it. All of a sudden, one day, this man in a Karen outfit with no shoes met me in the high school office and told me what happened. I'm so glad he did that. I had never heard of the Karen before that morning. (Anonymous teacher, personal correspondence, 2011, Georgia)

Such lack of awareness was a common theme expressed by teachers and a primary motivation for this chapter.

Findings

In order to better contextualize the Karen story in the U.S., I begin my findings section with background information on the process of resettlement from Thailand. The following section pertains to Karen educational experiences in the camps and resettlement to the U.S. based on the experiences of my focal Karen community.

Karen Educational Experiences in the Camps

One of the major reasons cited by Karen adults when asked why they chose to resettle to the U.S. was *education for their children*. One Karen father of three children expressed a common sentiment expressed by parents in regard to their motivations to resettle:

> Karen people they go to U.S. and Australia, somebody go Norway for kid. In camp they no have chance to go school, college, and learning. I want my kid go to school and learning. Here [U.S.] they can do. (Wah Htoo, 2012, Georgia)

Interestingly, the Sgaw Karen in particular have a long history with formal, westernized, education as evidenced by the establishment of the Karen Education Society in 1860 (Mason & Reynard, 1862). Most early missionary descriptions of the Karen offer some account of the

Karen commitment to education with the emergence of mission schools (Mason & Reynard, 1862; McMahon, 1876; Po, 1928; Smeaton, 1887). Such high regard for education is also found in more contemporary accounts (Baron et al., 2007; Moonieinda, 2010; Thawnghmung, 2012). Importantly, both boys and girls benefited from schooling as missionary schools were established for both.

In Mae La Camp, the largest of all refugee camps along the Thai-Burmese border, the Karen Education Department (KED) and the Karen Teachers Group (KTG) have created a relatively "good and diverse" education system according to Karen scholar Ardeth Thawnghmung (2012). She writes, "Mae La Camp supports 18 nursery schools, 13 elementary schools, three middle schools, four high schools, two Bible schools, and a continuing education program" (p. 81). Other camps have less education opportunities (Baron et al., 2007). For a glimpse into a typical camp classroom visit http://youtu.be/wAih5HTPpRE and for a look into the ad hoc Karen education efforts back in Karen State, Burma visit http://youtu.be/L96-F6ln22s. Schooling in the camps is very much unlike American-style teaching and learning.

Teacher is Boss

The teaching methods in the camps are based on what Moonieinda (2010) describes as "rote learning" (p. 42). One Karen adolescent's, Eh Htoo, account of his education in the camp school was indicative of many descriptions:

> Not like here. Everyone must say and copy teacher, like that. Here [the U.S.] teacher want you talk but in camp, never. You talk, you maybe get hit. They say like Bible with stick parent can do, it okay to hit. Teacher hit for many thing like be quiet, no listen, like that ... to me teacher is boss. (Eh Htoo (pseudonym), Age 19, Georgia, 2011)

As Eh Htoo suggests, schooling and classroom management are very different from their American classroom experiences. I have found Karen students to be highly respectful toward their teachers and unaccustomed to speaking in class. Importantly, many Karen attend Bible classes or Karen language classes conducted by Karen teachers in the evenings and weekends in the U.S. where similar teaching methods reinforce cultural preference for strict discipline and silence. Finally, as McBrien (2005) suggested such silence may be compounded by student's fear of ridicule and harassment for their non-native English accents (p. 343).

The *Silent* Karen

Those working with the Karen need to recognize Karen attitudes and cultural norms when it comes to self-expression, especially between youth and adults. The Karen I have worked with are not accustomed to expressing concerns, fears, or frustrations to those in authority.

In my experience I have found the Karen to be very reticent and unwilling to question or express themselves and, as one Karen adolescent put it, "They stay quiet, they want no trouble!" (personal correspondence, 19-year-old Karen male, Georgia, 2011). Their reticence is not surprising when we consider their historical oppression, flight from Burma, and protracted stay in refugee camps.

As a minority hill tribe in Burma long subjected to oppression, the Karen have long maintained distance and preferred to remain in relative isolation. This was further reinforced in the refugee camps where they were also taught the importance of avoiding Thai officials. Karen cultural mores also make communication an issue.

The Karen Communities Foundation (KCF), a Karen organization in the U.S. promoting Karen causes, offers a telling account of Karen cultural norms when it comes to asking for assistance:

> Karen people are extremely polite, considerate and deferential; this is even more important to those we perceive to have higher status. By virtue of being older, male, American, white, etc. you are of higher status. A Karen person does not want you to lose face by complaining about your help or to be seen as ungrateful for the aid they are getting by complaining. We also worry about burdening you with requests. The word to describe the cultural norm is "annade." "Annade" is best described as "I feel bad that you have to go out of the way to do something for me ... Not understanding our rights, not coming from a culture where individual rights are central, many Karen arrivals are unlikely to tell you if something is wrong unless it is extremely serious." (Karen Communities Foundation, 2011)

Consequently, Karen parents and students may avoid contacting or communicating with teachers, administrators, and other government officials. Interestingly, many Karen youth related stories to me told to them by their parents or grandparents about the dangers of drawing attention to oneself. In short, for the Karen, staying under the radar was a means of survival. However, such reluctance to ask for assistance or to question their child's teacher can lead to more Karen students falling through the cracks of the U.S education system.

The Language Divide

Most Karen children in U.S. schools speak Karen at home and most seem to prefer speaking Karen with siblings and Karen peers. However, many younger Karen will not be able to read and write any of the forms of Karen. Many parents complained about this loss of Karen literacy and a few communities have responded by offering Karen language classes for school-aged children.

Children, namely 1.5 and 1.75[7] *generationers* (those who resettled at earlier ages), also have limited speaking ability in Karen. Parents often rated their younger children's speaking proficiency with a score of five or lower (on a scale of ten)[8] and expressed frustration over communication issues such as the loss of spoken Karen and the inability of their children to read and write Karen. Moreover, it was not uncommon for younger Karen children to have very limited Karen vocabularies, compromising parent-child communication.

Studies suggest that this discrepancy in language ability between generations can further the gap between parents and children (Lee et al., 2010; Nguyen & Williams, 1989; Smith-Hefner, 1993). This *cultural dissonance,* where youth acquire language and understanding of the host culture faster than their parents, has been well documented in other immigrant communities. Like other Southeast Asian refugee groups before them (i.e. Hmong, Khmer, Laotian, and Vietnamese), Karen youth are acculturating faster than their parents. As younger children become socialized in schools, they are losing some of their heritage language. Studies on other Southeast Asian groups contend that such heritage language loss can be detrimental to academic achievement and healthy adaptation (Bankston & Zhou, 1995; Rumbaut & Ima, 1988).

Furthermore, there is widespread evidence that bilingualism has a positive effect on educational outcomes (Portes & Schauffler, 1994; White & Glick, 2000), regardless of immigration status, and that bilingualism may buffer the effect of coming from a lower socioeconomic background (Rumberger & Larson, 1998). More studies are warranted on the role heritage language loss is playing in Karen and other refugee communities[9].

Parent Involvement in Schooling

One of the major concerns of new immigrants and the schools attempting to accommodate them is the lack of parental involvement in their children's schooling. A large corpus of studies suggest that parental involvement is a key factor in immigrant student graduation rates (Anguiano, 2004), psychological well-being (Kia-Keating & Ellis, 2007), and overall academic achievement (Blakely, 1983; Henderson & Berla, 1994; Rumbaut & Ima, 1988; Siu & Feldman, 1996; Zhou & Bankston, 2000). Lack of parental involvement has been a major concern witnessed with Karen families in Sandville.

The disconnect between immigrant parents and schools has been well documented (Blakely, 1983; Hones, 2002; Siu & Feldman, 1996). Karen parents repeatedly expressed to me the desire for their child to do well in school and attend college. However, none of the parents in my focal community had ever attended a teacher-parent conference, and only one teacher had visited any of the children's homes. Parents cited lack of English speaking ability, knowledge about American style education, and transportation as the primary reasons for their lack of involvement. A corollary of this disconnect was that Karen students became solely responsible for their and their younger siblings' education.

The lack of parental involvement led to two troubling outcomes. First, students were found unprepared to navigate the school system on their own. Second, teachers and counselors were also unprepared to meet their unique needs. For example, students often missed important announcements or were unaware of school policies, course offerings, and the possibilities of participating in extracurricular activities. Students often signed their and their younger siblings report cards and other school documents.

The lack of parental involvement may be a cultural norm (see Blakely, 1983, on Southeast Asian parental attitudes towards school) as many Southeast Asian parents view schools as solely responsible for their children's education. Such a belief is exemplified when considering one American teacher's description of Karen parents. "Some parents [Karen] will discipline their children if we call, but for the most part they expect us to take care of everything" (High school teacher, personal correspondence, June, 2012). It is clear that Karen parents are marginalized from their children's education and that Karen children are often responsible for navigating the American education bureaucratic system alone.

Teacher Perceptions

Sgaw Karen students were reported to be well behaved and respectful by teachers interviewed. I found my Karen students to be respectful and deferential but unaccustomed to dialoguing with their teacher. They also spoke of saying little in their American classes. Although teachers expressed frustration with their lack of requisite skills, initially the Sgaw Karen students seemed well received in schools. Teachers reported only isolated instances concerning disciplinary issues.

As with Kenny and Lockwood-Kenny's (2011) study of Karen in the northeastern U.S., I found Karen academic performances to be very mixed. One community in Tennessee[10] with over 130 Sgaw Karen families is finding some encouragement from Sgaw Karen graduation rates. One teacher writes:

> We currently have a 100 percent Sgaw Karen graduation rate, with 16 students graduating last year. One of our students was in the top 10 percent of the graduating class, and we've been able to hire her as an assistant at the school. (Anonymous teacher, personal communication, July 3, 2012)

Such high graduation rates were not indicative of other communities. Again, like Kenny and Lockwood-Kenny's (2011) study, I found very mixed results related to graduation and dropout rates. Although this one community boasts excellent academic outcomes, I witnessed a great discrepancy between Karen students' grades and their actual academic abilities.

What is an A?

Many of the Karen children I worked with received high grades on report cards despite their lack of ability in the various disciplines. The case of one Sandville High School student best exemplifies this phenomenon. Ler Say (pseudonym) was a 19-year-old Karen adolescent who moved to the United States when he was 13 years old. Since arriving he has advanced to the succeeding grade every year. However, it was clear to me as his tutor that Ler Say was well below his grade level in reading and writing and that he struggled with spoken English. One study session demonstrated the discrepancy between his grade level and skill level.

One study session I had Ler Say and each of his siblings take practice exams. Whereas his brothers and sister were preparing for the Criterion Referenced Competency Tests (CRCT)[11] in advance of their scheduled state mandated tests, he was preparing to take the Georgia High School Graduation Test. Accidently, Ler Say took a copy of his brother's first grade reading test rather than his tenth grade test. It wasn't until he completed the practice test that I realized the mistake. I didn't inform him of the error and decided to see how he did, he missed four out of the ten questions. When we reviewed the test together I realized two important things.

First, Ler Say struggled with reading at a first grade level. Second, much of his confusion surrounded the title of the reading passage, "Setting the Table." As a young man coming from a culture that does not use utensils (the Karen eat with their fingers) and whose home language was not English, he had never been exposed to the expression "setting the table." Therefore, from the outset he was at a disadvantage, as he could not contextualize the reading passage the way an American child might. As an American child I was never formally taught to set the table; rather, I learned in context by watching my parents and siblings arrange the utensils, cups, and plates. The more I considered this example, the more I began to see similar cases with his siblings. It was clear that he and his siblings were unaware of the many idioms, phrasal verbs, and colloquialisms of "home."

At the time Ler Say was in the tenth grade, and each of his report cards indicated he was not only passing but excelling in school. However, his report card belied the reality that he struggled with basic skills. Whether his grades reflected his effort, the sympathy of teachers, his shy and deferential demeanor, or an unwillingness to retain him, Ler Say was not served by his high grades. He, like other older Karen in his community, ended up failing repeated attempts at mandatory state graduation exams and was unable to graduate from high school.

Ler Say's story is not unique to this community or to the many immigrant students' school experiences (Blakely, 1983; Rumbaut & Ima, 1988). One can empathize with teachers as well. Ler Say was a model student in many ways. He was well behaved, maintained perfect attendance, and worked hard. For me, the issue is less about teachers assigning unrealistically high grades and more about the system they are trying to work within. At some level, Ler Say was passed on because no one knew what to do with him. This issue will be taken up later in the implication section of the chapter.

What's in a Name?

Gunn, Brice, and Peterson (2014) contend that by learning students' names teachers can demonstrate respect for the student's home culture and help children "fit in." I have witnessed much confusion regarding Karen names and believe it is an important element in respecting home culture but also respecting individual students' identities.

Karen children may have a variety of names, some of which defy their ethnic origin. They may be given Burman, English, and Karen names, or a combination of them. For example, a Karen female may be named *Julie Paw* (Julie Flower) and her brother *Bright Htoo* (Bright Gold), while a third may simply be named *Wonderful*. Many of the Karen children born in the United States are given such mixed names.

According to Ananda Rajah (2002), many Karen have what are called "event names." These names describe "events" at the time of the baby's birth. For example, a boy born June 2 may be called June Two; while another boy, who was born while preparing to flee oncoming Burmese troops, might be simply named *Ready*. Other names may reflect favorable qualities, like Law Eh (handsome). Many Sgaw Karen names are taken from the Bible. Names like *Grace, Esther, Sara, Mo Say* (Moses), *Pol Lu* (Paul) and *Christ* are common. Other Karen names depict natural objects such as flowers, stars, money, and love (see Table 10.1).

TABLE 10.1   Sgaw Karen Names

Sgaw Karen (Gender)	English
Kayo Paw (Female)	Cherry Flower
Sa Ra (Female)	Sarah
Eh Ser Paw (Female)	Love Sweet Flower
Christ Mu Htoo (Female)	Christ Life Gold
Grace Taw	True Grace
Hser Gay Htoo (Female)	Sweet Good Gold
Ler Moo (Male)	True Life
Htoo Wah (Male)	White Gold
Sher Tah Taw (Male)	Sweet True Heart
Eh Taw (Male)	True Love
June Two (Male/Female)	June Second
Lucky Moon (Male/Female)	

Karen also use honorifics (Moonieinda, 2010) and most Karen children will be accustomed to referring to adults, especially teachers, with an appropriate honorific. The female honorific *Naw* prefaces a female name, such as Naw Kayo Paw (Ms. Cherry Flower). And the male honorific *Saw* is used with adult males, for example, Saw Htoo Wah (Mr. Gold White). Importantly, Karen students are accustomed to using the honorific *Thera* when addressing teachers and may be uncomfortable with less formal appellations such as Mr. Daniel or Ms. Maya. Nevertheless, most Karen refer to each other with a nickname or pet name usually designated by parents, grandparents, or a family friend. Such nicknames usually reflect special qualities or characteristics. For example, a common nickname for a diminutive Karen boy is *Chit Poe* (Little One). Other Karen may be nicknamed according to their complexion, weight, or character. Table 10.1 provides some sense of the variety and beauty of Karen names.

Significantly, the Karen do not have surnames. Their names are neither patronymic nor matronymic. When they arrive in the United States, the final syllable of their name becomes a surrogate surname on all official documents. Thus, someone named *Moo Tha Wah* becomes Moo Wah on all official documentation (Tha becomes a middle name). His brother, Moo Say Wah might have the same official name, Moo Wah. This can cause confusion and misidentification. Moreover, teachers and school officials need to recognize that students might be biologic siblings despite not sharing a common surname.[12] Those who work with the Karen should ask their students what they prefer to be called; usually the nickname is preferred as it is what they identify with at home and with friends.

Sgaw Karen Language

The Sgaw Karen writing system is relatively new. Prior to the introduction of a Karen script, devised by American missionary Dr. Wade in 1834, the Karen had no written orthography (Marshall, 1992; South, 2011; Thawnghmung, 2012). The American missionary enterprise was extremely efficient in educating the Karen in this new script and made literacy an early missionary goal (Falla, 1991; Lewis, 1924). Later, other Christian missionaries and Buddhist scholars divided the Karen along religious and linguistic lines by creating competing Karen writing systems (Delang, 2000; South, 2011; Smith, 1999). There are over 12 non-mutually intelligible but related Karen dialects with at least nine different scripts (Cheesman, 2002; South, 2007). Sgaw Karen has become the Karen *lingua franca* in the refugee camps (Baron et al., 2007; Brees, 2010) and post resettlement communities with Pwo and Sgaw Karen often interacting in Sgaw Karen (field notes, Karen New Year celebration, January 2012). The majority of Karen children entering U.S. schools will speak Sgaw Karen at home. The characteristics of the Sgaw Karen language are singular in the region and deserve a brief description. Despite the paucity of studies that address teacher awareness of language characteristics of their students' L1 (first language) in English as a second language class-rooms, the author argues that teacher awareness of certain linguistic features of their students may help address grammar and phonemic issues from the outset.

Harry Marshall's (1922) ethnographic work on the Karen provides some of the key linguistic features of Sgaw Karen that may help inform teachers working with Karen students. The Sgaw Karen alphabet contains 25 consonants and 10 vowels and has 6 different tones (Marshall, 1992). Unlike more recently created orthographies that use Roman script, the most commonly used Sgaw Karen script uses Burmese letters (Hayami, 2004). As such, the Sgaw Karen alphabet is "a perfect phonetic alphabet" according to Marshall (1922, p. 31). Consequently, Karen students struggle with the notion that English letters have various pronunciations.

Sgaw Karen orders sentences much like English with subject-predicate-object ordering. Accordingly, English syntax has not been found to be a major obstacle for Karen students. However, there are a few linguistic differences between English and Sgaw Karen that may apprise teachers.

First, in Sgaw Karen, there is an absence of final consonant sounds (Marshall, 1992). This absence of a final sound has been evidenced frequently during my work as a tutor with Karen students who often do not pronounce the final consonant of English words, adversely affecting their pronunciation. For example, the words *little, liter,* and *litter* will often be confused. For the fist few months I thought my students were simply mumbling, until I realized they were simply not pronouncing final consonants because they did not exist in their first language.

Second, Sgaw Karen verbs are "almost always transitive" (Marshall, 1992, p. 33) and, more importantly, there is no tense system. All of my older Karen students struggled with verb tenses (e.g., I eat yesterday. and; I doing homework every day.). Third, in Sgaw Karen there are no sounds compatible to the English letters g, j, v or z and therefore are frequently problematic sounds for Sgaw Karen students to pronounce. The Center for Applied Linguistics also notes that Sgaw Karen is monosyllabic and tonal and therefore difficult to Romanize accurately (Baron et al., 2007). Therefore, transliteration is not always possible or advisable.

Fourth, Karen script does not differentiate between lower case and upper case letters. I have found that the English rules for capitalizing to be a major obstacle for older Karen students. Invariably, Karen children will write their names in lower case letters. For example, *hser mu htoo* and *Hser eh taw* are common ways I have found my students writing their names. Such issues pertaining to writing were evidenced more with older (1.25 generation) Karen who read and wrote in Sgaw Karen and had limited expose to English.

Acknowledgement of these linguistic differences between Sgaw Karen and English may have implications for classroom teachers, curriculum designers, speech pathologists, ESL teachers, and tutors.

Gender

Women have traditionally played a very active role in Sgaw Karen village life and are important actors in Sgaw Karen social life (Falla, 1991; Zan, 2008). Since the arrival of American missionaries, Karen women have held important positions within Karen society. Many Karen girls were provided the same education as boys and have served important roles in the insurgency (Zan, 2008). Louisa Benson Craig, a former Miss Burma, was one of the many Sgaw Karen women who held important military positions within the insurgency and later in the Karen Diaspora community in the U.S. Today, Karen women, such as the award-winning author, Zoya Phan (see Phan, 2010), are important spokespeople in the Karen Diaspora community. However, like Watkins, Razee, and Richters' (2012) study of Karen women in Australia, I found some troubling trends related to Karen women and girls in the U.S.

First, I have found that Sgaw Karen adolescent girls are dropping out of high school at higher rates than boys. Four out of the five adolescent girls related to the community dropped out of high school before finishing grade 10. The sister and sister-in-law of one family, and two cousins all dropped out school in order to marry. This is not surprising in light of similar accounts at the camps related by Su-Ann Oh and Marc Van der Stouwe (2008). Their research on Karen education in the camps reveals high dropout rates amongst girls in camp schools. They write of Karen girls in the camps: "The threat of exclusion from education does not, however, discourage youths from marrying. ... Of the 28 young women in our sample, all but two women had dropped out of school because of pregnancy" (p. 601). Male dropouts were also documented, but in each of these cases, employment was cited as the primary reason for quitting school.

Adolescent girls were also more burdened with housework compared to brothers (Watkins et al., 2008). As in other Southeast Asian communities (see Zhou & Bankston, 2001 on the role of adolescent girls in the Vietnamese community), girls were responsible for caring for younger siblings, cleaning the house, and cooking, often at the expense of doing schoolwork. Again, more studies are warranted on Karen girls' education in the United States.

Conclusions and Implications

Josef Joffe, the publisher-editor of the German weekly *Die Zeit*, suggests in his new book, "The Myth of America's Decline," that the United States will continue to be a world leader because, in part, of its immigrants. It is clear to this author that the U.S. has benefitted from its diversity but that too often the first and second generations (and those in-between) are left behind because teachers, schools, and state education policies are not meeting their needs. The following offers suggestions for ways that schools and teachers can begin to address this latest immigrant population and concludes with ways in which teachers can begin to use these children's' funds of knowledge in their instruction.

First, schools must first recognize which ethnic groups under the label *Burmese* are being resettled in their schools. Teachers and school administrators need to acknowledge the unique history and culture of their Karen students. In urban schools, students from each of the Burmese ethnic groups (Chin, Karen, Kachin, and Karenni) may be arriving. Each of these groups is singular and Karen and other minority groups may be offended if referred to as Burmese because of the historical animosity and 60-year civil war. Schools need to acknowledge their differences and make a concerted effort to educate their staff, students, and community about their new neighbors, students, and classmates. Moreover, such cultural training should include stakeholders from the community.

By facilitating more interaction with parents, schools will help mitigate the negative consequences associated with parental marginalization, misunderstandings about school regulations and policies, and the lack of minority student involvement in extracurricular programs. Schools can begin by offering information sessions for parents about American-style grading, discipline, homework, report cards, state and national exams, and educational options post-high school. Parents must also be informed about ways in which they can supports their children's learning. Such programs can help parents regain some autonomy over their children's education.

Parents must also recognize their rights and responsibilities in their children's education and be shown ways they can participate and keep track of their child's progress. Too often, non-English speaking parents falsely assume their child is managing well because of their apparent English proficiency. Bridges must be built between immigrant communities and schools. News travels fast and I have witnessed how quickly information is shared within one Karen community. In every community visited, I was able to find at least one Karen adult who spoke English proficiently. These adults must be identified and utilized by schools.

Teachers must also recognize the burden these children face as they attempt to navigate their and their younger sibling's education without support. Awareness of their students' home life (i.e., parental education, employment status, housing conditions, etc.) can help teachers better understand and address their students' emotional, psycho-social needs (Bronstein & Montgomery, 2011).

Furthermore, schools need to address the mismatch between students' grades and their actual skill levels. As was demonstrated with the case of Ler Say, high grades and promotion to the next grade level only provided him and his parents with a false sense of success. His eventual inability to graduate led to feelings of hopelessness and limited employment prospects. Sadly, Ler Say's case has become the norm for many resettled refugee children who resettle in their early teens (Blakely, 1983). Ler Say is currently unemployed and reports that he "sleep all day and very sad with nothing to do" (personal correspondence, November, 2013). Schools need to acknowledge this phenomenon and find alternative methods to meet the needs of such students. The first step is awareness.

It was clear to me as the children's tutor that each of the children had few authentic language speaking opportunities outside of school. I contend that this, too, is a community wide issue, and that willing members of the community (American) should be utilized. Partnerships might be made between refugee communities and the surrounding community. The support of local churches, retirement homes, and universities may help build bridges. States and schools need to recognize the importance of healthy acculturation for the future of their children and communities.

Next, state departments of education must reconsider policies regarding universal graduation tests and recuse second language students from these tests. Such tests are inherently unfair and culturally biased (Wong, 2006). Alternative means of graduation should be made available (i.e., waivers) and, most importantly, explained to Karen students and their parents.

Schools should also consider ways to provide a blend of both sheltered and mainstream classes to English language learners. My opinion matches the findings of Kenny and Lockwood-Kenny (2011) who suggests that Karen students are often treated with "benign neglect" in schools after the novelty of their arrival dissipates. Overall, teachers and school officials need to recognize the manifold realities refugee families face as they cope with resettlement and to acknowledge and incorporate their *funds of knowledge*. Teachers are encouraged to view students' homes not only in terms of their physical condition but must recognize the *funds of knowledge* that are present in these homes. These *funds of knowledge* may be utilized to foster lessons or assignments that can draw on students' home life while valuing the student's home culture and immigration experience.

Ideas for Teachers: Utilizing Karen Funds of Knowledge

Teachers can use the students' cultural background or funds of knowledge in their curriculum. For example, with younger students teachers can use students names as a means to work on pronunciation, cross-cultural understanding, and, most importantly, to address the elephant in the room. Karen students continually reported being made fun of because of the uniqueness of their names. This is often the case with immigrant students and can heighten feelings of loneliness and isolation (Gunn, Brice, & Peterson, 2014). However, such ridicule can be eliminated if the name issue is addressed.

By addressing students' names teachers can "foster early literacy learning, and nurture children's sense of personal cultural identity through intentional planning of instructional activities that highlight children's names" (Gunn, Brice, & Peterson, 2014, p. 175).

Such nurturing is also crucial for other ages and can be accomplished simply by asking and observing students. Teachers can have students draw or paint artistic representations of their names and/or Karen students can help other students choose a Karen name based on their preferences. Also, teachers can use a naming jar (see Choi, 2013) as a means of acknowledging all students' names.

Teachers can also capitalize on the many strengths Karen students bring to class. In my time with the Karen, I have become aware of their appreciation for and ability in the arts, namely, drawing and music. Every home visited had at least one guitar and all males demonstrated some degree of skill. In each case, they were self-taught or taught informally by their father or a male relative. Although I only witnessed one Karen woman playing guitar, Karen girls and women are renowned for their singing.

Every Karen church visited had an active youth and adult choir. Surprisingly, the Karen often lose their shyness when singing or playing on stage. I have been amazed to witness some of my most reticent Karen students singing in front of an audience of many hundreds. Teachers and communities should try and incorporate music into their lessons and curricula. *Singable* books can be an excellent tool for incorporating songs as part of the reading curriculum for young children (see Haynes & Smallwood, 2008, for more information).

Moreover, Karen youth have become savvy in creating and disseminating their own music via the web (Gilhooly & Lee, 2014). Christian, pop, rock, hip-hop and heavy metal songs are all favorites of Karen youth. YouTube is replete with Karen-made music videos attesting to their musicality and adeptness at using new technologies. The children and adolescents I worked with also demonstrated great interest in drawing and painting. Art classes may provide Karen students another avenue to succeed in courses or after school programs that are not language focused. It may allow them opportunities to build affinity groups as well. Most importantly, they will have opportunities to socialize as well as demonstrate their abilities.

Sports may be another means of better integrating Karen youth in schools and communities. The Karen have a passion for soccer, volleyball, and cane ball and are learning to play basketball and baseball. Karen students would relish the opportunity to demonstrate cane ball to their classmates. Like music, such activities may entice Karen students to participate in extracurricular activities. In my focal community none of the children participate in sports or music programs despite their expressed interest. Schools can use the lure of musical instruments or musical production, art classes, choir, or band to entice Karen students to participate in extracurricular activities and socialize with American peers.

Agriculture or technology classes can also draw from Karen knowledge with farming and mechanics. As an agrarian people, the Karen are skilled at farming, hunting and fishing, and animal husbandry. Schools with agriculture programs can work on initiatives that draw on these traditional skills. Because of their protracted confinement in refugee camps the Karen have become very resourceful and demonstrate ability in small motor repair, appliance repair, as well as making and fixing an assortment of tools. These students would benefit from classes that help promote skills that can lead to direct employment.

No discussion of the Karen is complete without some recognition of the role of church within the family and community. The Sgaw Karen are very devout and the church is the center of many Karen villages in Burma, the camps, and communities in the U.S. They are also sites for multiple forms of knowledge. At church, Karen children not only learn doctrine but are encouraged to be involved in youth choir, Bible study, and community outreach where they help organize and conduct Karen functions. They also learn academic skills such as memorization, recitation, and public speaking that can help them in their school studies. I have found Karen students to be very capable in memorizing and reciting poems and songs. There rich oral culture may be integrated into English language arts classes or in public speaking.

Immigrant families like the Karen bring many abilities, knowledge, and stories to our classrooms and communities. They each come from rich cultural backgrounds that can enrich the school and wider community. This can only be achieved when educators gain awareness into the students' individual and collective stories. Therefore, culturally responsive teaching includes awareness of the complex cultural, historical, linguistic, personal, psychological, and social aspects that each student bring with them into our schools and classes.

Questions to Consider

1. In what way does knowing something about the history of a particular group inform us as teachers (in this case the Karen)?
2. What aspects of Sgaw Karen language do you think would most confuse learners of English?
3. How do Karen student attitudes toward teachers differ from the way we expect student to respond to teacher in the US?
4. What are two of the differences you might expect between a 1.25 generation student and their 1.75 generation sibling?
5. What are two reasons Karen parents were not involved in their children's schooling?
6. What are examples of some of the funds of knowledge Karen children demonstrate in this chapter?

References

Anguiano, R. P. V. (2004). Families and schools: The effect of parental involvement on high school completion. *Journal of Family Issues, 25*(1), 61–85.

Bankston, C. L. I., & Zhou, M. (1995). Effects of minority-language literacy on the academic achievement of Vietnamese youths in New Orleans. *Sociology of Education, 68*(1), 1–17.

Baron, S., Okell, J., Myat Yin, S., Vanbik, K., & Swain, A. (2007). *Refugees from Burma: Their backgrounds and refugee experience.* (No. 21). Washington DC: Center for Applied Linguistics.

Bauböck, R., & Faist, T. (2010). *Diaspora and transnationalism: Concepts, theories and methods.* Amsterdam, Netherlands: Amsterdam University Press.

Blakely, M. M. (1983). Southeast Asian refugee parents: An inquiry into home-school communication and understanding. *Anthropology & Education Quarterly, 14*(1), 43–68.

Brees, I. (2010). Burden or boon: The impact of Burmese refugees on Thailand. *Whitehead Journal of Diplomacy & International Relations, 11*(1), 35–47.

Bronstein, I., & Montgomery, P. (2011). Psychological distress in refugee children: A systematic review. *Clinical Child & Family Psychology Review, 14*(1), 44–56. doi:10.1007/s10567010-0081-0

Charmaz, K. (2006). *Constructing grounded theory: A practical guide through qualitative analysis.* London, UK: Sage.

Cheesman, N. (2002). Seeing 'Karen' in the union of Myanmar. *Asian Ethnicity, 3*(2), 199–222. doi:10.1080/14631360220132736

Choi, Y. (2013). *The name jar.* New York, NY: Random House LLC.

Corbin, J., & Strauss, A. (Eds.). (2008). *Basics of qualitative research: Techniques and procedures for developing grounded theory.* Thousand Oaks, CA: Sage.

Cusano, C. (2001). *Burma: Displaced Karens like water on the khu leaf.* London, UK: Luto Press.

Delang, C. (Ed.). (2000). *Suffering in silence: The human rights nightmare of the Karen people of Burma* (1st ed.). Parkland, FL: Universal Publishers.

Falla, J. (1991). *True love and Bartholomew.* New York, NY: Cambridge University Press.

Gay, G. (2002). Preparing for culturally responsive teaching. *Journal of Teacher Education, 53*(2), 106–116.

Gay, G. (2010). *Culturally responsive teaching: Theory, research, and practice.* New York, NY: Teachers College Press.

Gilhooly, D., & Lee, E. (2014). The role of digital literacy on refugee resettlement: The case of three Karen brothers. *Journal of Adolescent & Adult Literacy, 57*(5), 387–396. doi:10.1002/JAAL.254.

Glesne, C. (2011). *Becoming qualitative researchers: An introduction* (4th ed.). Boston, MA: Pearson.

Gonzalez, N., Moll, L., Tenery, R. M., Rendon, A., Gonzalez P., Amanti, C. (1995). Funds of knowledge for teachers in Latino households. *Urban Education, 29*(4), 443–470.

Gonzalez, N., Moll, L. C., Floyd-Tenery, M., Rivera, A., Rendon, P., Gonzales, R., & Amanti, C. (1993). Teacher research on funds of knowledge: Learning from households. Washington, DC: *Center for Research on Education, Diversity & Excellence.*

Gonzalez, N., Moll, L. C., & Amanti, C. (2005). *Funds of knowledge: Theorizing practices in households, communities, and classrooms* Mahwah, NJ: L. Erlbaum Associates.

Gunn, A. A., Brice, A. E., & Peterson, B. J. (2014). Ideas for the classroom: Culturally responsive teaching: Exploring children's names and cultural identities. *Childhood Education, 90*(2), 174–176. doi:10.1080/00094056.2014.894836

Harriden, J. (2002). "Making a name for themselves": Karen identity and the politicization of ethnicity in Burma. *Journal of Burma Studies, 7,* 84–144.

Hayami, Y. (2004). *Between hills and plains: Power and practice in socio-religious dynamics among Karen.* Kyoto, Japan: Kyoto University Press.

Haynes, E., & Smallwood, B. (2008). Singable books: Sing and read your way to English proficiency. *CAL Digest, 34,* 1–4.

Henderson, A. T., & Berla, N. (1994). *A new generation of evidence: The family is critical to student achievement.* Columbia, MD: National Committee for Citizens in Education.

Hones, D. F. (1999). Crises, continuity, and the refugee. *Journal of Contemporary Ethnography, 28*(2), 166–198.

Hones, D. F. (2002). *American dreams, global visions: Dialogic teacher research with refugee and immigrant families.* Mahwah, NJ: L. Erlbaum Associates.

Karen Communities Foundation. (2012). Considerations for individuals and agencies working with the Karen people in the United States. Retrieved from http://www.karensusa.org/index_files/Page762.html

Kia-Keating, M., & Ellis, B. H. (2007). Belonging and connection to school in resettlement: Young refugees, school belonging, and psychosocial adjustment. *Clinical Child Psychology & Psychiatry, 12*(1), 29–43.

Kenny, P., & Lockwood-Kenny, K. (2011). A mixed blessing: Karen resettlement to the United States. *Journal of Refugee Studies, 24*(2), 217–238. doi:10.1093/jrs/fer009

Lee, R. M., Choe, J., Kim, G., Ngo, V., Park, Y. S., Kim, B. S. K., & Ju, C. M. (2010). Asian American family conflicts scale. *Asian American Journal of Psychology, 1*(1), 67–79.

Lewis, J. (1924). *The Burmanization of the Karen people: A study in racial adaptability.* Chicago, IL: The University of Chicago Press.

Malseed, K. (2008). Networks of noncompliance: Grassroots resistance and sovereignty in militarized Burma. *Journal of Peasant Studies, 36*(2), 365.

Marshall, H. I. (1922). *The Karen people of Burma: A study in anthropology and ethnology.* Columbus, OH: Ohio State University Press.

Mason, E. H. B., & Raynard, E. H. (1862). *Civilizing mountain men: Or, Sketches of mission work among the Karens.* London: James Nisbet.

McBrien, J. L. (2005). Educational needs and barriers for refugee students in the United States: A review of the literature. *Review of Educational Research, 75*(3), 329–364. doi:10.2307/3515985

McMahon, A. (1876). *The Karen of the golden chersonese.* London, UK: Harrison and Sons.

Milbrandt, J. (2012). Tracking genocide: Persecution of the Karen in Burma. *Texas International Law Journal, 48,* 63–101.

Moll, L. C., Amanti, C., Neff, D., & Gonzalez, N. (1992). Funds of knowledge for teaching: Using a qualitative approach to connect homes and classrooms. *Theory into Practice, 31*(2), 132–141.

Nguyen, N. A., & Williams, H. L. (1989). Transition from east to west: Vietnamese adolescents and their parents. *Journal of the American Academy of Child and Adolescent Psychiatry, 28*(4), 505–515.

Oh, S. A., & Van der Stouwe, M. (2008). Education, diversity, and inclusion in Burmese refugee camps in Thailand. *Comparative Education Review, 52*(4), 589–617.

Phan, Z., Lewis, D., & Phan, Z. (2010). *Undaunted: My struggle for freedom and survival in Burma.* New York, NY: Free Press.

Po, S. C. (1928). *Burma and the Karens.* London, UK: Elliot Stock.

Portes, A., & Schauffler, R. (1994). Language and the second generation: Bilingualism yesterday and today. *International Migration Review, 28*(4), 640–661. doi:10.2307/2547152

Rajah, A. (2002). A 'nation of intent' in Burma: Karen ethno-nationalism, nationalism and narrations of nation. *Pacific Review, 15*(4), 517–537.

Refugee Processing Center (RPC). (2014). Refugee arrivals by region and country of nationality: Fiscal years 2001 to 2013. Retrieved from www.wrapsnet.org/Reports/InteractiveReporting/tabid/393/EnumType/Report/Default.aspx?ItemPath=/rpt_WebArrivalsReports/MX%20-%20Arrivals%20for%20a%20Demographic%20Profile

Richardson, L. (2000) Writing: A method of inquiry. In N. Denzin & Y. Lincoln (Eds.), *Handbook of Qualitative Research,* (2nd ed., pp. 923–946). Thousand Oaks, CA: Sage Publications.

Rumbaut, R. G., & Ima, K. (1988). *The adaption of Southeast Asian refugee youth: A comparative study.* San Diego, CA: San Diego State University.

Rumberger, R. W., & Larson, K. A. (1998). Toward explaining differences in educational achievement among Mexican American language-minority students. *Sociology of Education, 71*(1), 68–92. doi:10.2307/2673222

Siu, S. F., & Feldman, J. A. (1996). Patterns of Chinese American family involvement in young children education. *ERIC Document Reproduction Service No. ED399346.* Retrieved from http://files.eric.ed.gov/fulltext/ED399346.pdf

Smeaton, D. M. (1887). *The loyal Karens of Burma.* London, UK: K. Paul, Trench & Co.

Smith, M. (1999). *Burma: Insurgency and the politics of ethnicity.* New York, NY: St. Martin's Press.

Smith-Hefner, N. (1993). Education, gender, and generational conflict among Khmer refugees. *Anthropology & Education Quarterly, 24*(2), 135–158. doi:10.2307/3195722

South, A. (2007). Karen nationalist communities: The "problem" of diversity. *Contemporary Southeast Asia: A Journal of International & Strategic Affairs, 29*(1), 55–76.

South, A. (2011). *Burma's longest war: Anatomy of the Karen conflict.* Netherlands: Transnational Institute Burma Center Netherlands.

Stake, R. (1995). *The art of case study research.* Thousand Oaks, CA: Sage.

TBBC. (2008). *Scale and distribution of internal displacement*. Retrieved from www.tbbc.org/idps. htm#distribution

Thawnghmung, A. M. (2012). *The "other" Karen in Myanmar: Ethnic minorities and the struggle without arms*. Lanham, MD: Lexington Books.

Thawnghmung, A. M. (2008). *The Karen revolution in Burma: Diverse voices, uncertain ends*. Washington, DC: East-West Center.

Watkins, P., G., Razee, H., & Richters, J. (2012). 'I'm telling you ... the language barrier is the most, the biggest challenge': Barriers to education among Karen refugee women in Australia. *Australian Journal of Education (ACER Press)*, *56*(2), 126–141.

White, M. J., & Glick, J. E. (2000). Generation status, social capital, and the routes out of high school. *Sociological Forum*, *15*(4), 671–691. doi:10.1023/A:1007515100190

Wong, S. (2006). *Dialogic approaches to TESOL: Where the ginkgo tree grows*. Mahwah, NJ: Lawrence Erlbaum Associates.

Worldwide Refugee Admissions Processing Services (WRAPS). (2014). Refugee arrivals by region and country of nationality: Fiscal years 2001 to 2010. Retrieved from http://www.dhs.gov/files/statistics/publications/YrBk10RA.shtm

Zan, S. (2008). *Life's journey in faith: Burma, from rags to riches*. Bloomington, IN: Author House.

Zhou, M., & Bankston III, C. L. (2000). *Straddling two social worlds: The experience of Vietnamese refugee children in the United States*. (Evaluative Report No. 111). New York: ERIC.

Zhou, M., & Bankston III, C. L. (2001). Family pressure and the educational experience of the daughters of Vietnamese refugees. *International Migration*, *39*(4). 133–151.

Notes

1   Burma or Myanmar? The State Law and Order Restoration Council (SLORC) military junta officially renamed the country "Myanmar Naing-ngan" in 1989 (South, 2008). However, ethnic minority groups and some governments, such as the United States, still use the old designation "Burma." This study follows the traditional usage of "Burma" as it was the only designation used by the Karen contributors to this chapter.

2   Burmese refers to all minority groups in Burma whereas Burman refers to the majority ethnic group in Burma. Burmese is also the appellation for the Burman language, the official language of Burma.

3   Burman refers to the majority ethnic group in Burma whereas Burmese refers to all ethnicities from Burma.

4   The first Karen student, Theodore Thanbyah, graduated from an American university, the University of Rochester (New York) in 1871 (Martin, 2012).

5   Some Karen Buddhists and Karen Muslims are also arriving.

6   It is important to note that Karen armed groups, including the Karen National Liberation Army (KNLA) and Democratic Karen Buddhist Army (DKBA), have been accused of human rights violations, including forced conscriptions as a means to continue their insurgency (South, 2011, p. 15).

7   Drawing on Rumbaut's (1997) "decimal generations," 1.25 generation refers to those resettling from ages 13–17 and 1.5 as resettling between the ages of 6–12, and 1.75 refers to those who resettling 0–5.

8   This was an informal scale where I would ask parents to assess their children's language ability according to the following; 10 = excellent Karen, 5 = fair Karen, 0 = no Karen. I did not attribute any weight to the other numbers.

9   As of May 2014, my focal community has begun a summer Karen school where students of all ages are being taught Karen reading and writing.

10 I made the acquaintance of a teacher working with Karen students and we corresponded frequently and exchanged information about the respective Karen communities from 2011 to 2012.

11 All Georgia students from grades 1–8 took the CRCT until 2010–2011. From 2011–2012 the test is only given from grades 3–8. A passing score on the GHGT was mandatory for all Georgia students who entered high school before July 2011.

12 To complicate matters more, I have recently heard reports of how some families bought new identities from the camps in order to resettle. It seems that as fewer and fewer Karen and other minorities are eligible for resettlement, registration for resettlement has premium value to those looking to resettle. Therefore, some children may be entering the United States with names acquired by the illegal procurement of chapters in the camps.

Appendix A

First-Day Protocol Checklist for All Newcomers

Task	Ways to access information	Actions	Task completed
Identify child as an English language learner.	Schools often provide student information in advance. If not, most students can be identified early on by staff, fellow teachers, ESL coordinators, and/or fellow students. *Typically, schools provide a home language survey or language use survey that initially identifies a student's home language.	Begin to build a student biography and language needs assessment. Find time in the first days to talk with the student privately to begin creating a positive rapport. Begin assessing social, emotional, and academic needs.	
Find out how the student wants to be addressed and how to pronounce their name. Make sure the student understands how you want to be addressed. In some cultures students refer to teachers with an honorific like San or Maestro.	From the student or school interpreter or parent.	Have a new student routine (game or activity) that is low stress and effective in assuring everyone can pronounce the student's name. Include yourself and any co-teachers or support staff in the activity.	

(Continued)

Task	Ways to access information	Actions	Task completed
Review parental information.	Schools often provide student information in advance. If not, most students can be identified early on by staff, fellow teachers, ESL coordinators, fellow students, or via a quick chat.	Relevant information should be stored for each parent or guardian. Set up a time to meet parents and establish lines of communication.	
Assign an empathetic buddy to help transition newcomer student.	Partner your new CLD student with a co-ethnic student or appropriate empathetic partner.	Have a "go-to" set of students who you have trained on how to mentor new students.	
Create a welcoming but non-intrusive activity/icebreaker.	N/A	Have a "go-to" set of activities for when a new student arrives.	
When possible, address the student's arrival with the class prior to student's arrival and let them know your expectations in welcoming the new student.	N/A		
Assess the physical space.	Student projects, internet searches of famous co-ethnics of student	Creating a physical space that is inclusive can begin by decorating the walls of the classroom with people who resemble the CLD student. These images should represent a wide variety of "successful" people who look like the CLD students such as artists, scholars, scientists, writers, and athletes. Set up seating to promote one-on-one and group discussions. Include a section of multicultural authors in your classroom and school library.	

Appendix B

Activities for Day 1

Lower Elementary to Middle School

The Name Jar: Have the book the *Name Jar* (Choi, 2013) on hand in your classroom library. At the start of the year you can say and write each student's name in a jar. You could also have the child write his or her name in their native language. Having students write their name and the names of other students in their L1 can help validate the student's L1 in your classroom.

Students can draw a name from the jar, say the name, and identify the correct student. Such an activity can have many variations. The key is that all students' names are respected and included in the class. Importantly, some students may ask to be called a nickname or name other than the name that is provided on the class roster. Teachers should consider using the child's preferred name.

Find Someone Who?: Upper Elementary to High School

This is a standard activity in many ESL classrooms on the first day. Teachers make a list of student attributes (see example), and students find someone who matches the attribute. The first student to find a different student to match each attribute will read from their completed table. In the example, the student would read, "Amaya has a younger brother." The teacher can then confirm with Amaya that she has a younger brother, and the student continues down their list. This is a great way to get kids interacting and acts as a means for everyone to learn about each other. Teachers should join in and share about themselves. This activity can be modified based on grade level and class size. Teachers should also consider if this activity is language appropriate from their CLD students and modify accordingly.

Find Some Who ...	Student's Name	Correct Response
Has a younger brother	Amaya	Amaya has a younger brother.
Can speak a language other than English	Mi Hyun	Mi Hyun can speak Korean.

Middle School to High School

What does your name mean?

Students can engage in lively conversations around their names. Naming systems often differ across cultures, and names often have "cool" stories behind them. An activity where students share in the many meanings and significances of their names can be fun and can set an inclusive tone for class.

References

Choi, Y. (2013). *The name jar*. Knopf.

Appendix C

Computerized Technology for Teaching ELLs

Suggested Activity: Website Review

This activity is intended for you to think about the applicability of online spaces for your ELL students or for you as teachers. Before responding to any of the questions please take some time to play with/figure out the website you are assigned. Note, you may have to sign up for some of these, but they are *free*. After some trial and error and attempts at using the site, address the questions as you write your review. Please try and consider these from the perspective of a teacher working with ELLs.

1. **Weblink:** provide the link to the site you are reviewing
2. **Short description of site:**
   - Write a brief four- to seven-sentence description that would help teachers get an overall idea of the site's usefulness.
   - Which age or English level is the site best suited for?
3. **How might the site be used for working with ELLs? Be specific and descriptive. This section is the heart of the assignment (250–500 words)**
   - Is it for teachers? Students? Parents? All?
   - What domains might students be able to practice/develop on this site (reading, writing, listening, speaking) and how?
     o Describe how the site would be used to address one or more of these domains.
   - Would the site be used in class? Homework?
4. **How would you describe the site in terms of user friendliness? Navigability? What features did you like/dislike? What issues might arise with your future students? What issues did you have understanding and navigating the site?**

5. **How would you grade this site as a teaching tool? Please explain. Think of how students (ELLs) might respond to the particular technology.**
   - Grade: A–F

Suggested Activity: Digital Tools Repository

This activity is intended for you to think about the digital tools that you use. Please look at the provided class repository document prior to looking for resources. You may use any digital software or application (but it does have to be available on all devices, nothing iPhone specific, for instance). These should be available either online or through the app stores on mobile devices. After you find your resources answer the questions.

1. **Using the provided class repository document (Google Documents or something similar):** Locate a resource for each listed subskill of language learning. It is okay to have the same tool, but you need to provide your own description and activity.
2. **Your name:** Make sure to include your name and the resource title.
3. **Weblink:** Provide the link for the website or resource you are including.
4. **Short description of site:**
   - Write a brief four-to seven-sentence description that would help teachers get an overall idea of the site.
   - Which age or English level is the site best suited for?
   - Is it a paid site or free? Do you have to create an account? Do students need an account?
5. **Simple activity idea:** Post a simple four-to seven-sentence activity idea for your resource. This does not have to be detailed but should give an idea of how you would use the resource in a class.

Class Repository Document

Reading: Resources related to reading can be posted here.
Writing: Resources related to writing can be posted here.
Speaking: Resources related to speaking can be posted here.
Listening: Resources related to listening can be posted here.
Grammar: Resources related to grammar can be posted here.
Vocabulary: Resources related to vocabulary can be posted here.
General teacher resources: Resources related to any other ESL teaching skill can be posted here.